Practical Guide to
COMPUTERS IN EDUCATION

Practical Guide to
COMPUTERS
IN EDUCATION

PETER COBURN
PETER KELMAN
NANCY ROBERTS
THOMAS SNYDER
DANIEL WATT
CHERYL WEINER

ADDISON-WESLEY
PUBLISHING COMPANY

Reading, Massachusetts
Menlo Park, California
London • Amsterdam
Don Mills, Ontario • Sydney

THE ADDISON-WESLEY SERIES ON COMPUTERS IN EDUCATION

Intentional Educations, Series Developer
Peter Kelman, Series Editor
Peter Coburn, Technical Editor

Practical Guide to Computers in Education
Peter Coburn, Peter Kelman, Nancy Roberts, Thomas Snyder, Daniel Watt, Cheryl Weiner

Computers and School Administration
David Dennen and Carleton Finch

Computers in Teaching Mathematics
John Burton, Peter Coburn, Frank Watson

Other titles forthcoming

Library of Congress Cataloging in Publication Data

Main entry under title:

Practical guide to Computers in education.

(Computers in education)
Bibliography: p.
Includes index.
1. Education — Data processing.   2. Computer managed
instruction.   3. Computer assisted instruction.
I. Intentional Educations, Inc.   II. Series.
LB1028.43.P7   370'.28'54   82-1718
ISBN 0-201-10563-2   AACR2

ISBN 0-201-10563-2
  CDEFGHIJ-AL-89876543

Foreword

The computer is a rich and complex tool that is increasingly within the financial means of schools to acquire. Like any educational tool, it comes with inherent advantages and disadvantages, is more appropriate for some uses than others, is more suited to some teaching styles than others, and is neither the answer to all our educational ills nor the end of all that is great and good in our educational system. Like any tool, it can be used well or poorly, be over-emphasized or ignored, and it depends on the human qualities of the wielder for its effectiveness.

The purpose of the Addison-Wesley Series on *Computers in Education* is to persuade you, as educators, that the future of computers in education is in your hands. Your interest and involvement in educational computer applications will determine whether computers will be the textbook, the TV, or the chalkboard of education for the next generation.

For years, textbooks have dominated school curricula with little input from classroom teachers or local communities. Recently, television has become the most influential and ubiquitous educator in society, yet has not been widely or particularly successfully used by teachers in schools. On the other hand, for over one hundred years the chalkboard has been the most individualized, interactive, creatively used technology in schools.

Already, textbook-like computerized curricula are being churned out with little teacher or local community input. Already, computers are available for home use at prices comparable to a good color television set and with programs at the educational level of the soaps. If teachers are to gain control over computers in education and make them be their chalkboards, the time to act is now.

Each book in the *Computers in Education* series is intended to provide teachers, school administrators, and parents with information and ideas that will help them begin to meet the educational challenge computers present. Taken as a whole, the series has been designed to help the reader:

- Appreciate the potential and the limits of computers in education.
- Develop a functional understanding of the computer.
- Overcome apprehension and fear about the computer.

- Participate in efforts to introduce and integrate computers into a school.
- Use the computer creatively and effectively in teaching and administration.
- Apply a discerning and critical attitude toward the myriad computer-related products offered in increasing volume to the education market.
- Consider seriously the ethical, political, and philosophical ramifications of computer use in education.

Practical Guide to Computers in Education is the basic primer for the series. Its purpose is to introduce the novice to computers in the general setting of schools, including information on the workings of computers, their potential educational applications, and pragmatic suggestions on how to establish a computer resource in a school. The other books in the series deal with computer use in particular educational contexts: teaching mathematics, reading, writing, science, and social studies; working with special needs students; and performing administrative tasks in a school or school system.

It is my hope, as series editor, that the *Practical Guide* will get you, the reader, off to a good start in your consideration of the educational possibilities that computers bring to our schools, and that other books in the series may broaden and deepen your understanding and participation in educational computing.

Peter Kelman
Series Editor

Preface

This book is addressed to you who are concerned with the education of children — teachers, administrators, parents. In writing it, we have tried to imagine what you would need and want to know about computers in education. The book is organized and written to provide you with both a learning experience and a practical plan of action.

We begin in Chapter 1 by establishing an historical, social, and pedagogical context for computer use in education and by raising some perplexing issues that emerge from this context. While this may not sound practical, as the title of the book implies, our sense is that it provides the basis for serious reflection without which educational practice is mere action, devoid of purpose or meaning.

In Chapter 2, "The Computer in the Classroom," we provide a thorough overview, replete with examples, of computer applications in the classroom. It is our hope that this survey will spark your interest in the possible uses of computers in education and, at the same time, warn you of some of the limits and even dangers of such use.

Chapter 3, "Bits and Bytes," plunges you into the world of computers. Written in an informal, friendly style, it tells you all you ever wanted to know about computers (and perhaps even a bit more). Technical terms and computer jargon are carefully defined, but more importantly, they are used in clarifying contexts, usually of an educational nature. This chapter should provide you with a sufficient knowledge base and familiarity with computer terms, not only to make you comfortable reading the rest of this book, but also to enable you to understand and talk with more experienced computer users.

Chapter 4, "Choosing Your Computer System," should be particularly valuable to schools intending to purchase computers. It presents a unique analysis of types of computer systems currently available for educational use that should aid readers in making informed decisions about their computer needs. In addition, the chapter along with the appendix contains the first part of a buyer's guide, which is intended to help educators make appropriate selections of computer equipment and programs for their specific needs and budget.

Chapter 5, "Choosing Educational Software," provides educators with the second part of their buyer's guide to educational computing. While Chapter 4 provides guidelines for purchase of equipment and general computer programs, this chapter focuses on criteria for selecting computer programs and ancillary materials specifically designed for instructional use.

Chapter 6,"Introducing Computers into the School," addresses many of the political, financial, and personal issues that arise when educators decide to bring computers into a school. Vignettes and examples drawn from real cases are used to illustrate how such issues have been handled by others. Suggestions are offered to help would-be computer change agents to introduce computers into their schools.

Chapter 7, "Integrating Computers into the School," provides detailed practical suggestions for establishing and maintaining computer facilities in a school. These include: location, user access, rules and guidelines for use, necessary physical environment, maintenance, service, and security. To write this chapter we surveyed hundreds of school computer users across the country. They responded in true computer-culture fashion with lots of comments and suggestions, many of which we cite specifically.

Finally, in Chapter 8, "Issues and Choices in Educational Computing," we come full circle to address many of the issues raised in Chapter 1. Here, we ask you to join us in confronting the serious problems and great promises facing education in general and educational computing in particular.

Throughout the book, computer terms, both technical ones and jargon, are identified by a bold type face and underlining the first time they are used and when they are defined. All of these terms are defined in the glossary at the end of the book, as well as in the text. In addition, a large, useful, up-to-date, annotated list of resources and a bibliography are provided to help educators locate the kind of information they need in their efforts to incorporate computers into their educational endeavors.

We have tried in this book to avoid using the terms "microcomputer," "minicomputer," and "mainframe" to mean small, medium, and large computers. There are microcomputers available today that are more capable and powerful than most so-called minicomputers and which will outperform the state-of-the art mainframes of the sixties. Many people seem to feel that "micro" means low-powered and not capable. It does not. In a very few years _all_ computers will be microcomputers.

Although the recent growth of computers in schools is almost entirely in small personal computers such as the Apple and the TRS-80, our opinion is that this will not remain so. These personal computers have given us a taste of the power of the computer as a teaching and learning tool, but the feast is only beginning. If the personal computers as we know them today survive at all in the next phase of expansion of educational computer use, it will be as parts of complex networks of small computers. In this book we have tried to give equal weight to the smaller systems currently in vogue and the larger ones that will surely come.

Throughout the book, we have used descriptive vignettes to illustrate more concretely the ideas we are presenting. All of these are based on real events, people, and settings. However, we have made slight editorial modifications so as to provide clear examples free of unnecessary situational details. In all cases, we have changed or omitted names to protect the subject of the vignette from being inundated by inquiries, as has happened to many of the schools pioneering in educational computing. For the same reason, we have also done this for references to schools using computers.

As we approached the task of writing this book, we each reflected on our experiences as teachers. As a current teacher, Tom Snyder talked over ideas for the book with his colleagues at the Shady Hill School in Cambridge, Massachusetts. As teacher trainers, Nancy Roberts and Dan Watt discussed issues for the book with their students (most of them teachers) at Lesley College and the Technical Education Resource Center (TERC) respectively. As a former member of the Computer Assisted and Managed Instruction (CAMI) Project Team at McGraw-Hill, Cheryl Weiner visited with numerous people in instructional project teams in school districts, universities, publishing, the military, and informal educational settings. All of us communicated with friends, colleagues, and contacts involved in educational computing for their input. We feel that we benefitted enormously from these interactions and owe these people a debt of gratitude, although none of them should be held responsible for the views presented in this book. Those who have been particularly helpful to us include: Adeline Naiman of TERC; Ludwig Braun of S.U.N.Y Stonybrook; Karen Billings of Teachers College, Columbia University; Bill Carlsen of Mascoma Valley Regional H.S. in Canaan, N.H.; Richard Hoffman of Miami University of Ohio; Martha Rich of Dartmouth College; and William Davis of Miami University of Ohio.

There are also people whose technical expertise and skill made the publication of this book possible, most notably, Peter Gordon and Sue Zorn of Addison-Wesley, David Crocker and Oscar Dalem, and the entire Intentional Educations support staff, especially Newton Key, Ricki Pappo, Laura Koller, Ann Fisher, Carol Trowbridge, Sandy Edmonds, Debbie Galiga, Peggy Newell, Pam Lodish, Barbara Nielsen, Missy Goldberg, Mickie Rice, Debbie McGonagle, Kevin Watts, and Jane Manners.

Finally, we would like to thank our understanding families who missed us when we were off working on the book.

March, 1982

Peter Coburn
Peter Kelman
Nancy Roberts
Thomas Snyder
Daniel Watt
Cheryl Weiner

Contents

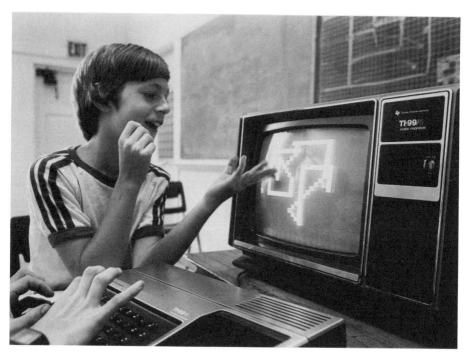

Photo: J.D. Sloane

The Computer Goes to School

Chapter 1

The computer revolution is here! All across the land the arrival of a computerized society is being announced. From the pages of news magazines and daily papers, in countless brochures and advertisements filling our mailboxes, on radio and television, we hear the same message: Prepare yourselves; the computer revolution is here now!

Indeed, computers appear to be revolutionizing every aspect of our lives. The stores in which we shop, the offices where we work, the cars we drive, the banks that handle our money, the games we play, even the television sets in our homes are being radically altered by computers.

Incredibly, a single technological breakthrough, the silicon chip, is largely responsible for both the computer revolution and the larger microelectronics revolution of which it is just one part. Chip technology has made possible the construction of electronic components that are much smaller and cheaper than before. For the computer industry, this has meant the development of miniature computers called **microprocessors**, which reside on a single thumbnail-sized silicon chip and which are the technological basis of the well-publicized downward plunge in the size and price of computers over the last several years.

Yet, according to some futurists the computer revolution our society is currently experiencing is but a tremor, presaging a worldwide upheaval that could transform our entire civilization. Such futurists envision a cataclysmic change in lifestyle, family structure, work habits, and education emerging out of technological breakthroughs such as the chip and spurred on by rapidly diminishing sources of fossil fuels. In one such vision of the future, described in detail in Alvin Toffler's book *The Third Wave*, people would stay closer to their homes and families. They would no longer commute to work, but instead "communicate" their work on computers over telephone lines. They would no longer travel long distances to shop and visit, but do so over computerized videophones. They would no longer go to school for their education, but instead learn through interactive computer systems, linked to other people and information sources. And these are but a few of the changes envisioned by some futurists.

However, many of us haven't yet caught up with the current computer revolution, mere tremor though it may be, and we are certainly not prepared to consider future social upheavals of the magnitude predicted by Toffler and others. So, for the remainder of this book, let us stick to the present revolution in computers and the challenges that it presents to us, as educators. This should keep us busy for some time to come.

WILL COMPUTERS TRANSFORM THE SCHOOLS?

Computers are changing the face of business, both on the assembly line and in the office. They are altering the way many Americans, especially children, are spending their leisure time. They have revolutionized the ways information is generated, stored, and transmitted in our society. But will they transform the schools?

Among today's advocates for educational computing are a number of optimists who would answer an unequivocal yes. They see computers as slowly but surely bringing about many of the changes in schools long sought by educational reformers and concerned citizens. In their view, school people are beginning to take advantage of the power of the computer to make significant improvements in the conduct and effectiveness of the school. These optimists cite some of the marvelous features of even today's first-generation micro-computers: video, color, high-resolution graphics, animation, sound, speech synthesis, speed, accuracy, and the capacity to manipulate vast amounts of data. Computers are already beginning to free teachers from the drudgery of repetitive managerial tasks, so they can give their attention to the more personalized aspects of teaching. Further, a growing number of teachers are using the computer as a tool with which children can think and learn in new and exciting ways. Still other teachers are using computers to augment and make more effective their regular curriculum and methods.

This optimistic view sees the current flurry of interest and activity in educational computing as leading eventually to the development of a new generation of computer systems specifically designed for use in schools. Equipped with these new systems, educators would then be able to develop even more effective ways of using computers to accomplish long-standing educational goals and objectives such as improving basic literacy and computational skills, teaching students concepts, promoting student inquiry, individualizing instruction, mainstreaming special needs children, matching teaching and learning styles, and compensating for deficiencies in students' environments. Computers would be used to address the learning needs of students who are physically handicapped, bilingual, learning disabled, mentally retarded, unmotivated, emotionally disturbed, gifted and talented, homebound, chronically absent, delinquent, school phobic, or geographically isolated. This is indeed a bright and hopeful view of what could be done with computers in schools.

But is it realistic? Others in the educational community are far more sceptical about what will happen when computers go to school. They regard the optimistic vision described above as being naive about computers and about schools. They cite grave deficiencies in the current generation of computers — machines that don't work properly and are hard to get serviced; computer programs that won't run on different machines even of the same make; programs that stop working when a user makes even minor input errors such as striking the wrong key on the computer keyboard; the limited number of people who can use a small personal computer at the same time, and the high cost if large numbers of such computers must be purchased; the quickly reached limits of the inexpensive personal computers to handle large amounts of data; and the often unclear, overly technical instruction manuals for computers and their programs. According to the sceptics, if teachers encounter such problems in their early experiences with computers, they will quickly sour on them and remain disenchanted for a long time to come, no matter how much computers are later improved.

As if this were not enough, the sceptics observe that schools and teachers are no more ready for computers than the machines are ready for them. Given the other demands of teaching, most teachers have neither the skill, the time, nor the inclination to develop or modify existing computer materials. When teachers do create their own programs, most of these seem to involve trivial uses of the computer and student materials that are little more than electronic ditto sheets or, at best, video textbooks. The sceptics continue: just as educational television programs used in schools were unable to capture children's attention despite their addiction to T.V., educational computer programs used in schools will be unable to capture their attention despite their love for space invaders computer games. Still worse, some argue that even though the computer is becoming as ubiquitous as the television in our society, many teachers and students seem to regard computers as threatening and alienating. To them the news that "the computers are coming" sounds more like an ominous warning than the announcement of a bright new day.

Most educational computing advocates are unimpressed by the arguments of the sceptics. Some retort simply that if schools are not responsive to the educational potential of computers, the schools will shrivel up and die out as institutions of education in our society. They will be replaced by learning networks of home computers and public information sources.

Most knowledgeable educators, including many computer advocates, find this retort to be both irresponsible and naive. Schools perform too many invaluable functions in our society to be abandoned in favor of home computers and utopian learning networks. They are crucial instruments in the process of developing good citizens and an appropriately trained workforce; they socialize children to become adults and to carry on the cultural traditions of our society; they are custodians of our children while we work; they provide compensatory attention to those who may lack a proper diet, hygiene, medical care, basic literacy skills, or the ability to speak English; they are the primary route to economic success in our society. As long as there are societies, there will need to be schools. While some affluent families now and in the future may supplement their children's learning with home computers, it seems unlikely that even they would wish to deprive their children of the important formative influences experienced in schools.

COMPUTERS WILL AFFECT THE SCHOOLS

Despite sharp disagreements among educators concerning the revolutionary potential of computer use in schools, there would seem to be few who would dispute the assertion that computers will affect schools in some fashion and to some degree. Just as the widespread use of the automobile, the telephone, the airplane and the television changed the face of society and therefore of schooling as well, so too is the increasing computer presence in our society likely to alter, at least indirectly, the nature of schools. These earlier technological innovations created the conditions for the emergence of a country of relatively prosperous suburbanized metropolitan areas and regionalized rural areas, all with architecturally similar schools, an emerging national curriculum, and a kid culture, shaped by the media. Television, in particular, seems to have contributed to creating a student body that many teachers find to be extremely homogeneous, worldly but jaded, relatively passive and uncreative, barely literate, all too often violence prone, and largely unimpressed by the experiences we nonelectronic teachers can offer them.

In light of these past indirect effects of technology on schools, some of us have mixed feelings about the possible fallout the schools may experience as a result of a computerized society.

When we are feeling optimistic, we see:

1. Schools drawn into the large-scale information networks that are almost certain to emerge soon, allowing students and teachers ready access to a quantity and quality of information heretofore too expensive to obtain.
2. Family bonds becoming stronger, as computers allow more people to work at home, leading to less alienated children and greater parent interest in their children's school experiences.
3. The re-emergence of smaller, more local schools, although now through computers, without the resource disadvantages from which small schools once suffered.
4. An end to problems with the basic skills of reading, writing, and arithmetic, as these become unnecessary in the forms we know them and as people master new computer based basic skills by using them in their lives.
5. Computers becoming an antidote to many of the ill effects of television, as their use promotes active, creative, individualized behavior in children.

On the other hand, when we are feeling pessimistic, we see:

1. A further decline in necessary computational skills as computers handle more and more of our daily uses of numbers.
2. More resistance to learning and more truancy from schools which cannot provide the immediate excitement of computer games.
3. More violent behavior in schools as students spend more time killing space invaders in quarter arcades.
4. An erosion of the print-based culture on which schools are based as more time is spent with computers and less with books and magazines.
5. New and greater pressures on schools to provide equal opportunity in a society in which computers are likely to widen the gap between the rich and the poor, the powerful and the powerless.

Unfortunately, there appears to be little we, as educators, can do about such computer fallout in the schools except to prepare ourselves and our students for the possibility of its occurring. One way to do so is to use computers in schools to promote our educational goals in the best way we know. This book has been written with that task in mind. By reading it and engaging in some of the activities we suggest, you should begin to get a sense of the possibilities and the limits of computer use in schools. You will then be ready to decide what, if any, uses you will make of computers in your school.

SOME COMPUTER VOCABULARY
FOR BEGINNERS

Modern civilization (of which computers are an outstanding manifestation) is a naming society. Names, labels, definitions, and distinctions are considered essential for understanding. To start you off on your quest for knowledge and understanding about computers, we will provide below a few simple definitions of computer terminology. Later, in various places in the book (especially in Chapter 3) we will add to your growing vocabulary. All computer terms appear in boldface and are underlined when first introduced and/or explained. They are also defined more formally in the Glossary at the end of the book.

Basically a **computer** is an electronic device that manipulates symbolic information according to a list of precise (and limited) instructions to perform a few very simple operations. A **computer system** is what most people mean when they say "computer." A computer system consists of a computer, additional devices for controlling and communicating with the computer, and adequate lists of instructions for performing some specific assigned task or tasks (such as printing payroll checks or quizzing students). The collection of devices is called **computer hardware** or just **hardware** and in most computer systems includes: some sort of **input** device such as a keyboard that allows the computer user to feed information to the computer, some kind of **output** device such as a video screen by which the computer reports results to the user, and a **peripheral storage device** of some sort such as a regular audio cassette tape recorder/player which is a means of storing small or large amounts of information in a form that can be played back by the computer.

The lists of instructions that are part of a computer system are called **computer software** or just **software**. It is software that transforms the non-specific computer into a specialized teaching machine, paycheck printer, or record keeper. Like curricula, software comes in many shapes and sizes, but it all has in common that it delivers its instructions, called a **program**, electronically rather than through the printed page. These programs are written by people called **programmers**. Educational software is usually accompanied by a range of ancillary materials, including teachers' manuals, ditto sheets, workbooks, and tests. This total package of programs and ancillaries is often called **courseware**.

Programs are written in special languages that have rules analogous to grammar and syntax in spoken and written languages like English or Spanish. However, the rules for most computer languages are much tighter, and the vocabulary is very limited and specialized. For example, to get many computers to obtain a program and follow its instructions, they must be told to **LOAD** the program. That command causes the computer to bring the program into its memory from its peripheral storage device. To cause the computer actually to perform this list of instructions, it must be told to **RUN** the program. As the computer runs through the instructions on the program that has been loaded into its memory, we say that the computer is <u>executing</u> the program (executing here means "performing" not "putting to death"). If you make changes in a program and wish to preserve the new version, you would tell the computer to <u>SAVE</u> the program. This causes the computer to record the current version of the program on its peripheral storage device.

With these few words and their simple definitions you are now ready to enter the subculture of educational computing. Welcome!

A BRIEF TOUR OF THE SUBCULTURE OF EDUCATIONAL COMPUTING

Within the larger culture of schools, there is an emerging subculture of educational computing that is filled with stories of the struggles and accomplishments of its members. Hearing some of these stories may help you to understand better the potential and the limits of computer use in schools. So, before going on to a more systematic and practical discussion of educational computing, we will devote the remainder of this chapter to telling these stories, as they were told to us, adding commentary and raising questions for your consideration after each.

A Tale of Two Teachers

Samantha Tanner is one of those junior high school math teachers who is both respected by her community as a math whiz and loved by even her most "mathophobic" students. Her classes promise humor, an unending series of intriguing puzzles, gentle explanation, and high academic expectations. Her response to students confused by a mathematical concept is to present them with a host of everyday examples until the students relax into understanding. She likes to have her first-time programmers write a flowchart of the operation of making a peanut butter and jelly sandwich.

Richard Allen is an equally beloved math teacher working with Samantha in the same small, advantaged junior high school. He joined the math department after ten years of teaching art to elementary students. He is an irrepressible tinkerer and math ponderer. His classroom is lined with colorful charts, graphs, and illustrations. The shelves are piled high with rods, blocks, old student-made abacuses, and wooden lab balances. Attending his classes is a very active experience, as one must constantly shift in a chair to follow his animated lectures around the perimeter of the room. He never attempts a math explanation without the aid of several colors of chalk at the chalkboard.

The close friendship and complementary teaching styles of Samantha and Richard help create a very successful though small math department. When in 1978, they first introduced computer programming into their curricula, again their partnership led them in two different but mutually supporting paths. Since, over the course of three years, both of them teach math to every junior high school student on an alternating basis, their differences in approach with the same students create an interesting picture, as we shall see in the two brief accounts that follow.

*   *   *   *   *

Jimmy did not particulary like math when he first came to Richard Allen's class in the seventh grade. However, once he started learning how to program the computer he became fascinated with computer graphics images that could be drawn on the screen. Mr. Allen usually assigned problems that read something like, "Make the computer draw a series of six square boxes, each one inside the next. Be sure to sign up for enough computer time!" In previous years, Jimmy would take one pass at a math problem, hand it in to find out whether it was correct, and then, when it was not, he would rethink his logic only under duress. For Mr. Allen's assignments, Jimmy did not need such constant pressure. Drawing boxes inside of boxes is a graphics problem that requires considerable manipulation of numbers, but a student does not need a teacher's input to know whether the solution is correct. The instant feedback on the computer screen encouraged Jimmy to stick with a math problem.

The following year in Ms. Tanner's class, Jimmy was surprised to discover that she viewed graphics enthusiasts as little different from "space invader and tube freaks." Of course, she did appreciate all of Mr. Allen's students' interest in graphics and was ready to work with them on that. However, her assignments read quite differently from Mr. Allen's. A typical example might be "Write a program that draws six boxes, one inside another, starting with the largest box. On Friday, after the program is written we will type it into the computer for a trial run." Ms. Tanner even kidded Mr. Allen in front of students about always having his students work right at the computer. "You don't necessarily do your best programming when you are at a keyboard, Richard. In fact, it can give you some rather bad habits in problem solving." He would jokingly reply that she didn't know what she was missing.

Jimmy attacked Ms. Tanner's problems by pretending that he was the computer as he read through the steps of programs that he wrote out on paper. He could usually tell whether or not one of his programs would work long before he put it on the real computer. But, given a little free time, he still preferred to work with the machine itself.

*   *   *   *   *

Ginny is a hardworking student who has never really had a problem with math, but prefers to spend her free time reading fiction. In Ms. Tanner's computer class she especially enjoyed assignments to write programs relating to her own life. Once she wrote a program that calculated how long her commute to school each day should take, given factors such as route, time of day, weather, and even (for fun) her mood. She had to research each factor's effect, test the resulting program's accuracy, and make proper adjustments. Ms. Tanner was thrilled with Ginny's completed program. Her next assignment for Ginny was to redo the same program keeping two points in mind. First, some of the pieces of the program were considerably longer than they had to be. Ginny should shorten them. Second, a person looking at the written program for the first time would not see clearly how the program was meant to work. Ginny should add thorough remarks to name and explain each section. "Make your programs as elegant and efficient as possible," Ms. Tanner would gently encourage her students. Sometimes she would have students from different classes exchange printed-out programs to see whether or not they could understand without using a computer what someone else's program was meant to do. Only very clearly written programs could survive that test.

Later, when Ginny took math with Mr. Allen, she was pleased to see that he loved her well-documented, elegantly structured programs. (He noticed all of those good problem-solving habits that Samantha had told him about!) Since Ginny was already quite skilled on the computer, Mr. Allen gave her a relatively sophisticated problem to solve using the computer. At first she balked, not knowing how to get started. She was amazed to hear him tell her just to start anywhere, to "mess about" until she had a feel for some of the difficulties involved. "But what if I start doing it some ridiculously long way?" she asked him.

"Two things," he replied, "One, you can polish it up later if you like and, two, who cares if it's a little long? Look, the computer is your servant — it's here to dance for you, not vice versa. This machine has plenty of storage capacity, so just get started without a lot of fretting about the perfect program. Don't worry if your program is a little inefficient. Have some fun with it."

"Oh, Richard," Samantha would taunt, "How can you provide such a sloppy model to your young programmers?" In fact, she knew that he worked miracles with most of his students.

"Samantha," he would answer, "What about letting your young programmers do a little unstructured exploring in mathland? They'll find things that we didn't even know were there." In fact he knew that many of her students were discovering new things on computers all the time.

If computers are to be used successfully in schools, it will be up to imaginative, energetic teachers like Richard Allen and Samantha Tanner to use them well. They will have to know as much about computers as a good French teacher must know about French language, culture, and history, and they will have to "speak the language." Schools considering the creation of a significant computer facility must enlist such teachers from the start, taking careful note of their intuitions, their imaginations, and their cautions.

But how typical of teachers are Samantha Tanner and Richard Allen? For that matter, how typical is their small, advantaged junior high and their eager young students, Jimmy and Ginny? This story may bear little resemblance to the classrooms that many of us have known. Is it possible to be a Samantha or a Richard if you must manage a class of thirty or more restless preadolescents while teaching them a prescribed curriculum with outdated and boring materials? When we hear stories about successful uses of computers in schools, what kinds of schools are these? Are they only wealthy suburban or private schools, or do they include poorer urban or rural public schools as well?

These questions must be addressed by those who are promoting computer use in education, as well as those who are considering it.

A Story About a Teacher and Her Machines

Denton Day School had been given several thousand dollars by a group of parents who felt that the school should enter the computer age by offering courses in computer programming. The principal, delighted with the gift and intimidated by the subject, gave full responsibility to Jean Munroe, the elementary math teacher. Since she had taken a course in computer programming recently, he asked her to buy the computers and to put together a good little programming course for the fifth graders.

The four-color promotional brochures from each of the major micro-computer companies all claimed their machines were "easy to use," "reliable," and "educationally sound." The manufacturer of the computer Jean chose promised a powerful library of educational software and a wealth of teacher understanding. The retail store, the Computer Factory, promised prompt delivery and continuous support.

When the computers first arrived, Jean was so delighted she came in to school on Saturday morning to see her "new toys." She could hardly wait to type in her first program, which would write the name of the school across the computer screen in big letters. The sixteen cardboard cartons, some of them marked "COMPUTER" were all surprisingly light, a fact that always strikes first time personal computer users. In all, Jean was expecting four computers to be delivered. She opened one of the larger boxes to find a familiar-looking keyboard. The accompanying book of instructions congratulated her on her choice, and then proceeded to give explicit directions and warnings concerning assembling it.

"DO NOT CONNECT MONITOR/CPU CABLE OR INSTALL DISK DRIVER CARD WHILE POWER IS ON." Where, suddenly, was the wealth of teacher understanding? Jean couldn't understand a word of the directions. There was no way that she was going to install any mysterious thing called a disk driver card into a CPU, whatever that was. "IF THE SERIAL NUMBER ON YOUR CPU DOES NOT END WITH A "1," USE THE 32 PIN CONNECTOR PROVIDED."

A telephone call, more anxious than angry, to the Computer Factory produced speedy results. A woman named Diane arrived after lunch, and, to Jean, she seemed to know an unbelievable amount about personal computers. Taking about forty-five minutes per computer, she soon had three of the four machines up and running (one of the keyboards had to spend some time back at the Computer Factory to be adjusted). During this time Jean heard Diane mumbling mysterious phrases such as, "Oh, of course! The 2.4 DOS only does a cold boot if you press RESET with a control key." Jean wondered how much of this she would have to know.

After Diane left, Jean remembered that she had bought a little treat for herself — a computer Adventure Game for her cassette based computers from a company in Minnesota. Alone at last with her computers, she read the loading instructions for the cassette on which the game was stored.

"INSERT CASSETTE IN RECORDER AND REWIND FULLY . . ."

That she understood.

"WHEN PROMPTED BY THE COMPUTER, TYPE IN THE MEM NUMBER PRINTED ON THE CASSETTE LABEL. (IF NUMBER ON LABEL DOES NOT MATCH NUMBER PRINTED AT TOP OF INSTRUCTIONS, CONVERT TO HEX AND ENTER.)"

Of course the number on the label did not match, and incidently, nobody at the Computer Factory knew immediately how to "convert to hex," but they said they would call back. Jean telephoned the software company in Minnesota who sold the game, but they didn't answer.

Nevertheless, within two weeks, groups of fifth graders were regularly found sitting at the four machines, learning to program. Jean had managed to grasp the essential syntax and idiosyncracies of this particular computer. She could make it store student programs or her own demonstration programs. She could make it print out a student's program on a small printer. That took two trips to the store — one to buy the printer and one to exchange the connecting cable for a slightly different model since, of course, the serial number on her CPU did not end with a "1."

Plugging the cable into the computer required removing a cover from the back of the keyboard. Jean hated to admit to herself that she was apprehensive about touching the computer's inner parts, but her caution prevailed, and Diane came to Jean's rescue again.

In June, Jean announced that because of an unexpected opportunity to teach abroad, she would be leaving the Denton School. This was a difficult decision to make since over the past three months she had enjoyed the growing admiration of her colleagues. Privately, she was concerned that her reputation as "the computer person" on campus was undeserved. There was so much that she had yet to learn about computers. She still did not know what "convert to hex" meant. But her school was extremely grateful to her because the students were learning to program and were enjoying themselves in the process. Parents and teachers alike felt that Denton's first year with computers had been a success.

The computers were stored in the walk-in closet for the summer. Jean had, of course, left a copy of her basic computer programming curriculum for the teacher who would take her place next year. She also left reassembly instructions taped to the boxes in the closet. They were simple. "Call the Computer Factory."

We may wonder whether Denton Day School's computers will ever emerge from the closet again. How many teachers would have Jean Munroe's programming training or her patience with the idiosyncracies of the machines? Where could Denton Day find a replacement who would also have the necessary dedication and expertise to run the programming courses? For how long will the Computer Factory respond to anguished calls for help? In some ways, Denton Day's first year experience with computers was a very lucky one. Other schools have encountered many more difficulties with equipment and servicing.

By the early eighties over 50 percent of American schools had provided their students with access to computers in classrooms and resource rooms. There were between a quarter of a million and half a million microcomputers in schools. Parents, computer stores, and teachers like Jean Munroe helped numerous schools develop enthusiasm for computers and engendered the notion that schools are ready for this new technology. But are the computers themselves ready for the school environment?

Despite the promotional claims of manufacturers, it is doubtful that many computers can yet be considered a comfortable tool for the average classroom. It is difficult to imagine most teachers or students coping with systems that arrive needing to be assembled, masses of wire connections, delicate components, instructions written for experts, finicky cassettes, or machines that won't accept programs developed on earlier versions of the same machine. Willing and enthusiastic teachers appear ready to invite computers into their schools. However, unless computer manufacturers become sensitive to the special demands that school use places on equipment, those same machines may soon find their way into closets.

The State of the Art and the Art of the Possible

As a chemistry teacher in a large urban high school, Karen Hardy had always loved the lab on fractional distillation. The first time she taught it eleven years ago, Karen did precisely what the chemistry lab manual prescribed. Everything had worked well. She enjoyed watching her students make the clear, predictable connections derived from the data. Each year since, she had improved on the experiment in small but important ways. She changed the paired partners into larger groups. She created a special bulletin board format for better display of their results. But her ultimate enhancement of this favorite lab came a few months after the science department bought a microcomputer.

In the first month with the computer, Karen learned enough about programming to write a simple educational game in which students used clues to fill the elements into a periodic table. All five of her chemistry classes enjoyed running through the game a few times, but Karen had little interest in applying this game to other topics in the curriculum.

One morning between class periods as Karen was tinkering with the computer, she had an inspiration. She would create a program to assist her in the teaching of the distillation lab. Her enthusiasm increased as she began to realize that the computer would allow her to set up an exciting learning environment that, in the past, would have been too complex to manage. Now the computer would tend to the repetitive details.

As has happened with many a computer buff, Karen sat at the computer for hours at a time, often late into the night, working on the project. Her programming was not elegantly structured, but it did the job. She enlisted her students to test each successive version of the program. When she was satisfied with her new program's performance, Karen turned to her other teaching methods to complete the package she was developing. She designed ditto worksheets, wall charts, and even wrote some fiction to further motivate students' interest in the experiment/program.

When completed, her computer-assisted lab worked superbly with a class of twenty eager chemistry students, seated at five prearranged lab tables. A message on the computer screen at the front of the room instructed each of the five groups to begin setting up their beakers and solutions as described in the workbook, and to proceed with part one of the experiment. Soon, someone noticed that the screen had a new message requesting several kinds of data from any table/group that had finished part one of the lab. Eager to see what the computer had in mind, the lab groups in turn entered their information into the machine, which then instructed each group to proceed with part two of the lab. When all five groups were working on part two, the computer beeped three times. Five color graphs, derived from the class's data for part one, appeared on the screen. Students ran to the computer to look for their graphs, then to compare them with the other groups' graphs.

This process continued throughout the lab. Sometimes when the computer beeped, it was calling for just one specific group. It might have told them their most recent data had values twice those of any other group, or that their group and another group had very similar or very different data. Before each group started the last part of the lab, the computer requested that each group enter specific data predictions for what would happen. The computer was staging a little contest.

The students loved this approach. They asked if the computer could help on more of their chemistry labs. Right away, Karen Hardy started thinking about the experiments on changes of state that were coming up next. Maybe the computer could simulate changes of state for various compounds where each group would . . . .

*   *   *   *   *

Donald Riggs was excited that his high school tutoring program had finally been given the money to buy two computer word processing systems. He knew that the freedom to type words into a computer would be a great incentive for his students with severe handwriting problems. Also, the ability to add words, to erase words, to flip words around on the screen would encourage all kids to be more experimental with their writing.

The word processors in Donald's tutoring department lived up to his expectations. And despite the predictions of a few sceptical teachers, the students' appreciation of the machines did not appear to be based solely on electronic fascination. They were writing more and enjoying it more. But Donald was worried about Raymond, a tenth grader bursting with literary ideas, eager to commit them to paper, and quite incapable of proceeding further.

The word processor did help enormously with Raymond's old tendency to quit when the frustrations of handwriting overcame him.

Suddenly relieved of that great physical burden, he started to compose great volumes of prose. But his letter reversing and syllable omissions were as bad as ever, and eventually his discouragement returned. Donald suspected that the computer was capable of doing more for Raymond than simple word processing.

Here was as good an excuse as any for Donald to teach himself to program. He bought a programming guide for children. He was comforted by the low-key style and by the pictures of little computers with arms and legs running over the keyboard, telling him about the ENTER button. He discovered that a very good way to learn programming was to have a definite and important project in mind from the start, a project such as the revised word processor for Raymond. At all hours of the night he would telephone friends to ask computer questions, and he gladly accepted suggestions from student programmers. It seemed to Donald that every time he learned a new computer command, he would have a new idea for Raymond's program.

Approximately three months from the beginning of his programming career, Donald's first educational system was up and running. The time had come for the acid test. Raymond entered the tutoring room, as usual, at 10 a.m., and proceeded to load the standard word processing program into the computer. Donald interrupted him, saying, "Wait a minute, Raymond, I want to try something a little bit different today. I have a new program called . . . SMART-WRITER, and I'd like you to give it a try."

Donald sat at the keyboard and told Raymond to dictate something to him — anything — a story, a letter, a joke, anything. Raymond thought for just a moment and announced that he would dictate a humorous letter to be sent to the school paper. "Dear Sir," he began, "It has recently come to my attention that . . . that nobody wears leather shoes these days. Find me a student without sneakers and you've found a member of an ever-increasing minority. . . . "

Donald typed in Raymond's dictation and then suddenly stood up from the keyboard and motioned to Raymond to sit there. "Type your name and then push the RETURN button," Donald instructed. Raymond did so, and the screen immediately went blank. Then it wrote out the line,*

Dear Sir, It has recently come
NOW, RAYMOND, IT'S YOUR TURN TO TYPE IN THAT LINE.

Note: In the example above and throughout the book, wherever a program is presented as it would appear on a computer terminal being used, the user's input will appear in bold type, while the computer's output will appear in regular type.

Then the screen went blank again. Raymond looked up at his teacher who shrugged his shoulders saying he'd be just down the hall. Raymond looked back at the screen which now read:

HERE, LET'S HAVE ANOTHER LOOK AT THAT LINE. . . .
Dear Sir, It has recently come

Then the screen went blank. Raymond started to type in the line:

Daer

The computer beeped once and the screen said:

OOPS! YOU MISSPELLED THE FIRST WORD. LET'S LOOK AGAIN.
Dear Sir, It has recently come

Raymond smiled when he realized that there was no one around to make him feel embarrassed about the mistake. When the screen went blank he tried again, this time misspelling "recently." On his third try he typed the line correctly and the computer said:

NICE GOING. NOW TRY THIS LINE.
to my attention that nobody wears

When Raymond had correctly typed the entire short letter, the computer congratulated him and asked if he wanted the printer to make a copy for him. He typed that he did. And there it was — a letter that he had composed, perfectly typed with no spelling mistakes, and he had done it all on his own. When Donald returned to the tutoring room Raymond was ready for his next letter. Donald had been thinking to himself that there was probably a way to make different kinds of word processors for different kinds of student language problems. He was on the verge of jotting down a few ideas when Raymond started dictating his next letter. "To whom it may concern . . . ."

Many teachers like Karen Hardy and Donald Riggs are not waiting for someone else to supply new, effective ways of using computers in schools. They are creating their own computer curricula. And their ideas often address classroom management issues and student learning problems with a sensitivity missing in most commercially prepared materials. Teacher approaches tend to deal creatively with problems such as limited computer availability or servicing a large class with only one computer. Teachers know better than anyone how to gently integrate new technology into a cautious, structured educational environment. At the same time, is it realistic to expect teachers, in general, to be responsible for the demanding and time-consuming task of creating computer programs for our schools? And, if not the teachers, then who will create appropriate, high quality software? Thus far, few software publishers have managed to provide it. Yet, without it, educational computing seems almost bound to fail.

We leave the educational computing subculture now to begin a systematic inquiry into the nature of educational computing. Throughout the book we will return to the issues that have been raised in this chapter, and we will confront them head on in the final chapter, "Issues and Choices in Educational Computing."

Photo: Texas Instruments, Inc.

The Computer in the Classroom

Chapter 2

The computer is a jack-of-all-trades. It can be a workbook page or a science laboratory, a teaching machine or a personal tutor, a four-dimensional model or a fantasy world to be explored. It can compute grades for an entire class and generate reports that analyze the progress of every student in that class. It can teach and be taught. It is, indeed, a tireless servant at the command of the teacher who wishes to use it.

The computer can also be a horror. A printed workbook is always there to rely upon. If the lab experiment goes wrong, there is usually a way of figuring out why. A teacher can put grades and written reports in a locked file. A human tutor can respond sensitively to student learning problems. No such certainties yet exist with computer use.

The single guarantee is that a computer always interacts with its user. Regardless of what is done to it, it responds: either it does what is expected, or it gives back a message that says it can't do it, or it stops dead in its tracks.

In seeking to maximize this interactive capability of computers in schools, educators confront a challenge, not only to their capacity to use computers, but also to their use of more traditional instructional materials. To begin with, uses of computers in schools defy the usual labels educators like to apply to classify and codify their world. The situation is a bit like the old story of the six blind men who each, touching a different part of an elephant, believed it to be a different thing: a rope, a spear, a blanket, a snake, a tree, and a wall. To some educators, computers are instructional aids, like movie projectors or blackboards, and their programs are teaching materials and methods, like workbook drills or demonstrations. To other educators, computers are objects to think and learn with, like cuisenaire rods or terrariums. To others, computer operation is a skill to be learned, like typing or reading. Others see knowledge of computers and their operation as the content of instruction, like biology or history. Still others still see computers as part of the cultural landscape to be appreciated and understood, like art or music. Some educators, particularly administrators, see computers as parts of educational management systems, like files or grade books. And still others see computers as unlike anything currently used in schools, yet rich in their potential for students to learn in totally new ways.

The computer is really all of these things and probably more. In Chapter 1, we suggested that at its most fundamental level a computer was an electronic device that could perform a few very simple operations. Beyond these basic operations, the nature of computers has been defined and redefined continuously by the myriad applications people have developed for them. In this chapter we will explore the current range of such applications in classrooms, mentioning in passing some non-classroom administrative uses of computers as well. This discussion cannot be comprehensive or the last word since new computer applications and new notions of what a computer can be in an educational setting are emerging every day.

To facilitate the discussion of how computers may be used in schools, and because as educators we do like to classify the inhabitants of our world, we have sorted the many educational uses of computers into five major categories: computer assisted instruction, instructional/learning tools, computer managed instruction, programming, and computer literacy. We will discuss each of these, in turn, citing many examples to give you a glimpse of their possibilities and their limits. This particular division of educational computer applications is our own. There are, as yet, no agreed-upon classification schemes in the educational computing world, although some clever and even poetic labels have been suggested, such as Robert Taylor's "tutor, tool, tutee" and variations on this theme by others to include "toy" and "toolmaker." Other more systematic schemes have also been proposed, such as Northwest Regional Educational Laboratory's "computer as: instructor, laboratory, calculator, object of instruction, and instructor's aide."

Before launching into our discussion of classroom computer applications, we offer one word of caution: it is quite important to distinguish between the potential applications of computers and the manner in which teachers use them. Just as chalkboards, textbooks, typewriters, and cuisinaire rods may be used in many types of school settings, and just as facts, concepts, and skills may be treated in many different ways, ranging from traditional teacher-centered large group instruction to more "open" child-centered individual inquiry, so too may the computer be used in a variety of settings and treated in a variety of ways governed by differing educational philosophies. Because we believe that no computer application should be considered the exclusive domain of a particular teaching philosophy, we will cite a range of settings in which teachers can use computers in various ways. On the other hand, because we also feel that some computer applications are more appropriate in certain settings than in others, we will highlight these uses in our examples.

COMPUTER ASSISTED INSTRUCTION

Computer Assisted Instruction, known in the educational computing world as CAI, represents probably the largest single category of computer use in the field of education. In schools, in the military, in the business sector, and in other institutions with educative goals, those considering a role for computers in their efforts most often see them as instructional aids, facilitating the attainment of existing educational goals via more or less traditional educational methods. In schools, this view most often results in computers being used as teaching machines or versatile audiovisual devices to teach students facts, skills, or concepts in the regular school curriculum. Occasionally, CAI may employ less traditional methods, such as simulations or instructional games, but for the most part the basic CAI diet consists of drill and practice, tutorials, and demonstrations. Computer applications in each of these five methods of instruction are discussed below.

Drill and Practice

Drill and practice programs are probably the most common, best known, and most disparaged educational application of computers. Such programs are used for exactly the purpose implied in their name. Teachers assign students to use them for drill and practice in performing particular sets of discrete skills in math, reading, spelling, or other basic skills areas. They are criticized by many educators for being narrow in their pedagogy (stimulus-response), unnecessarily boring, and even at times for reinforcing incorrect learning.

Defenders of drill and practice acknowledge that some programs have been poorly designed, particularly those written by educators with poor programming skills or by programmers with little or no understanding of how children learn or even of the skills being presented. But they insist that drill and practice can be extremely effective if applied imaginatively to take full advantage of the capabilities of the computer. In this view, computers can take the drudgery out of routine and inherently boring activities such as practicing skills.

When a student starts a drill and practice program, the computer usually asks where he or she would like to begin in the skills sequence. In some programs, the computer already has a record of the student's most recently achieved level of skill mastery, so it automatically starts the student reviewing that level or beginning on the next. In some programs, the teacher chooses the level at which the student enters the program. Let us look at the interaction between computer and student in a typical drill and practice program, starting with the computer's request for information.

HOW MANY PROBLEMS DO YOU WANT TO DO?

10, 15 or 20?

15

WHAT LEVEL DO YOU WANT—DIFFICULT, AVERAGE, EASY?

AVERAGE

The computer then presents problem sets, either one problem at a time or a column of problems, as in a workbook. The student types in his or her response to the first problem. The computer checks the response and immediately informs the student if he or she has gotten the correct answer. In this way, students do not go on to the next problem practicing incorrect processes. If the answer is right, the computer presents the next problem. If the answer is wrong, the computer generally directs the student to try again. If the student types in the wrong answer repeatedly, the program may instruct him or her to seek help.

6 x 5

30

RIGHT! 9 x 6

56

NO. TRY AGAIN. 9 X 6

54

VERY GOOD. 3 x 8

26

NO. TRY AGAIN. 3 x 8

23

YOU SEEM TO BE HAVING TROUBLE WITH THESE PROBLEMS.

ASK YOUR TEACHER FOR SOME HELP.

In some drill and practice programs, when a student misses a particular type of problem repeatedly, the computer may provide a brief explanation of how to do problems of that sort.

```
LETS REVIEW SOME OF OUR MULTIPLICATION FACTS
6 x 2 = 12     6 x 3 = 18     6 x 4 = 24     6 x 5 = ?
30
RIGHT. 6 x 6  = 36     6 x 7 = 42     6 x 8 = ?
48
```

A pedagogically and technically more sophisticated drill and practice program might use the graphics capabilities of the computer to present the student with an alternative method of approaching the problem, as follows:

```
HOW MANY ROWS OF BOXES DO YOU COUNT?
3
RIGHT. HOW MANY COLUMNS OF BOXES ARE THERE?
8
RIGHT. HOW MANY BOXES ARE THERE?
24
RIGHT. HOW MUCH IS 3 X 8?
24
RIGHT. 8 X 3?
24
VERY GOOD. NOW LET'S RETURN TO THE PROBLEMS
THAT GAVE YOU TROUBLE.
```

When the student has completed a problem set successfully, some programs will summarize the student's performance. Others simply inform the student that he or she has finished the set and ask if he or she wants to go on to the next set.

YOU HAVE FINISHED THIS SET OF MULTIPLICATION PROBLEMS.
WOULD YOU LIKE TO SEE HOW WELL YOU DID?
YES
YOU GOT 6 OUT OF 10 PROBLEMS RIGHT ON THE FIRST TRY.
YOU STILL NEED MORE PRACTICE ON THIS KIND OF PROBLEM.
WOULD YOU LIKE TO TRY ANOTHER SET OF MULTIPLICATION
PROBLEMS?
NO
OK. BYE.

Even though such drill exercises can be dull, various computer capabilities can increase their effectiveness significantly. As suggested, providing instant feedback so that students do not practice incorrect processing adds value. Another important feature of many such programs is that they encourage students who have mastered a skill to go on to the next set of problems, thereby removing some of the tedium associated with doing set after set of already mastered materials, as so often happens with workbooks. Some programs that run on computers with a lot of storage capacity even send students automatically to other problem sets based on their progress or difficulty with a given set. Such features allow students to spend their drill time more effectively and more efficiently.

There are also features that may be added that allow teachers to use their time better. Some drill and practice programs have built into them a management system that allows the computer to keep track of the progress of a whole class of students through the practice sets. At the end of a day, a teacher then has available a report that can be used to place students for small group instruction on the following day.

Finally, when graphics, sound, and animation are added to routine drill and practice exercises, there is little question that they become more appealing to students. However, bells, whistles, or elaborate graphics of a little animal jumping up and down saying "good" can also become distracting and diminish the effectiveness of the lesson.

Proponents of drill and practice suggest that even extremely simple versions of such programs, perhaps teacher designed, can provide useful educational experiences for students. In this view, ten minutes a day reviewing and practicing basic skills with a patient drillmaster that says an answer is right or wrong and moves on to the next question may contribute considerably to increasing student achievement in such skills. Other educators challenge such claims and ask whether such use of limited computer resources should be a priority. There is no consensus on this issue in the educational computing community.

Although there is a temptation to do so, drill and practice programs should not be associated exclusively with traditional teacher-centered classrooms. Just as more child-centered classrooms often feature workbooks in the "math center" in which students may practice their skills at their own pace when they elect to do so, so too may drill and practice programs be available to students to be similarly used.

On the other hand, there is probably cause for concern when drill and practice is used to substitute for primary instruction by the teacher. In the first place, none of these programs is sophisticated enough to instruct students as well as most teachers. Their basic pedagogy is limited to repetitive drill. But, more importantly, extensive use of such programs in the place of human interaction is bound to become extremely boring to students and may turn them off to all educational computing. This is partly what happened with school use of television in the sixties and seventies. Many students were required to attend closed circuit live or prerecorded video lectures that were poorly produced and difficult to watch on small, often distant classroom monitors. Some of these students then associated these boring presentations with any school use of T.V., so that later more sophisticated uses of television were never given a chance to engage their interest.

One last comment about potential uses of drill and practice programs may be intriguing. As the computer culture spreads in a school, many students become fascinated with figuring out how programs work and may even learn to modify them for some given purpose. Teacher-designed drill and practice programs, particularly poorly constructed ones, may provide exciting challenges to such student inquiry. When was the last time you saw a student working to rewrite a workbook?

Tutorial

As the name implies, in a tutorial the computer instructs the student in some area of knowledge in somewhat the same way a teacher would in a one-on-one situation. There are crucial differences, of course. The computer is not human. It is a machine that has been programmed to carry out the instruction in a humanoid but severely limited fashion. Most tutorial programs resemble Socratic dialogues in which the computer presents some information about which it then asks a series of questions, each with a fairly limited range of possible responses. The student types in a response that the tutorial program has prepared the computer to anticipate. Depending upon the nature of the response, the computer provides more information and asks further questions.

HI! TODAY WE'RE GOING TO INVESTIGATE THE CONCEPT OF DENSITY. LOOK AT THE TWO GLASSES PICTURED BELOW. NOTICE THAT EACH CONTAINS A LIQUID.

OBSERVE WHAT HAPPENS WHEN WE DROP AN ICE CUBE IN EACH GLASS.

WHAT DID YOU SEE HAPPEN?

ONE FLOATED. ONE SANK.

O.K. WHY DO YOU THINK THAT MIGHT HAVE HAPPENED?

ONE CUBE WAS HEAVIER THAN THE OTHER.

IF WE PUT TWO PIECES OF WOOD IN THE WATER AND ONE WAS
HEAVIER AND THE OTHER LIGHTER WOULD ONE SINK AND ONE
FLOAT?

I THINK SO

WELL, LET'S SEE. THE BLOCK ON THE LEFT WEIGHS 1
POUND AND THE ONE ON THE RIGHT WEIGHS 1/4 POUND.

WHAT HAPPENED?

THEY BOTH FLOATED.

WHY?

THEY WERE BOTH LIGHTER THAN WATER.

AHA! NOW WE'RE GETTING SOMEWHERE.

This is a pretty sophisticated tutorial, containing moving graphics (sinking and floating objects), as well as a provision for recognizing responses as tentative as "I think so" and as complex as "They were both lighter than water." Nevertheless, such sophistication is possible both in terms of computer technology and pedagogy.

Of course, the programmer has to anticipate most of the potential responses that the student might make in order to create a meaningful dialogue. This is extremely difficult to do, requires more space than is available in most small

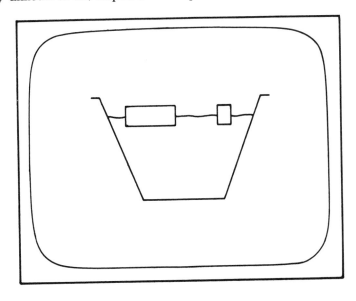

computer programs, and takes a lot of field testing to make sure that appropriate free responses have been anticipated. For this reason, most dialogues are much more highly constrained than in this example and most questions to the student are in a multiple choice format. Nevertheless, there have been some impressive tutorials originally designed on large computers, primarily for college-level use, but now available on smaller computers as well, such as those developed by Alfred Bork at the Educational Technology Center of the University of California at Irvine.

As might be expected, critics of drill and practice are also often critics of tutorials. Again, the charge is "limited and limiting pedagogy" ("Guess what's on teacher's mind?"), but added to this criticism is a concern about trivializing important concepts. The argument is that the limits of the computer's "intelligence" force the program designers to channel students into a narrow range of possible responses that keep them from exploring the complexities of the concept.

Tutorial enthusiasts respond that this is the case only if computer tutorials are the sole mode of instruction employed in teaching a given concept. They are quick to point out that the same criticism might be leveled at such time-honored instructional methods as the lecture, the textbook, and the demonstration. It would appear again that the real danger in using tutorials lies in using them inappropriately, not in using them at all. Even tutorials that are more con-strained than the one described above may be very useful in introducing or reviewing a topic. They may be just the thing to assign a student who has missed a key lesson on a topic and needs to catch up quickly. Under certain circum-stances some tutorials may even teach a concept better than the teacher. After all, with a tutorial students may enjoy a one-to-one student-"teacher" ratio, they may proceed at their own rate, and they get the opportunity to respond to every "teacher" query, not just the one or two per lesson that depend upon the teacher calling on them at the right moment. Nevertheless, as with drill and practice, educators must ask themselves about the value of allocating limited computer resources to applications that do nothing that a teacher can't do as well or better.

Demonstration

Demonstrations are one of the main features of a traditional teaching repertoire in such subjects as science and math. Yet, all but the simplest ones require a good deal of teacher preparation or an expensive kit, and they are still notorious for not working just when they are needed. Using a computer can raise demonstrations to undreamt heights of sophistication, and at the same time make them failproof and easy enough to use to be appealing to even the most disaster-prone science-shy elementary school teacher.

Utilizing the color, graphics, and sound potential of most small computers, software manufacturers are rapidly developing demonstration packages that will soon make the overhead projector as obsolete as electronic calculators made the slide rule. Imagine a computer program to demonstrate the relationship between the variables associated with a sine curve. The teacher or student can manipulate any one variable, say amplitude, and watch the effect on the other variables in a visual representation of the curve. No more need for different colors of chalk to indicate changes in shape. No more constant erasing of old curves and redrawing of new ones, misshapen at best. No more piles of transparency overlays. Just type a key and a new curve appears. Hit another key and the old one disappears. If you want to display several curves simultaneously in different colors, a couple of key strokes more and you've got it.

Think of the possibilities: Demonstrations of planetary motion; atomic structure; the circulatory system; the relationship between distance, velocity, and acceleration; geological processes; genetic relationships; balancing chemical equations; the area under a curve in calculus; ocean currents; the food chain; and on and on.

And, of course, demonstrations now take on the added dimension that students can use them without a teacher's intervention, if so desired. Computer demonstrations have a much richer potential to be interactive than chalkboard or overhead projector demonstrations. Variables are more easily manipulated. Effects are instantaneous. The graphics are clearer than chalk marks and the working surface cleaner than a board full of erasures.

However, let's not get carried away. Elaborate graphics and a high degree of interaction require sophisticated and time-consuming programming, so that most such demonstration packages are beyond the capacity of teachers to create and are fairly expensive to buy. As a result, most demonstrations may be much more modest than the examples we just imagined. Some are preprogrammed to run through a sequence without intervention, much like a filmstrip accompanied by a tape containing both narration and electronic signals advancing the strip. Some lack color, sound, or moving graphics, thus closely resembling black and white overhead transparencies. And some are little more than illustrated tutorials.

Nevertheless, computer demonstrations, even the more modest ones, can be used effectively by teachers in a variety of educational situations. They are probably most appropriate as an aid to the teacher in the primary instruction of students and as an aid to students when they review material.

One important characteristic of demonstration programs, as well as drill and practice and tutorial programs, is that with some programming experience teachers can create their own very simple versions of such programs. That is probably not true for the next two types of CAI to be discussed, simulation and instructional games.

The potential of teacher-created or teacher-modified programs adds a whole new dimension to a computer environment. Not only can teachers tailor programs to the needs of their students, but by example they may encourage students to create their own programs! Thus, even these traditional approaches to instruction—drill and practice, tutorial, and demonstration—when implemented via computer can promote unusually advanced and innovative learning experiences for students, such as creating educational computer programs for themselves and their classmates. However, teachers considering the design of their own programs or having students design programs themselves should be prepared to spend many hours of their own time and computer time. Again, educators with limited computer resources need to ask themselves about priorities.

Simulation

A simulation model imitates a real or imaginary system based on the modeler's theory of the operation of that system. One of the original uses of computers in the military and government was to simulate a particular environment and then test the effects of various interventions on that environment. Such simulations required large sophisticated computers. Meanwhile, in schools and homes, simplified simulations have been enjoyed for years in board games such as "Monopoly," "Diplomacy," "Ghetto," and "Life." Now even small computers have the capacity to simulate reasonably complex systems. They can be programmed in advance to respond to certain inputs in predictably "realistic" ways, and they can process large amounts of data. As a result, educational computer simulations are able to incorporate greater complexity, and hence realism, than is possible with board games. For example, in a simulation of life after high school, a computer can generate a future scenario for a "player" who has made certain life choices, such as getting married or getting a job, based on actual population statistics for persons having made similar decisions in real life.

Popular, commercially available computer simulations include models of the Three Mile Island nuclear reactor, the human circulatory system, the running of a lemonade stand, and the ecosystem of a lake. (See the Bibliography for articles about other computer simulations.) Since reality is not fully represented by any model, simulations focus students' attention on certain aspects of the real-life process under investigation. Students then test their hypotheses about problems in the simulated environment by manipulating variables to see how behavior changes in the model under various circumstances.

At times, there may be a fine line between computer simulations and computer demonstrations, on the one hand, and computer simulations and popular computerized fantasy games on the other. However, such distinctions do not seem very important. For example, it is probably the case that many fantasy games can be as instructive as simulations explicitly designed for educational purposes, since the real power of simulation seems to derive from the advanced thinking and problem-solving skills required, not from the mastery of content. Good simulations aid in developing those high-level skills as the students interact with the model. Well-designed computer simulations combine graphics, animation, text, and a realistic problem to solve in a rich learning environment that is varied each time the student returns to it.

The utility and quality of a simulation depend upon several elements. The designer has to limit the complexity of the model to allow students to manipulate variables in manageable contexts. However, if the simulation model is not accurate or becomes oversimplified, it loses both its descriptive and its explanatory powers. The design and programming of good computer simulations is very difficult. It is probably not within the reach of most classroom teachers to create their own. In fact, to date many commercially developed computer simulations for elementary and secondary schools leave much to be desired. However, many excellent computer simulations have been developed for use in higher education, and we anticipate that adaptations of these programs will soon trickle down to the schools.

Computer simulations can be used in many classroom situations to promote a range of educational goals, from mastery of skills, to learning content, to concept development, to promoting inquiry, to motivating student interest in the subject. In science, the computer can simulate experiments and natural systems. In social studies, simulations can explore cause and effect relationships, develop strategic thinking, and examine interactively social, political, and economic systems. In mathematics, simulations can promote an understanding of self-contained axiomatic systems. Simulations may be interdisciplinary, such as simulations of business environments, societies, and natural environments.

Using a computer to simulate a chemistry laboratory can add value to a course of study while reducing cost and inconvenience. Students can "mix" reagents quickly and easily and can analyze results that "occur" immediately. This saves money in terms of chemical supplies as well as time waiting for results. The frustration resulting from errors in lab procedures or measurement is entirely eliminated. Complex multiple hypotheses can be tested easily. Of course, by "heating" a test tube on the computer, a student doesn't learn how to use real equipment like Bunsen burners. But, after all, simulations are intended to reinforce and extend the lab experience, not to replace it. If educators mistakenly use computers in place of lab work, students will lose an important learning experience.

Simulations can also be powerful learning tools in studying events that could not be otherwise examined owing to danger, expense, or lack of time. For example, a series of simulations on ecological systems allows students to "pollute" various environments and then watch the effects of this pollution on plant and animal life. In a number of simulations in genetics, students can "watch" fruit flies, people, and plants proliferate, exhibiting latent traits, mutations, and dominant gene characteristics, all according to probability formulas. In another dramatic simulation, students cause nuclear explosions and calculate the half-life of the radioactive fallout.

In most science simulations, the major processes under investigation have precise operating rules so that learning how to succeed in the simulation means understanding and mastering both the content and the rules. Unfortunately, the limitations of the computer also restrict most nonscience simulations to precise rules and predetermined outcomes, despite the fact that reality isn't often like that.

Many social studies simulations recreate actual historical events, but also include fictionalized content to personalize these events for the students. For example, one simulation follows American settlers going west. Only limited resources are available and certain dangers exist along the way. Hostile forces attack. Food runs out. But the ways that the events occur to the individuals playing the roles in the simulation do not replicate any particular real expedition. Nor is learning based on mastering a certain content or even a particular model. Rather, students are intended to absorb a more general sense of what exploration and survival were like within a particular historical setting.

In using simulations, it is important that the model represent, as accurately as possible, the reality being simulated. For example, if a science experiment is simulated, the results should be the same as they would be if an actual experiment were run. Students should be taught to question and explore the validity of models through more traditional research methods such as reading or experimenting. They should also recognize the difference between a simulation that is used to explicate aspects of reality and reality itself. The assumptions used in creating a model should always be clarified when debriefing the simulation, so that students understand why the model reacted in the ways it did.

Simulations are the most unconventional teaching method we have discussed so far. Drill and practice, tutorial, and demonstration, whether computer-based or not, are all variations on the methods of education that have been practiced by most teachers in most schools for most of the duration of American education. Simulations and the next application to be discussed, instructional games, are relative newcomers to education in general, and are much less widely used both on and off computers.

Instructional Games

Instructional games constitute the last category to be discussed in what is ordinarily considered Computer Assisted Instruction. Computerized instructional games are quite unlike fantasy games or other games developed for the home computer market. Yet they are classified as games principally because they run by a clear set of rules and usually have a winner at the end. Instructional games are designed to be fun for students and thereby increase the chances of their learning the concept, knowledge, or skill embedded in the game. They come in all shapes and sizes, so that it is hard to specify any distinguishing characteristic other than that their explicit goal is learning. At one extreme, "gaming" is simply a motivational strategy employed to achieve that end. At the other extreme, a game can itself provide a student with a rich and complex learning environment.

In one-well known instructional game, students engage in a problem-solving exercise that requires them to apply various rules of logic. To play, students have to discover who murdered someone by putting together sentences that describe relationships between facts. They can try to guess who the murderer is at any point. For example, they are told the following facts by the computer:

MR. JONES WEARS A RED SUIT.
MRS. BROWN LIVES NEXT DOOR TO THE MURDERER.
MRS. BROWN LIVES NEXT DOOR TO MR. JONES.

Given these clues, a student may wish to guess the identity of the murder and so types in:

MR. JONES IS THE MURDERER.
NO.
THE MURDERER WEARS A BLUE SUIT.

From the computer's response the student can now see that while it is true that Mr. Jones lives next door to Mrs. Brown, he wears a red suit so he is not the murderer.

By playing this game, students can learn about language, thinking, and reading. They learn how to process facts and make logical inferences while solving a problem that is interesting to them. Unfortunately, this game, like so many other computer games, deals with a violent event, a murder. It is disturbing enough to recognize that children are fascinated by violence without finding that educational game designers reinforce this by their choice of content.

Traditional educational goals such as teaching basic skills may also be addressed by instructional games. In one well-known computer instructional game, "Darts," students have to figure out the location of a balloon on a number line marked off in fractions and mixed numbers. To do this, students must estimate distances and convert equivalent fractions. Students type in the fraction at which they think the balloon is located. This activates a dart that strikes the designated point and pops the balloon if it was indeed at that point. The popping balloon provides reinforcement for the student's performance as well as a graphically pleasing display. The sequence of screens on the following pages shows the results of two student attempts to locate the balloon.

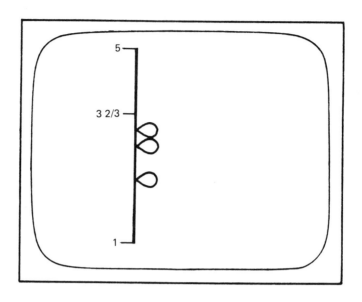

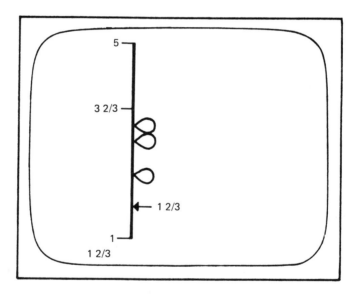

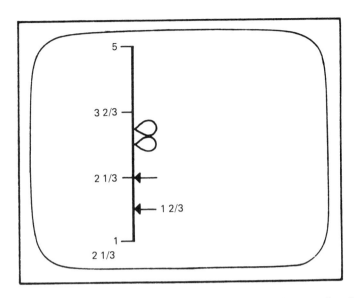

Like most other computer applications in education, instructional games often yield unintended educational outcomes that are as important as the intended ones. For example, a research study reported by Dr. Thomas Malone on the learning outcomes for students using "Darts" indicated that students did not learn about fractional equivalents any better than students taught by another method. Yet informal observation showed that students playing "Darts" did improve their abilities to solve problems and develop estimation strategies. (See the Bibliography for annotated reference to this study.)

As with simulations, the power of the computer allows such games to be far more complex than comparable noncomputer instructional games. As a result, a single game can teach multiple skills and concepts, usually of a more sophisticated nature, and in such a way that students do not readily get tired of the game. Of course such complexity requires sophistication in both curriculum design and computer programming. For commercial software houses, hiring such expertise costs money that, so far, it appears few have been willing to pay. On the one hand, less complicated drill and practice programs are much cheaper to develop and appear to have a proven audience for the education audience. On the other hand, if substantial money is to be spent developing games, the market for noneducational adventure and fantasy games would seem to be much larger than for educational games.

Unfortunately, creating complex instructional games is also beyond the ability and available time of most teachers. However, some relatively simple games that work well have been created by adventurous teachers. One such game that was written up in an educational computing magazine along with a complete program listing helps students learn syllabification. To play the game, students move syllables around on a four-by-four grid to make words. Points are awarded by the computer for every word made. The game is set up by having the computer choose several two- or three-syllable words from a class list of words. The words must have a total of fifteen syllables, which are then randomly assigned to positions in the grid, leaving one position open. As students play the game, they move syllables into the empty space to make a word. The computer keeps track of the students' turns and scores for correct words. Like many teacher-designed games, this one is an adaptation of an educational card game and, in fact, can be played quite as easily in a card game format. This once again raises the question if such a use of limited computer resources is worthwhile.

Of course, commercially developed games are usually far more complex than teacher-developed games, but that doesn't necessarily mean they are better. It all depends on the instructional goals of the teacher. For some teachers, games provide a ten-minute break from more routine work. For others, games may be a primary mode of instruction that takes up hours or even days of classroom activity time. One commercially available game that might be appropriate in this latter case is "Snooper Troops."

Imagine an entire classroom caught up in problem-solving activities that are so engaging that the students don't want to do anything else. That's "Snooper Troops." Students receive a dossier on a crime (once again!), complete with newspaper clippings, eyewitness reports, photographs and descriptions of key people associated with the crime, a worksheet for storing clues, and a list of phone numbers to call for further sources of information and clues. Different groups receive different sources. In turns, student groups are allowed up to the computer where they type in the number of their group and receive information. Students can raid sources, tap files, and discover new sources by using computer clues effectively. In the process they read, write, think, and solve a mystery.

The kind of learning that "Snooper Troops" fosters is extremely powerful. Not only do students have to gather facts, make inferences, and test hypotheses, but they also have to anticipate outcomes, plan alternative strategies, and negotiate with group members based on processing information. These are the essential elements of most reading, writing, and thinking in the real world.

One key element of "Snooper Troops" and games of this type is that they foster activity, discussion, and problem solving away from the computer. The computer is used only when its special characteristics are needed. The designers of such games apparently recognize the premium placed on computer time.

New educational games are slowly appearing on the market. Teachers interested in using instructional computer games should watch the various magazines and software catalogues for descriptions and evaluations of them. (See the Resources section: Periodicals and Software Catalogues, as well as several specific books and articles on games in the Bibliography.)

Summary of CAI Applications

The term Computer Assisted Instruction has been used in a variety of ways by those concerned with educational computing. Some have applied it only to the first generation of educational computing materials that emerged in the sixties: large-scale drill and practice and tutorial programs. Others apply it to any educational use of computers. We have adopted its usage somewhere in the middle. As discussed above, CAI refers to computer applications involving conventional educational methods used in pursuit of traditional educational goals. In this context, the computer is an electronic aid to teachers, and CAI programs are the teachers' instructional materials in which are embedded their teaching methods.

In the next section we discuss some very different educational applications of computers: instructional/learning tools. These tools are employed by teachers and students in ways that bear little resemblance to conventional educational methods, although the educational goals being pursued may be quite similar to traditional ones.

INSTRUCTIONAL/LEARNING TOOLS

The vast majority of computer applications are not in the field of education but rather in business, industry, medicine, the military, government, the media, communications, and basic research. Thus, most computer research and design of both hardware and software has always been focused on these other areas. Not surprisingly, then, workers in these fields have developed the most powerful ways of using computers, the most sophisticated hardware options, and the most elegant software. Educational applications of computers have generally been outgrowths of these more global computer applications. Simulations, as has been discussed, is a dramatic case in point.

Educational computing has continued to draw its inspirations from computing in other fields. At this time some of the more promising applications being "borrowed" by educators are the real-world computer tools such as word processors, numerical analysis programs, data processors, instrument monitoring devices, high resolution graphics software, and sound synthesizers. As educators continue to examine developments in the rest of the computer world, there will undoubtedly be other promising applications for education. For now the challenge is to appropriate those that have been identified as potentially useful, and, as with simulations, translate them wisely so that educators may make them their own.

Such appropriation of general purpose computer tools for educational uses has proceeded along several different paths. Some tools, like statistical analysis packages or graphics software, have been simplified for classroom use, but are used in essentially the same way as they are outside the school. Conversely, the basic nature of some tools, like text-editors, high-speed printers, and sorting programs is unaltered, while the ways in which they are used in classrooms are rather different from their use outside of schools. Recently, computing educators have taken two other approaches to educational computer tool development. In one, CAI is "piggy backed" onto a real-world tool such as VisiCalc (a numerical analysis program) to teach students how to use that tool for various purposes. In the other, the broad word processing and numerical analysis capabilities of computers are tapped to write specialized CAI/tool hybrid programs focused on particular educational goals like working with learning disabilities or solving physics problems. Examples of all of these types of educational computer tools are described in this section.

Word Processing

Word processors have been used in offices for a number of years, but only recently have computer manufacturers developed text-editing software packages that essentially convert small computers into the equivalent of simple word processors. As a result of this recent development, teachers and students with access to small computers, accompanied by text-editing software, can now organize, enter, edit, format, and print out anything they might write. A simple text-editor allows the user to compose on the computer's video screen before committing words to paper. Revision requires no erasing, cutting and pasting, and no tedious retyping of subsequent drafts. All changes can be made on the screen first, before printing out copy. Word processing programs existing for most machines provide printed material that is automatically formatted, with margins observed left and right, words properly hyphenated, titles centered, footnotes properly placed, and pages numbered.

These ordinary word processing functions can be applied in classrooms to yield some extraordinary educational outcomes. They can be used by students to outline papers and write to that outline, to revise and keep track of changes in the revision process, to accumulate and automatically alphabetize and format bibliographic material, to keep track of and properly place footnotes, to write in iambic pentameter, Haiku or any other programmable poetic form, in short to improve their writing process and their written product. Schools using word processing programs have found that even young children will revise their work to correct punctuation, spelling, word selection, sentence structure, and the dozens of errors common to student writing, such as word and letter juxtaposition. Using word processing programs encourages students to write who might otherwise avoid writing. All students using such programs tend to write longer, more detailed stories and essays. As a side benefit, learning to use such programs properly often results in the students' overall improvement in following directions.

In addition to these classroom uses of the word processing capabilities of computers, teachers and administrators are finding word processing invaluable for creating error-free, perfectly formatted dittoed worksheets; for inexpensively printing in-house student publications with a professional look; for writing and sending out personalized mass mailings to parents, teachers, students, and sponsors; for storing and easily revising annually updated documents like the school handbook; for printing daily notices; and on and on. The potential educational applications of these word processing capabilities, in both administration and instruction, are limited only by the imaginations of educators and the available computer resources.

However, one important consideration in allocating computer resources to word processing is that such use requires a tremendous amount of computer time and space on peripheral storage devices. At present, few schools have the resources to make word processing an option to all who might want it. This raises several related and serious questions. When schools do allocate computer time for word processing, how much do they allocate and to which students for what purposes? What can be done about the differential access to word processing between schools in different socioeconomic areas and within schools between students from different socioeconomic backgrounds? For example, some students will have access to word processing on home computers; others clearly will not. Should schools become involved in compensating for such discrepancies?

Beyond these applications in schools of well-established text-editing functions, there are some exciting and innovative adaptations of the word processing capabilities of computers for uniquely educational purposes. One example of such an adaptation was the SMART-WRITER program developed by Donald Riggs in Chapter 1. Other programs that have been developed or adapted are designed to help students improve their spelling, use of punctuation, paragraph construction, and even writing style. More and more attention is being paid to word processing programs to address the difficulties of learning disabled students and other special needs children. Teachers may expect a great deal from these research and design efforts in the future. Paul Goldenberg, one of the pioneers in computer applications for special needs children, sees the computer being for many of these children the equivalent of eyeglasses for millions of us. He feels that appropriately designed computer tools may allow many heretofore handicapped individuals to lead much more normal lives.

Numerical Analysis

Perhaps the best-known real-world use of computers involves storing and processing vast amounts of numerical information in designated ways. We are all familiar with the election eve computer projections of results, based on surprisingly small percentages of final returns. Although such projections are occasionally off base, what surprises most of us is how accurate they are so much of the time. This accuracy is due not to the computer itself but to the sophisticated statistical programs that have been written for it. Now, many such programs exist for much smaller computers, as well.

In addition to statistical packages, there are accounting and other numerical business application software packages available for even the least powerful personal computers. And, of course, all computers can be programmed to tirelessly, rapidly, and accurately perform extremely complex calculations for virtually any purpose.

As with word processing, these numerical analysis capabilities have almost limitless applications for instructional and administrative purposes, including use in social studies classes to analyze demographic and other population statistics; use in biology and chemistry labs to analyze results of experiments, particularly those requiring extrapolation, interpolation, and/or error analysis; use in math classes to compute numerical results of solved problems and to study probability, statistics, and number theory; use by the athletic department to store and analyze individual and team statistics; and use by the administration to do pupil attendance projections, to analyze reading scores, grades, and basic competency testing results, and to keep track of inventory, individual school budgets, purchasing, or other aspects of school finances. Some schools have even combined administrative functions with the instructional goals of the business and vocational education departments, so that students in these courses learn computerized accounting procedures by using accounting packages to help manage the school's financial affairs.

Although using "number crunching" packages, as these numerical analysis programs are affectionately called, does require a bit more mathematical understanding than using a word processor, many such programs are so well designed that the users' main task is simply to know what questions they want to ask the computer to answer. There is little, if any, need for users to become involved with the mathematical formulas themselves, except insofar as they need to understand or interpret the numerical results obtained. One of the principal benefits of using the computer as a super calculator is that it allows students to engage in certain concept learning activities that they could not have done before because of the tediousness and difficulty of the calculations.

However, again as with word processing, the most exciting applications of the numerical analysis capabilities of computers probably arise from uniquely educational adaptations, rather than from these more well-established applications. Two types of educational number crunching applications deserve special mention.

First, are the emerging packages in which CAI is piggy backed onto a numerical analysis tool such as VisiCalc. VisiCalc is an electronic worksheet used by accountants, financial analysts, engineers, and scientists to solve problems in their fields. However, it can also be used by individuals to balance their checkbooks, maintain their budgets, compute their taxes, project costs of loans, test out the implications of alternative financial strategies, compute personal athletic statistics, correlate changes in personal calorie intake with weight loss, and so forth. In a school setting, then, students may be taught how to use VisiCalc to perform any of these functions. The piggy backing feature involves building a tutorial program around VisiCalc, so that students may be instructed by the computer as to how to use the program and may practice using it at the same time. The educational payoff of such programs is not that students learn how to balance their checkbook with VisiCalc, but that they learn to balance their checkbook...with or without VisiCalc. Programs like this use computers to instruct in ways that teachers cannot, in contrast to traditional computer tutorials, which provide a pale imitation of a teacher-student educational interaction.

The second type of uniquely educational numerical analysis tool is exemplified by the **Sem**antic **Cal**culator (SemCalc), developed by Judah Schwartz of M.I.T. This is a hybrid of CAI and a numerical analysis tool designed to help students solve and understand "word" or "story" problems, estimation problems, and some simple algebra problems. The following example illustrates how a student might use SemCalc.

SemCalc presents the student with an electronic scratch pad, set up with two columns and any number of rows, to be used to solve any word problem on which the student is working. The student fills in the magnitudes and the units of measurement of the data given in the problem and what mathematical operation he or she wishes to perform with these quantities.

	HOW MANY?	WHAT?
A	**2.50**	**$/HRS**
B	**40**	**HRS**
OPERATION:	**A X B**	

To this input, the computer responds:

THE UNITS OF THE ANSWER ARE $
DO YOU WISH TO CARRY OUT THE CALCULATION? (TYPE Y)
OR INDICATE A DIFFERENT OPERATION? (TYPE N)

The student types Y if he or she decides that dollars are the units of the result sought, in which case the computer carries out and displays the calculation:

2.50 $/HRS. X 40 HRS = 100 $

Let us see what would happen if the student indicated a different operation, as follows:

OPERATION: **A / B**

THE UNITS OF THE ANSWER ARE $/HR/HR

In this case, one would hope that the student would recognize that the operation A / B does not yield the desired result. Of course, if the student does command the computer to carry out the operation A / B, it will do so, reporting a mathematically correct but illogical result.

2.50 $/HR / 40 HR = .0625 $/HR/HR

The program does not indicate to the student that anything is wrong with the problem. The student must discover that himself or herself. The SemCalc program is a tool in the hands of the problem-solving student, not a tutor or drillmaster instructing the student in problem solving and testing mastery of the material.

However, SemCalc does have several tutorial-like features, such as a unit conversion sequence that is automatically activated in situations such as the following:

	HOW MANY?	WHAT?
A	**200**	**GRAMS**
B	**5**	**KILOGRAMS**
OPERATION:	**A + B**	

CAN GRAMS BE CONVERTED TO KILOGRAMS OR CAN
KILOGRAMS BE CONVERTED TO GRAMS? (TYPE Y OR N)
Y
A. HOW MANY GRAMS IN ONE KILOGRAM OR
B. HOW MANY KILOGRAMS IN ONE GRAM? (TYPE A OR B)
A
HOW MANY GRAMS IN ONE KILOGRAM?
1000
200 GRAMS + (5 KILOGRAMS X 1000 GRAMS/KILOGRAM) =
200 GRAMS + 5000 GRAMS =
5200 GRAMS

The unit conversion sequence has been programmed to offer another feature that, while simple, may have real educational value to students whose problem-solving strategies are too rigid. It results from the proverbial, but as we shall see, untrue maxim: You can't add apples and oranges.

	HOW MANY?	WHAT?
A	**9**	**APPLES**
B	**14**	**ORANGES**
OPERATION:	**A + B**	

CAN APPLES BE CONVERTED TO ORANGES OR
CAN ORANGES BE CONVERTED TO APPLES? (TYPE Y OR N)
N
APPLES AND ORANGES ARE BOTH WHAT?

Ahh, a flash of recognition strikes the student.

FRUIT
9 FRUIT + 14 FRUIT = 23 FRUIT

But let us suppose the student was a bit mischievous:

HOT DOGS

9 HOT DOGS + 14 HOT DOGS = 23 HOT DOGS.

Once again, we see that SemCalc is a tool controlled by the student, not an instrument of the teacher for controlling the student. SemCalc has other interesting features, but the ones cited should be enough to give you a sense of what can be done to use the capabilities of the computer to design CAI/tool hybrids. SemCalc is currently still under development and is not yet commercially available.

Data Processing

Along with word processing and numerical analysis, the capacity of computers to store and manipulate vast quantities of information is what makes them such powerful instruments of our modern civilization. This function of computers, known as **data processing,** is the most common use of computers by businesses, government, the military, and virtually every major institution in a bureaucratic society. Data processing is used to extract information from the U.S. Census, to characterize economic conditions based on various economic indicators, and to keep track of inventories, people, money, weapons, books, files, and records of every conceivable kind.

As one of the largest American institutions, schools have for some time utilized the data-processing capabilities of computers, although primarily for administrative purposes as opposed to instructional ones, including most notably pupil course scheduling, systems analysis, budgeting, and grade reporting. Until recently, the sole instructional application of data processing has been to teach it, as a skill, in business education courses. In some schools,

advanced business education students even carried out most of the data processing tasks for the school on computers.

However, as with the other tools we have discussed, imaginative educators
are beginning to devise ways of adapting the data processing capabilities of computers to enhance student learning. Two examples are especially worth
mentioning: one grand, the other modest.

Massive **databases** on almost any topic now exist or are currently being
developed. Many of these databases are accessible by people with microcomputers equipped with some sort of communications device. This puts
quantitative and qualitative primary data in the hands of students and teachers
who are seeking such information. In a sense, databases may be the
encyclopedia-almanac-library of the electronic age. Students growing up with
computers may be much more comfortable in calling a computer database than
using a library card index or thumbing through the *Readers Guide to Periodicals*.
In fact, many libraries are doing away with print-based indices in favor of computerized databases of their collections and sources they can communicate
with via computer. However futuristic this may sound, the fact is that information networks like the Source and other databases are functioning right now and
are accessible to people or institutions with computers. (See the Resources section: Online Sources and Databases.)

A more modest but perhaps more profound classroom application of data
processing involves students in creating and using their own smaller databases,
such as a list of books in the classroom library, or items in their own stamp or doll
collections. The importance of such activities is not to devise a better record-
keeping system for one's belongings or to develop prevocational data processing
skills. Rather, the significance of creating one's own database system is to gain
insight into how data, which is to say knowledge, is structured. For students who
will grow up in a world in which knowledge and hence reality is likely to be
defined by the contents of massive databases, it is important to understand that
knowledge may well be determined by the ways in which information is
structured, stored, and retrieved.

For example, the state of the nation's economy is defined by a range of
economic indicators derived from analysis of various databases. We are in a
period of inflation or recession only when the indicators tell us we are, not when
we feel it in our personal lives. These economic indicators, in turn, are determined by the way various pieces of economic data are stored, structured, and
retrieved in economic database systems. These database systems were constructed by people operating under certain assumptions about economics in
general and our economy in particular. Thus, the reality of our economy is, in
some senses, defined by assumptions held about it. It is not at all clear that such
heady stuff is recognized by students constructing their own databases, but it is
a start in a direction that appears worth pursuing.

Instrument Monitoring Devices

Most people are probably aware of computerized monitoring and control devices in aeronautics (space flights), medicine (fetal heart monitors), and basic research (you name it). These applications have often been designed for very large computer systems, but recently engineers have developed similar ways of monitoring and controlling much smaller instruments, such as thermostats, electrical appliances, and car engines. Following such developments, it hasn't taken long for science educators to spot the potential for similar applications in the science lab, where even the most modest personal computers can now be hooked up to instruments that allow them to measure, record, and analyze time; electric current, voltage, and resistance; temperature; radioactive decay; light and sound frequency and wave length; and many other physical and chemical quantities. Nor are these applications limited to high school classrooms. In one third-grade classroom, heat and light measuring instruments were plugged into the game paddle outlets of an Apple microcomputer. Data were collected continuously by the computer, enabling the teacher to create an authentic mini-laboratory in her classroom.

And this is only the beginning. Just as with the word processing, numerical analysis, and data processing capabilities of the computer, educators are figuring out ways to adapt the instrument monitoring capabilities of computers to develop uniquely educational tools, some of which like SemCalc are CAI/tool hybrids. Among such tools developed for science teaching are programs that test integrated circuits, generate electromagnetic wave functions, measure angular acceleration, simulate geological sounding experiments, effectively convert the computer into a storage-type oscilloscope, perform a Fourier synthesis on waves, analyze pulse heights of spectra, and calculate the half-life function of emissions from a Geiger tube. Perhaps most amazing of all is that the additional cost of all these applications is very small for science departments that already have access to a microcomputer.

High Resolution Graphics and Sound Synthesizers

Computers that can generate complex, colored, dynamic graphic designs are in wide use in a variety of industries, most especially the media. Similarly, computerized sound synthesizers are in heavy use in the music industry. These kinds of computer applications are becoming more and more available on inexpensive personal computers, largely to enhance the excitement of commercial computer games. Home use of computers for creative arts is beginning to flourish, and it is probably only a matter of time before the art and music departments of many schools will be taking advantage of these computer applications.

Summary of Instructional/Learning Tools

During the last several years instructional/learning tools have emerged as innovative and promising developments on the educational scene. While it is too soon to tell, these tools seem to have the potential to change classroom practices in fundamental ways. So rapid has been the development of such tools, that this section describing them is likely to double in size by the time the next edition of this book is published.

COMPUTER MANAGED INSTRUCTION

New tools, old tools. While computerized instructional/learning tools are relatively new to education, computerized educational management tools are not. Schools have used the data processing capabilities of computers for years for district-wide administrative purposes. However, it is not within the scope of this book to discuss such uses of the computer. For a thorough treatment of the subject, see *Computers and School Administration* by David Dennen and Carleton Finch, also in the Addison-Wesley Series on Computers in Education.

Here we will focus primarily on computer use to manage classroom instruction. However, since there are considerable areas of overlap between classroom management and the building-level management of student academic records, we will touch upon the latter as well.

With the advent of the competency-based education movement and the call for a return to the basics, the management of instruction has become a more routinized and important part of teachers' responsibilities. For example, records must be kept on student mastery of objectives, individual educational plans (IEPs) must be generated and monitored for special needs students, reports must be generated to receive funding, and evidence of achievement has to be given to parents at conferences. Consequently, teachers have found themselves barraged with paperwork that is time consuming and may often seem counterproductive to the primary task of teaching.

To alleviate the burden of this record keeping and reporting, **computer based testing (CBT)** and **computer managed instruction (CMI)** systems have been developed by a number of educational publishers. These systems are intended to be used by teachers and administrators to measure and keep track of student performance and activity in a variety of areas.

There are two basic types of computer based testing (CBT) programs. In one, test results are used exclusively for administrative purposes and often are not even shared with teachers. In the other, testing is seen as a support for classroom instruction. In the latter case, test results are made available to teachers to help them determine the best course of study for their students.

The former type of CBT is familiar to most educators. Students are periodically given commercially produced standardized achievement tests. The students' answer sheets are sent to a testing service where they are read and scored by optical scanning machines that feed the information into a computer to analyze the results. The school, and sometimes the teachers, get back score reports prepared by the computer. Both the test questions and the set of instructions that are used by the computer to analyze the results are prepared by the testing service. Neither the teacher nor the student manipulates the computer in any way.

With the advent of inexpensive microcomputers, a whole different approach to testing and its uses is now possible. Several companies have produced computer programs in which the student takes a test that is scored at the school on a small classroom computer which can then prescribe instruction on the basis of the test results. Such computer based testing is the foundation of many computer managed instruction programs.

There are four basic types of CMI program: two are testing based, two are not. In the first testing based type of CMI, student responses are put on computer cards or optical scanning sheets and fed into a card reader or scanner for scoring. The information is then sent on to the computer, which prescribes the needed instruction. In some of these CMI programs, the students enter their answers directly on sheets that are scored; in others, another person must transfer student answers to such sheets or cards. School districts employing such CMI programs generally use teacher aides, parents, volunteers, clerical staff, or older students to perform this function.

The other type of testing-based CMI program just beginning to emerge is more exciting than this traditional approach to testing and prescription. Here, the student actually takes the test on the computer which then calculates, stores, and analyzes performance data almost instantaneously. In such programs, the students are informed while they are taking the test as to whether or not their answers are correct. As a further embellishment, some CMI programs are being linked to tutorial programs so that students are tested and then placed by the computer directly into an appropriate computerized lesson on the basis of the test results.

A few programs are under development that are even more sophisticated, but for now they also require larger computers with more room to store information. These remarkable test programs ask questions, and based on analyzing the student's answers, they generate the next appropriate question. In this way, for example, students do not have to suffer through a reading achievement test that is above their reading level. In addition, because the computer selects the questions that give it the most information about a student's actual achievement, it can use fewer questions. Such CMI programs maximize the information received from students in the least amount of time with the most accuracy.

The third and fourth type of CMI have no computer based testing components. They are primarily record-keeping programs. The most elaborate versions of this type of CMI program envisioned would store all relevant information about students and their academic records and allow for constant updating of this information. Some administrators and teachers view such extensive CMI programs as the panacea for resolving many of the problems associated with the preparation of report cards, Title I evaluation reports, IEP's, and other periodic reporting requirements that have become a regular and tedious part of their jobs.

For now, however, the purpose of most operational CMI programs is simply to aid the classroom instructional process. CMI programs, now available on microcomputers, allow teachers to structure the way students will move through a computerized instructional sequence. To do this, the teacher must input student assignments and set up a computerized record-keeping chart before the students can begin the lessons. A sample that explains the type of information teachers need to put into such a CMI program follows.

The computer program begins by requesting the teacher's name and the classes that will use the instructional program. Whenever the teacher wants to use the program, he or she must type in the class with which it is being used.

WHAT IS YOUR NAME?
MS. SUSAN WERNER
THE CLASSES ARE:
1. **MATH 1**
2. **MATH 2**

The teacher then has a table of contents of options to choose from.

A. STUDENT MANAGEMENT PAGE
B. CLASS MANAGEMENT PAGE
C. REVIEW SEQUENCE AS A STUDENT
WHICH LETTER?
A.
PRESS "RETURN"

In most CMI programs, the teacher must use the teacher's manual in order to understand the abbreviations used and to know which assignments are appropriate. For each student, the teacher fills in all of the numbers for every assignment to be made.

STUDENT MANAGEMENT PAGE
WHICH NUMBER? **6**
SALLY

ASSGN	BEG	END	ML	FL	MP	STATUS
2	5	30	0	40	8	**NONE**

PRESS "RETURN" WHEN FINISHED.

As this illustration suggests, setting up the management sequence for a whole class of students can be time consuming and even confusing. In this particular program, the student proceeds through the activities on the computer according to the assignments the teacher makes. The computer automatically keeps track of the student's performance. When the teacher checks the records at the end of the day, the student's scores are listed. In this way, routine drillwork on the computer can become more effective than presenting the same exercises in a workbook. The computer can provide immediate feedback about right or wrong responses, can branch students automatically to more appropriate sequences of problem sets or questions, and can keep track of the mastery level information and progress without requiring teacher intervention.

The final type of CMI program is the simplest. Here the computer is used for record keeping only, not for instruction. Students do most or all their work with traditional materials, but the teacher enters progress on the computer, which acts in effect like an electronic gradebook. Such CMI systems are easy enough for teachers with a little bit of programming experience to design for themselves.

Although CMI is most often associated with traditional classroom structures and goals, it need not be seen in such a limited way. Progressive-minded teachers are recognizing the value of CMI programs to save them and their students lots of time in covering the basic skills, so that they may spend more time on student-centered concerns and activities. Moreover, CMI is seen by many as making feasible the once unreasonably idealistic goal of individualizing instruction.

Nevertheless, there are many strong critics of CMI. Some decry the diminution of student-teacher interaction. Some assail the behaviorist assumptions on which most CMI is based. Others criticize the quality of most CMI programs. However, in the last analysis, as with all other computer applications we've discussed, the basic question is whether or not this should be a priority use of limited computer resources.

PROGRAMMING

Although computer programming has been offered as an elective course in many high schools for some years, the advent of microcomputers and the dramatic increase in computer use by schools leads us to reexamine the importance and significance of learning to program computers as part of a student's basic school experience.

At present there seem to be three major justifications for increasing and extending the teaching of computer programming in grades K-12. These are: to prepare students for jobs and for postsecondary education, to prepare students for citizenship in a computer-based society, and to use computer programming to enhance a student's general intellectual abilities.

The most traditional argument for students learning to program is preparation for computer-related careers. More and more jobs in society involve use of computers, many calling for actual programming skills. Even for those jobs that do not directly deal with programming, some understanding of how programs work can be very helpful. So, according to this reasoning most, if not all, high school students should have at least one course in programming, usually taught using a programming language called BASIC (Beginners All Purpose Sequential Instruction Code).

As the name suggests, BASIC is a language developed for the specific purpose of giving computer novices a tool they can quickly learn and use for a variety of purposes. Indeed, BASIC has proven to be just that. It is a simple enough language that bright elementary school students can be taught the rudiments of it, while high school students can learn enough in an introductory course to provide them with some ability to create interesting programs. Another strength of BASIC is its availability, in some form, on most computers manufactured today.

Many high schools and junior high schools now include introductory programming in their curriculum as a required or elective course. Small, very inexpensive microcomputers such as the new hand-held computers are well suited for teaching large numbers of students simple programming in BASIC. The cost effectiveness and the simplicity of instruction when using such machines allows almost any school in the country to offer programming courses.

Along with prevocational training goes academic preparation in computer science, a discipline that is becoming as important as the traditional sciences— biology, physics and chemistry—to a student's precollege academic career. The Elementary and Secondary Schools Subcommittee of the Association for Computing Machinery has outlined goals and objectives for a computer science course that they recommend be taken by almost all students in the first or second year of high school. The course would be comparable in scope and significance to the type of biology course taken by most high school students today.

Many schools will feel a need to go beyond introductory courses as they expand their capability to provide vocational and academic training for their students. A school engaged in serious prevocational or preacademic training will want to include courses in several of the more widely used languages such as FORTRAN (used in scientific programming), COBOL (business programming) or Pascal (used in training computer scientists).

Schools moving in this direction should be aware of two serious problems they will undoubtedly encounter. Industry and business are changing more rapidly than schools can usually repond to changed needs. Schools going into prevocational preparation should recognize that their courses will need continual review and reevaluation to insure that they are meeting real training needs. Second, teachers who can teach intermediate and advanced courses in computer programming and computer science are increasingly likely to leave teaching for higher paid positions in high technology industries. It is an ironic and disturbing fact that at the same time industry and business are decrying the lack of skilled workers to fill existing jobs, they are recruiting away from schools the teachers who could help train the workers they need. These difficulties should not deter a school from offering introductory programming courses to all students who want them, however.

A second prominent argument that has emerged recently for teaching programming relates to the notion of <u>computer literacy</u>. Although this term has been used by different people in many different ways, we will take it to mean the general range of skills and understanding needed to function effectively in a society increasingly dependent on computer and information technology. Our concept of what computer literacy might include is developed later in this chapter.

The reason for including programming as part of a computer literacy program is not so much prevocational as it is precitizenship. According to this rationale, so many facets of our lives are computerized that some understanding of computer programming is necessary for the exercise of the rights and responsibilities of citizenship. While such a view may seem questionably futuristic to some, there are educators and some schools who take it seriously. Computer literacy courses and units that include programming have been developed for students from kindergarten through college.

Elementary school children can be introduced to programming by using programmable toys and learning a child-appropriate computer language such as Logo, which is discussed below. Junior high, middle school, and high school students can all learn enough of a programming language like BASIC or Logo to create programs of their own.

When developing an introductory programming course in the context of a computer literacy program, it is often effective to emphasize projects of intrinsic interest to the students, such as graphics, animation, and computer games, as well as real-world data processing tasks. More advanced courses could make a conscious effort to engage students in using computers to solve problems that exist within the school system so that they can carry their projects to completion and actually see their programs implemented. Some high school computer teachers even have their classes developing simple CAI programs for other students in the system. Other high schools assign administrative programming tasks to their advanced students or use paid student programmers in their administrative work. Of course, this places much more responsibility on the programming teacher than does a normal teaching load. Nevertheless, it appears that in most cases the teacher is pleased to be involved in such useful projects.

A third argument for teaching programming is the contention that learning to program a computer can enhance a student's intellectual functioning. To educators who hold this view, learning to program offers more than a route to jobs and citizenship. It can help us to learn to think better, more deeply, more clearly, and more profoundly.

This view has been most widely held among mathematics educators in the past and has accounted for the infusion of computer programming activities into high school algebra classes in many school districts. Since the actual behaviors involved in "thinking better" tend to be difficult to describe and evaluate precisely, we tend to lump them into vague categories called "logical thinking" or "problem solving." Thus, although programming has been included in some schools' math classes since the early seventies, there is little objective evaluation data confirming this contention. A growing body of anecdotal and observational data supporting it indicates that there are positive cognitive and affective benefits for many students learning programming, however difficult these effects may be to measure. For example, recent studies at the University of Massachusetts have examined student behavior in solving algebraic word problems. The results show clearly that students attempting the same problems have a much higher degree of success on their first attempt when a problem is expressed as a computer programming task than they do when it is expressed in a more conventional word problem format.

One of the most prominent and eloquent advocates of the view that computer programming can enhance intellectual functioning, even for young children, is Professor Seymour Papert of M.I.T. For more than a decade, he and his associates have worked to develop some concrete mechanisms for attaining this goal. The Logo language already referred to, together with a growing repertoire of commercially available features, including "turtle geometry" and "sprites," have provided children, older students, and teachers with unique ways of being with and learning from computers.

In his book *Mindstorms* (see Bibliography), Papert describes how Logo enables children to enter "mathland," a place where they can explore sophisticated, advanced mathematical concepts such as differential geometry, but in terms and ways that they understand and enjoy. For example, programming in Logo involves giving the computer commands and inventing new commands to teach the computer, rather than creating a long sequence of instructions in logical order, as is done in most other computer languages.

The best known Logo activity is called turtle geometry. Here, the learner controls a simulated robot turtle that can move around and draw pictures on a TV screen. Using common expressions like "forward," "back," "right turn," and "left turn," a student can create exciting geometric designs and cartoon drawings. The immediacy and concreteness of the output—the lines drawn by the turtle—remove programming from the sphere of the abstract, and make it accessible to very young children. When problems occur, learners can "play turtle," placing themselves in the turtle's place and asking "If I were the turtle, what would I do next?" Working with the turtle, students develop a strong intuitive sense of its geometric world, laying a cognitive foundation for future studies in such areas as formal geometry, trigonometry, calculus, and physics.

In a Logo activity, students must learn the specific subject matter needed to program the computer to carry out tasks in a particular domain. The learning process is much like that a teacher experiences in teaching a subject for the first time. "Teaching" a computer to carry out a task forces a programmer to develop a clear, well-articulated description of the task, which helps build an understanding of the task domain. The fact that a student must create a special language—a set of new commands—to describe each task and its constituent parts makes the teaching/learning/programming process easier, more personal, and more coherent.

Here's a simple example of what can actually happen as a student learns to program a computer using the Logo turtle, which appears as a small triangle on the computer's screen.

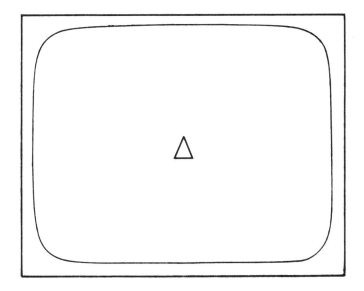

The turtle responds to simple commands typed at the keyboard: FORWARD 100, BACK 50, RIGHT 90, LEFT 45, and so forth. FORWARD 100 moves the turtle forward "100 turtle steps," drawing a line on the screen in the process. LEFT 45 makes the turtle rotate 45 degrees to its own left.

To make the computer draw a square, the student learns or discovers that the turtle must be turned the same amount, 90 degrees at each corner of the square, and that all four sides must be the same length. Eventually, the student succeeds in making the turtle draw a square.

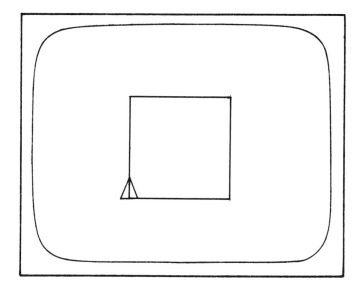

After the student has drawn a square and wants the computer to remember how to do it, he or she may type the command:

SQUARE

to which the computer responds:

YOU HAVEN'T TAUGHT ME HOW TO SQUARE.

The young programmer now must describe the procedure for drawing a square in terms the computer understands.

```
TO SQUARE
FORWARD 100
RIGHT 90
FORWARD 100
RIGHT 90
FORWARD 100
RIGHT 90
FORWARD 100
RIGHT 90
END
```

Or the programmer may discover a shortcut.

TO SQUARE
REPEAT 4 FORWARD 100 RIGHT 90
END

Now, when the student types the command, SQUARE, the computer carries out the new command, drawing whatever the sequence of commands tells it. SQUARE is now a word in the student's own computer language. (It didn't have to be called "SQUARE." It could have been called "BOX," "MARY," "SQ," or even "SQAURE," and the computer would still "understand" it.) SQUARE can now be used with other commands to draw other, more elaborate designs:

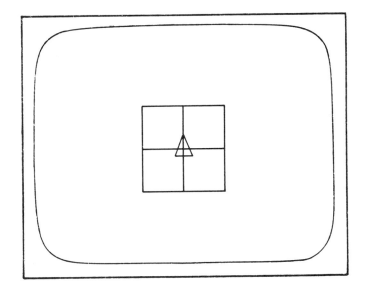

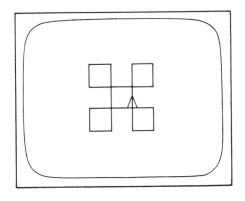

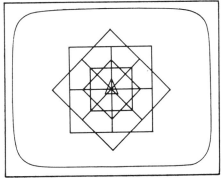

Students learning about squares in this way are having a very different kind of experience than has been possible without computers. It is certainly very different from learning the definition of a square as part of a geometry unit in a math class. They are also learning to program a computer in a friendly, natural way—gaining skills, understandings, and values that should help them function successfully as adults living in an age of computers.

Until 1981, Logo was only available on relatively large computer systems, and its use was limited mainly to students involved in university-based research projects. Now, however, Logo is available for microcomputers, and school systems are beginning to use it in computer literacy and programming courses at elementary, junior high, and high school levels.

If we follow the thinking of Logo's developers, we will recognize that there is much more implied by the use of this approach than just a neat way to teach programming. We now have the opportunity to rethink the entire math curriculum. Logo has also been used to help students learn music, art, physics, biology, and language. Rather than asking, "How does an approach like Logo fit into our existing curriculum?" we might begin to ask the more profound question, "How can our curriculum be changed to take advantage of radically new approaches to the learning of content and process made possible by computer-based learning environments like Logo?"

COMPUTER LITERACY

We conclude this chapter on classroom computer applications with a discussion of one of the major justifications for introducing computers into schools in large numbers: the broad set of goals that are sometimes lumped together under the term computer literacy. The very broadness of the term has led to a great deal of controversy about how it should be interpreted by schools.

As defined earlier in our discussion of programming, we consider computer literacy to imply all the skills, understandings, and values needed to function effectively in a society permeated by computer and information technology. The operational meaning of this for education may become clearer if we briefly consider the role of language literacy within our present society and educational systems. To be literate in our society, a person must be able to use written and oral language for a wide range of purposes. Literate people have a set of skills, knowledge, values, understandings, and relationships that allow them to use language, particularly reading and writing, on the job, at home, in school, while traveling, and so forth. A nonliterate person is, in many ways, a nonfunctional person in our society.

How does a person become literate? Most simply, by growing up in a literate society and attending literate schools. Before a child enters school, he or she has already learned most of the language skills needed for a lifetime. Language skills are taught in school, but more importantly, they are also used as a critical part of education and of daily life. As a child learns to read and write, literacy skills are used every day, in and out of school. Every teacher and virtually every adult a child encounters uses, values, and promotes literacy. Schools teach literacy, but they also exude it. Literacy is the very fabric from which a school is built. It would be hard to imagine schools in our society that did not use literacy as the essential element of the learning environment.

Literate citizens of a computer-based society would be literate with computers in the same way that people in our society are literate with language. This includes several broad abilities:

1. Computer literate people would be able to program computers to achieve a wide variety of personal, academic, and vocational goals. They would also be able to assess, understand, and if necessary modify computer programs provided by others.
2. Computer literate people would be able to use a variety of preprogrammed computer applications in personal, academic, and professional contexts; judge the suitability of particular software tools for particular purposes; and understand the assumptions, values, and limitations inherent in particular pieces of software.
3. Computer literate people would understand the growing economic, social, and psychological impact of computers on individuals, on groups within our society, and on society as a whole. They would also realize that computer applications embody particular social values and can have different impacts on different individuals and different segments of society. Such people would be able to play a serious role in the political process by which large- and small-scale decisions about computers are made, and to transcend the dependent roles of consumer or victim.
4. Computer literate people would be able to make use of ideas from the world of computer programming and computer applications as part of their strategies for information retrieval, communication, and problem solving.

It should be clear that no one would become computer literate simply by taking an introductory course labeled "computer literacy." Existing computer literacy courses vary widely in their goals and methods. Some merely teach about computers, their history, the mechanics and electronics of their operation, their functions in the business world, and their impact on society. There is no hands-on experience. Other courses combine such learning about computers with some learning on computers. Still others place almost all emphasis on student hands-on experience, using and programming computers.

Courses of this type offer one way of starting a broad computer literacy program within a school, but they should not be thought of as ultimately satisfying the long-range goal of educating computer literate citizens. Rather, the concept of computer literacy offers educators a useful framework for considering all of the educational computer uses described in this chapter. As student access to computers increases, in and out of school, and as educators become more familiar with many educational computer uses, the broad goal of computer literacy can give coherence to a school's use of computers, while allowing for a healthy diversity of particular applications.

CONCLUSIONS

As we have seen in this chapter, the computer is a versatile and powerful device for teachers to use with students in their classrooms. How teachers choose to use the compuer, if they do, will be largely a function of their teaching philosophy and the availability of computer resources. Since, for the present at least, few schools will have unlimited computer resources, school people will be forced to establish priorities for computer use. As educators, you will have to base your priorities on a knowledge of the real capabilities of computers for various applications and on your judgments about the educational value of these applications. This chapter was intended to lay the foundation for making such judgments, by introducing you to a wide range of educational applications of computers and by discussing some of the limits and potentials of these applications. In Chapter 5, we will return to this issue by discussing procedures and criteria for selecting educational software.

Bits and Bytes

Chapter

3

This chapter might have been entitled "More Than You Ever Wanted to Know About Computers but Were Afraid to Ask." Its task is to help you understand how computers work. We have tried to steer a middle course between the twin perils of the overly general description that explains nothing and the overly technical description that explains too much. It is intended to be a useful introduction to computers, a basis from which you can acquire more knowledge readily. It is not the last word, but a beginning.

Do not worry about learning everything contained in this chapter the first time you read it. Your familiarity with computer systems will surely grow over time. Just try to get a basic feel for the subject; that should be enough for now. You can always come back to this material for reference later on.

It is impossible to know it all — nobody does. So do not be embarrassed to state your unfamiliarity with a given subject and openly to seek advice and information on any topic.

If computers seem bewildering, it is perhaps because they are such non-specialized tools. To name but a few applications, we find computers running the fuel systems of our automobiles, writing our paychecks, producing our tax returns, and playing against us in chess. It is a completely variable tool, ultimately capable of any task that can be broken down into a finite number of steps. We are accustomed to defining our tools by what they do. With computers, that's a questionable approach.

Yet the ideas behind computers are possible for the layman to grasp despite the complexity, diversity, and technological ingenuity with which these ideas are applied. Once the idea of a computer is understood, the vocabulary of the field is not hard to learn, and one can begin to think and communicate intelligently about computers. One warning: many of the terms used to describe computers and their operation have no precise definition. The jury of lexicographers is still out, and the words and meanings seem to keep changing almost as fast as the technology.

In this chapter we try to define technical terms when we first encounter them. Sometimes this is difficult to do, as in the case of "memory" below. If you encounter such an undefined term, try to ascertain its meaning from the context in which it is used or look it up in the glossary. Eventually the term will be explained in the text as well.

As defined in Chapter 1, a computer electronically manipulates symbolic information according to a list of instructions given it. Manipulating symbolic information is a little scary: it is very close to some of the processes we call thinking. Computers do in fact perform some of the functions we have formerly associated only with human mental process — playing a pretty strong game of chess, for example. But the amazing thing about a computer playing chess is that some human has previously thought up the list of instructions that allows the computer to do so. Computers, for all their power, are entirely stupid, useless, and helpless without instructions from you and me. At its most fundamental level a computer can perform very few operations. Basically, a computer can:

1. Obtain numbers from its memory.
2. Return results to memory as numbers.
3. Execute a list of instructions in memory.
4. Compare two numbers and execute different instructions depending on whether or not the numbers are equal.
5. Add two numbers.
6. Change zeros to ones and vice versa.

Not very remarkable, is it? So what's so great about computers? Three things: first, these simple operations can be combined to make much more powerful operations. Second, computers can perform these very rapidly. Adding two numbers is not particularly impressive; performing 100,000 such additions in a single second is very impressive. Third, these numbers that the computer manipulates can be interpreted as codes for letters, punctuation, and control characters, such as advancing the screen or paper on a terminal, the result being that the computer can manipulate text data as well as numbers.

COMPUTER SYSTEMS

The common electronic calculator is, in fact, an extremely simple computer system. You input numbers (data) and operations (instructions) via the keys, the computer calculates the result from step to step (processes each instruction as it is received) and outputs results on the display. This input-process-output cycle is typical of most computer operations. The procedure a person might follow to obtain a result from a calculator is analogous to a program on a computer. In that sense, the following is a "program" to compute the average of two numbers on a calculator:

1. Turn on the calculator.
2. Press CLEAR key.
3. Enter first number.
4. Press + (add) key.
5. Enter next number.
6. Repeat steps 4 and 5 until list of items to average is exhausted.
7. Press ÷ (divided by) key.
8. Enter number of items you are averaging.
9. Press = (equals) key.
10. Read result on display.

Let's see how this calculator procedure might appear on a simple computer system. The program has been loaded into the computer and is ready to run. You, the user, type the first command RUN to which the computer responds. Thereafter you and the computer alternate responding to each other.

RUN
PROGRAM TO CALCULATE SUM AND
AVERAGE OF A LIST OF NUMBERS.
HOW MANY NUMBERS TO AVERAGE?
3
ENTER 3 NUMBERS, SEPARATED BY COMMAS:
67.5,82.5,90
SUM IS 240.0
AVERAGE IS 80.0
AGAIN (Y/N)?
Y
READY

In the example on the previous page the computer system has been program-med to perform the simple, repetitive task of averaging several numbers. The program prompts the user for input, adds the numbers, divides the sum by the number of items being averaged, and prints the result. The outputs of the pro-gram are the prompts and the final result. As an added feature, the program is ready to continue averaging sets of numbers until the user wishes to stop averaging numbers.

A major difference between the computer and calculator examples is the degree of visibility of the process to you, the user. In using the calculator, you are involved with each operation and see each intermediate result as it is generated. Once you have accepted the minor marvel that the calculator does indeed perform its operations correctly, the whole thing becomes routine and trivial. In the case of the computer example, all of the calculation is concealed from you: you enter the numbers, it gargles them and regurgitates an answer. The process by which the result is achieved is hidden. This is both good and bad. On the one hand, you, the user, are spared much that is boring, trivial, and repetitive; on the other, you are denied access (at least at this level) to the process by which your result is obtained. This often has the effect of making the computer seem more distant, forbidding, and magical than it really is. The user is potentially isolated from the process, and this isolation can be alienating.

This somewhat natural suspicion of unseen processes is not unfounded. Someone had to write that set of instructions to produce averages; except by careful testing of results, you have no way of knowing that the programmer did so correctly. It is easy to have a program announce a result with confidence; that confidence does not necessarily reflect accuracy. Many programs have errors in them, sometimes quite subtle ones (errors in programs are often referred to as **bugs** and the process of correcting a program is known as **debugging**). You should cultivate a certain wariness of computer results, however imposing and reliable they may appear. The efforts of the people who program the computer make it a marvelous machine; those same people are as subject to human error as you or I.

However, it is possible for you, the user, to examine the program that allows the computer to compute averages. Then if you have some knowledge of pro-gramming, you will understand how the results were obtained. If there were a bug in the program, you might find it by examining a **listing** of the program. To display the actual program listing on your computer's output device you type the command:

LIST

As a result the computer displays its program listing.

```
10   REM AVERAGE
20   REM PROGRAM TO DETERMINE SUM AND AVERAGE
25   REM A SET OF NUMBERS SUPPLIED BY THE USER.
30   REM AUTHOR: JANE T. GRAHAM
40   DIM A(100)
50   PRINT "PROGRAM TO CALCULATE SUM AND"
60   PRINT "AVERAGE OF A LIST OF NUMBERS."
65   LET T = 0
70   PRINT "HOW MANY NUMBERS TO AVERAGE?"
80   INPUT N
90   PRINT "ENTER 3 NUMBERS, SEPARATED BY
     COMMAS:"
100 FOR I =1 TO N
110 INPUT A(I)
120 T = T = A(I)
130 NEXT I
140 PRINT "SUM IS";T
150 PRINT "AVERAGE IS";T/N
160 PRINT
170 PRINT "AGAIN (Y/N)?"
180 INPUT A$
190 IF A$ = "Y" THEN 65
200 STOP
```

READY

Now, let us consider a more sophisticated example. Suppose your school has an administrative computer which has on its peripheral storage device a file of records — one for each student — including name, address, class and some sort of identification number. Each school day, a list of absentees is entered into the computer which outputs the result to another file containing the student's ID number and the date absent. When an attendance report for each student is wanted at the end of some period of time, we run a program that does the following:

- Sorts the absentee file in student ID order (remember it was entered in date order).
- Prints the name and address of each student.
- Prints the dates each student was absent (if any).
- Prints the total number of days each student was absent.

The above is an example of data processing, a process that a simple calculator cannot emulate.

As with stereo equipment, one can buy computer systems as integrated packages or as separate components. Unlike stereo equipment, which all plays sound no matter how it is set up, the choice of computer hardware and software can result in very different computer systems designed for very different tasks. At a minimum, however, a computer system needs the following:

- A computer.
- A peripheral device for storing programs and data between sessions on the computer (e.g., a tape player/recorder).
- Peripheral devices for putting instructions and data into the computer and receiving results back from the computer (e.g., terminals).

We shall now discuss each of the above components.

THE CENTRAL COMPUTER

Pictured is a printed circuit board for a computer. Each rectangular block is a plastic or ceramic package containing a chip, which is basically a lot of electronics packed into a small volume, capable of responding in certain predefined ways. Significantly, chips are cheap to build and buy.

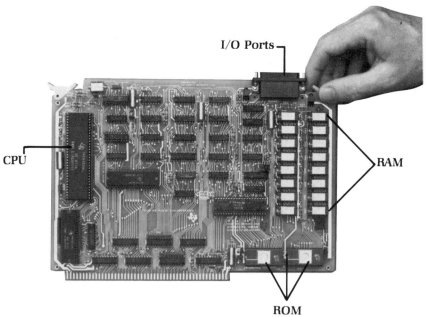

Printed circuit board
Photo: Texas Instruments, Inc.

The Central Processing Unit (CPU)

That largest rectangular block at the left of the board is the **Central Processing Unit (CPU)**. The CPU is the "brains" of the operation. It is this little device that can perform those basic opeations we listed earlier.

Building all of these functions of the CPU into one chip was the major technological breakthrough that has spawned the astounding price revolution in computers during the past few years. A **microprocessor** is a computer with a CPU in a single chip. A **microcomputer** is a computer whose main CPU is a microprocessor. What distinguishes microcomputers from older technology computers is not so much speed and power as price and size.

In order to process information, the CPU uses codes somewhat like the Morse code of the telegraph that are interpreted as letters, numbers, punctuation, and control characters. But instead of the long and short pulses of the telegraph, the CPU uses electronic signals called **digital signals** to represent binary numbers, which are sequences of zeros and ones. Groups of binary digits are then used as codes for instructions, for text letters and numbers, for punctuation marks, and for control characters. When you enter "The quick brown fox" into your computer, it is represented internally as a set of tiny digital signals. A single zero or one is called a **bit** (short for **bi**nary dig**it**) and is the smallest unit of information in the computer. In the old days of digital computing, bits were represented by vacuum tubes that were either off or on, representing zero or one.

Communicating by code, whether it be Morse or computer, requires some clever manipulation of very limited variables. For example, how does the CPU know that one string of bits is a line of text, another a series of integers, another instructions, and so on? It knows the same way that people know to interpret "bear right at the intersection" as a direction to follow rather than the location of a large animal: by context. If you tell the computer to run a certain program, it looks for instructions to execute. If you ask it to accept some numbers you are going to type in for summing and averaging, it expects numbers. You can confuse the computer by slipping it letters instead of numbers when it is expecting numbers.

Another requirement for communication by code is to indicate the division between letters. In Morse code this is done by pausing briefly between letters. In computer codes this is done by assigning a specific number of bits to hold a text character. The choice of this number is up to the manufacturer of the computer and is called a **byte**. Usually it is a group of eight bits (though not always). When the context of its processing is text, the CPU knows to process the bits in byte-sized chunks, thus eliminating the need to pause between letters. Eight bits turns out to be a useful size for coding one text character, be it a digit (0-9), a letter (A-Z, a-z), punctuation mark (e.g.:;,.-!$%.), or a control character (e.g., enter, return, linefeed). There are 256 combinations of eight zeros and ones from 00000000 (0) to 11111111 (255). Currently, the full set of <u>ASCII characters</u> (American Standard Code for Information Interchange, pronounced "as-key") uses 128 of these. "A," for example, is 01000001 in ASCII. Generally speaking then, a byte is eight bits and is capable of representing one text character. A short table of examples of ASCII computer codes follows:

CHARACTER	ASCII CODE
A	01000001
a	01100001
8	00111000
?	00111111
linefeed	00001010
delete	01111111

Reference to "8-bit CPUs," "16-bit CPUs," and "32-bit CPUs," indicates the amount of information that a computer processes at a time. Whether it obtains 8, 16, or 32 bits of data from memory at one time depends on the electronic architecture of the chip. The number of bits processed at one time by the CPU is called a <u>word</u>. Although the 8-bit word is the one implemented by most manufacturers of microcomputers, some 16-bit micros are already available, and there is a wave of 32-bit micros on the horizon. Neither do all computers have words that are powers of 2 ($8 = 2^3$, $16 = 2^4$, $32 = 2^5$) there are some 12-, 24-, and 36-bit word machines lurking about (mostly from Digital Equipment Corporation). But there is a widespread feeling that computers were intended to have words that are integer powers of 2.

Why the different word sizes? A CPU that processes information in 16-bit chunks is roughly twice as fast at processing information as one that looks at 8-bit chunks. This means that in assessing the performance of a CPU, word size must be considered as well as instruction rate. Comparing CPUs is a little like comparing trucks: you must not only consider the speed of their operation, but also how much they can haul in a given load.

The CPU performs all of its logical and arithmetic functions internally, using special places called <u>registers</u> to hold numbers within the CPU. The registers have very limited capacity for storing information. To do its work the CPU transfers information stored in its memory (see discussion of memory in next section) to and from its internal registers. Memory is usually separated from the CPU; physically it is an array of chips. One portion of memory might contain a series of instructions to the CPU, another portion might contain data, the rest might be unused. For example, commanded to perform a set of instructions to add two numbers, the CPU will bring the first instruction into its internal instruction register. This instruction typically tells the CPU to load a number from memory location A into an internal register. Having done so, the CPU then fetches the next instruction, which causes the CPU to load a number from memory location B into another register. The CPU then gets the next instruction, which tells it to add the contents of the two registers. Finally, the last instruction causes the CPU to store the result in memory location C. Pretty tedious, isn't it? Don't worry, most people never deal with the CPU at this level. Be thankful for computer languages that shield you from all this tedium and for applications programs that insulate you even more.

Memory

The easiest way to think of computer **memory** is as a long string of bits that are accessible in word-sized chunks (e.g., 8, 16, or 32 bits at a time). The CPU can get one word of information from anywhere in that long string (the 1st word, the 10th word, the 324th word, or the 52,401st word). The location of the word in that string is given a number (1, 10, 324, 52,401), which is called its **address**. One of the most important things about computer memory is that the CPU can access the information in any address directly, without having to pass any other addresses. This is a very powerful, very important feature of memory (think how convenient it would be if you could go directly to any address in a large city without passing any other addresses).

Computer memory (also called **main memory**, **core memory**, or **main storage**) comes in several flavors. All, however, have this direct access feature, which in the computer world is called **random access**. The most common type is in fact called **Random Access Memory (RAM)**. This is somewhat misleading, since all computer internal memory is random access. Random Access Memory has the following characteristics:

- Data may move directly from any RAM address to the CPU (this is called **reading from memory**).
- Data may move directly from the CPU to any RAM address (this is called **writing to memory**).
- When you turn off the power to the computer all data held in RAM is lost (the information in RAM is thus called **volatile**).

In the photograph of the circuit board shown previously RAM is the sixteen chips arranged in two columns at the far right of the board.

The other type of memory is called **Read Only Memory (ROM)**. It has the following characteristics:

- Data may be read from ROM into the CPU.
- Data may not be written from CPU to ROM.
- Data in ROM is fixed, not volatile (when you turn off the power, the information is not lost).

In the photograph of the circuit board ROM is the two chips at the bottom right of the board.

RAM is the computer's general purpose memory. It is workspace for your programs and your data. Nothing stays there very long. Everytime you turn on your computer, you must reload RAM with the programs and data that you need. ROM usually contains special programs that will either be used very often or provide a limited set of simple commands that will allow the user to load more powerful programs as needed. On some microcomputers, the BASIC language is often provided in ROM to save the rather lengthy time it takes to load the language from a cassette tape.

ROM comes in several variations. Normally it comes from the factory with its programs already in place (manufacturers call such preprogrammed ROM firmware). There is a version called **Programmable Read Only Memory** (PROM), which can be set up by you, the user, with whatever programs are particularly important to you. Once you have programmed it, though, that's it. No substitutions, as the waiter says. There is also a version called **Erasable Programmable Read Only Memory** (EPROM), which can be erased (cleared to zeros) by a special process and then reprogrammed with a new code. But the basic distinction between RAM and ROM remains the same: RAM is volatile and you can write to it; ROM is nonvolatile and you can't write to it.

So with RAM for a workspace and ROM to store all your programs, you're all set, right? Wrong. While the price of computer memory has been dropping steadily in the last decade or so, it is still an expensive commodity. Putting any kind of large group of programs in ROM would be prohibitively expensive. Furthermore, most small computers are not capable of addressing (accessing) more than about 64,000 (64K) 8-bit bytes of RAM and ROM together. 64,000 (64K) bytes or text characters may seem like a lot, but it turns out to be very, very limited in its potential for storing a library of programs. As a workspace, it's fine. The solution to the problem is to store your library of programs and data files in another way: via peripheral storage devices.

PERIPHERAL DEVICES FOR STORING DATA

We introduced peripheral storage devices in Chapter 1 as a means of storing programs or other information in such a way that the information can be either recorded by or played back to the computer. Information stored in this fashion is said to be **machine-readable**. Once again, the advantage of having information stored in this form is that you don't have to reenter the information everytime yourself (e.g. via a typewriter-like keyboard). The gain in time and convenience, even with relatively slow peripheral storage devices, is immense.

Peripheral storage devices tend to fall into three broad categories: those that use paper as a medium (now antiquated), those that use magnetic tape as a medium, and those that use magnetic disks as a medium. We will describe the two modern methods.

Magnetic Tape Devices

As practically every stereo buff knows, the nice thing about magnetic tape is that one can both record on it and play back from it. The same is true with the tape systems used by computers. There are several varieties. The cheapest and simplest is the audio cassette system in which a standard audio cassette player/recorder (pictured) is attached to the CPU via a special connection that converts the digital signals of the CPU into audio tones. These are then recorded on a tape cassette. When played back, the audio signal of the tape is converted to the digital signal of the CPU. The advantage of the audio cassette system is that it is cheap. Cassette recorders are available from $40 to $80 each, and the cassette tapes are approximately $2 each. The disadvantages of the system are that it is both relatively slow and somewhat unreliable. The more reliable cassette systems only operate at 30 characters per second, which means it can take several minutes to load a large program from the tape into memory. Unreliability is even worse than slowness, however. The frustration of finding that you cannot retrieve a long and complex program you thought you had saved on tape is very great, for it means that you will have to reenter the program manually. Thus there is a trade-off between price on the one hand and speed and reliability on the other. Not surprisingly perhaps, better performance tends to cost more.

There are also **tape drives** made specifically for storing computer output as a digital signal (rather than as an audio signal) such as the digital cassette player/recorder pictured on the following page. These are much faster, much more reliable, and, alas, cost much more than audio tape player/recorders (anywhere from several hundred to several thousand dollars, depending on the speed and sophistication of the drive). The more sophisticated magnetic tape drives are widely used in large computer installations as an efficient means of storing very large volumes of information. These drives such as the reel-to-reel drive also pictured on the following page tend to use half-inch-wide tape and take reels up to 16 inches in diameter. On the less expensive side are devices like the Exatron Stringy Floppy, which records and retrieves digital signals on a small continuous loop magnetic tape cartridge.

Audio cassette player/recorder
Photo: Sharon A. Bazarian

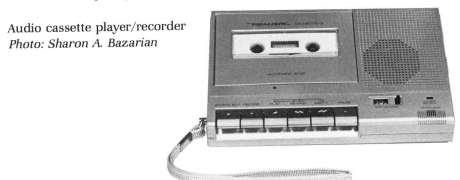

Digital cassette player/recorder
Photo: Sharon A. Bazarian

5¼″ floppy disk with disk drive
Photo: Texas Instruments, Inc.

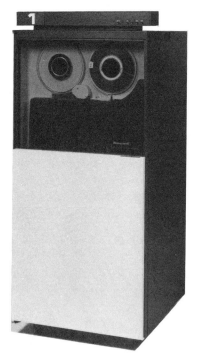

½″× 16″ reel-to-reel tape drive
Photo: Honeywell Information Systems, Inc.

Anyone who has used tape with stereo equipment knows that tape has an intrinsic design limitation: you cannot directly access any particular spot on the tape; you have to go forward or rewind until you find the place you want. This is fine if you want to play the whole tape, but if you want only a couple of items here or there, skipping around to find them can be tedious. One of Murphy's Laws assures us that any program we want to access will be at the opposite end of the tape at the time we want it most.

Magnetic Disks

Magnetic disks are the answer to this access problem. Instead of using a long tape as a recording medium, information is recorded on the surface of a round, flat disk coated with the same surface material as magnetic tape. **Disk drives** rotate the disk very rapidly. Playback/record heads are fixed on an arm that can be positioned anywhere along a radius of the disk. The operating principle is very similar to a record player in an audio system. Like a record player, the access to any spot on the surface is much faster than access to any given spot on a tape. Access times for disk systems are usually measured in thousandths of a second.

Magnetic disk drives come in two distinct forms: **floppy disk drives** and **hard disk drives**. The floppy disk (or **diskette**) was developed by IBM to replace punched cards, but it has been widely used by the small computer industry as a fast, efficient, and highly cost-effective approach to peripheral storage for small computer systems. The hard disk is similar to the floppy in operation but is about ten times faster in access time and holds about ten times as much information in the same space. It is currently the most cost-effective approach to peripheral storage for larger systems.

The floppy disk is so called because it is made of a thin, flexible plastic that bends easily. Floppies come in two sizes: 5 1/4-inch diameter and 8-inch diameter. They are permanently protected by a paper envelope that has a window in it through which the heads of the floppy disk drive contact the surface of the floppy disk. (See photograph of a 5 ¼" floppy disk with disk drive on the previous page.) There is a great variety in current disk technology. Depending on the manufacturer and system software chosen, a 5 1/4-inch floppy disk can hold anywhere from about 80,000 characters of information (80 kilobytes or 80K) to about 800,000 characters (800 kilobytes or 800K). The differences come from the density with which the information is recorded and the number of sides it is recorded on. (Some floppy disk drives work on both sides of a floppy disk, an option called **double-sided**.) Eight-inch floppy disks can hold from about 250,000 characters to over a million (1 megabyte or 1M). Access times (the time it takes to access any given spot on the disk) and transfer rates (how fast information can be read or written once the starting point has been found) vary widely as well.

Hard disks are made of rigid aluminum and are coated with a magnetic recording surface. They can operate much faster and can store characters more densely than floppy disks because the heads can read from or write to their surface without actually touching it. This means the heads must be very close to the surface, and therefore machinery of a very fine tolerance is required for reliable operation. A speck of dust can jam between a head and the surface and cause great damage. Thus hard disks are often sealed in special containers and rarely, if ever, exposed to a normal atmosphere. Until very recently hard disks were only affordable by those purchasing large computer systems, but a recent breakthrough known as **Winchester technology** has brought the price of these items down dramatically. (See the photograph of a Winchester hard disk drive.) As with floppy disks, recording densities and access times vary tremendously but are at least ten times the densities and speeds of floppy disks. Hard disks are available from 5 million characters (5M) to well over 100 million characters (100M).

At this point, we have discussed the central computer and peripheral storage. So far all we've got is some electronic devices talking to each other. The item missing from this cozy arrangement is you, the user. You need a way to communicate with the CPU and memory, both sending information (instructions or data) to the CPU and receiving results back. The section on peripheral storage devices was about communications between the computer and its library files. This next section is about communication between the computer and you.

Winchester hard disk drive
Photo: Honeywell Information Systems, Inc.

PERIPHERAL DEVICES
FOR THE USER

Some peripheral devices provide communication between the computer and the user. Examples include input devices such as keyboards, light pens, game paddles, bar code readers, optical character readers, and mark sense readers; and output devices such as cathode-ray tube monitors, printers, plotters, voice synthesizers, tone generators, and AC line controllers. Increasingly, some of these devices are combined into **input/output (I/O) devices**. For example, a keyboard and a video screen are often combined into a **video terminal**, such as the one pictured or a printer and a keyboard combined into a **hardcopy terminal**, such as the one pictured. The actual computer itself is often so small

Video terminal
Photo: Digital Equipment Corporation

Hardcopy terminal
Photo: Nixdorf Computer Corporation

that it is easily tucked away in a box largely dedicated to a peripheral device, such as a video terminal. Several manufacturers now make a video terminal unit that contains not only a computer, but also a pair of floppy disk drives and connections for a printer and other peripheral devices.

Terminals

Virtually all terminals use typewriter-like keyboards as their input component. Each time the user strikes a key, the terminal sends off to the computer a set of electronic pulses that are eventually changed into a one byte digital signal that reaches the CPU. If the CPU is accepting information from the user at this point, it will put the character received somewhere in its memory and send a copy back (by way of confirmation) that is reproduced on the output device.

Terminal keyboards vary in style and quality. Some have actual typewriter keys and, some work via a flat touch-sensitive panel. Some keyboards will have an additional numeric keypad for faster entry of numbers and/or a set of special function keys that can be defined according to the needs of the user. Some are easy to use, however some are very awkward. Worst of all, there are keyboards on the market that malfunction sporadically. A keyboard that will occasionally give you two letters for one keystroke (a phenomenon called keyboard bounce) is not much help.

Terminals vary in their output component which may be a TV screen (otherwise known as a **monitor** or **Cathode Ray Tube (CRT)**) or a **hardcopy printer** of some sort. Video terminals are usually capable of receiving information at a much faster rate than a hardcopy device, are much quieter, and don't chew up reams of paper unnecessarily. Also, a video terminal can be a much more flexible medium for graphics, as you can move the **cursor** anywhere on the screen with relative ease, and draw and erase lines readily. On the other hand, hardcopy devices provide you with an ongoing record of your entire terminal session (which is often more than you really want). However, most users do want results printed out at some point, and it is cheaper to buy a hardcopy terminal than to buy both a video terminal and a printer, which is why many people suffer the disadvantages of hardcopy terminals.

Video terminals have screens of varying size. Most good quality terminals provide an 80-column by 24-line screen, which is virtually the industry standard. Some more expensive models provide even more of a screen, and there are some that, alas, provide much-reduced formats. Some video terminals are capable of graphics (which simply means you can draw pictures as well as display text), some only handle text.

Most terminals these days are **intelligent**, which means that they have a microprocessor inside them to handle the terminal's functions and communications with the host computer. The so-called **dumb terminal** leaves all the chores to the host computer.

Printers

A <u>printer</u> is an output device (that is, the computer can send information to it but not receive information from it). It allows you, the user of the computer, to receive output from the computer on a piece of paper so that you can read it, analyze it, mark it up, file it, or dispose of it. The main difference between a printer and a hardcopy or printing terminal is that a printer lacks a keyboard. There are, however, several printing devices on the market that can be purchased with or without a keyboard. This option is usually indicated by the acronym **KSR** (**Keyboard Send/Receive**) or **RO** (**Receive Only**). The KSR printer is, of course, a hardcopy terminal.

As with everything else in this chapter, printers such as those pictured come in seemingly infinite variety. They vary in:

- The process used to produce a character on paper (dot matrix, daisywheel, ink jet, laser, thermal, electrostatic).
- The forms of paper handled (rolls, continuous pin-feed, single sheets).
- the width of paper handled (from 4 1/2 inches to 15 3/4 inches).
- The speed of printing (from 10 characters per second to over 200 characters per second).
- Price (from a few hundred to several thousand dollars).

But the purpose of all printers is the same: to transfer computer information to the printed page. Three different types of printer are shown in photographs on this page and the following page: dot matrix, daisywheel, and ink jet).

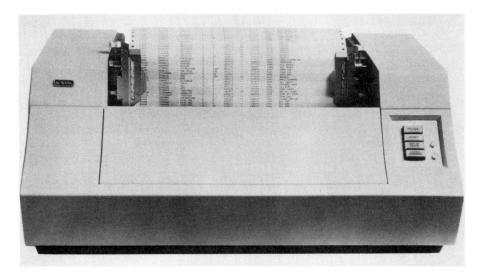

Dot matrix printer
Photo: Wang Laboratories, Inc.

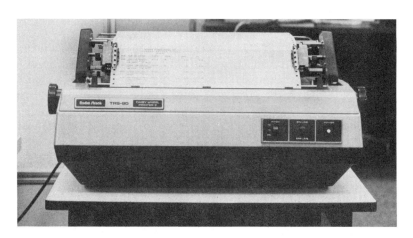

Daisywheel printer
Photo: Sharon A. Bazarian

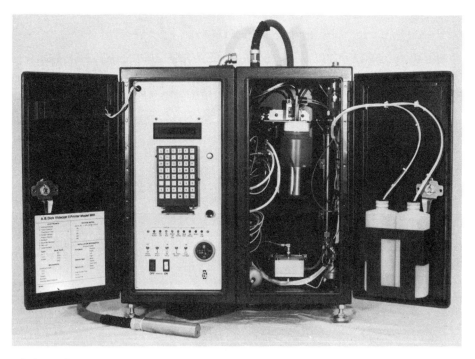

Ink jet printer
Photo: A. B. Dick

INTERFACES, CONTROLLERS, I/O PORTS

You may have been wondering exactly how the CPU communicates with the various peripheral devices we've discussed. After all, the CPU only understands patterns of electronic pulses or digital signals. How do such signals become typed letters on a video screen or a printer? The missing pieces are <u>interfaces</u> that change the signal of the CPU to some other kind of signal that the peripheral device in question can recognize, and vice-versa. The interface for a video screen is different from that needed for a printer and different again from the interface needed for a tape drive, and so on. In addition to simply converting the signals back and forth, interfaces perform other functions like resolving different device speeds. (It is no good sending a signal to a device faster than it can process it — compare the lightning speeds of the CPU with a 10 character per-second printer.) The interfaces themselves are connected to the CPU via chips and connections called <u>input/output ports</u> (an I/O port is pictured projecting out from the top right of the circuit board shown previously). A port is just a way in and out of the CPU.

Although different devices require different sorts of interfaces, the industry has managed to standardize two such interfaces: the RS232-C Serial interface and the Centronics Parallel interface. A <u>serial interface</u> transmits or accepts information one bit at a time. In contrast, a <u>parallel interface</u> accepts or transmits information a computer word at a time, by having eight wires to carry the eight bits simultaneously. Parallel is obviously potentially faster; serial is more standard and much more widely used. All communications over the telephone lines are serial (eight or more telephone lines would be required to support a parallel interface).

Finally, what ties all these things together (central processing unit, memory, input/output ports, interfaces, and so forth) is a set of parallel wires and connections called a <u>bus</u>. One of the breakthrough concepts in recent years has been to standardize bus structures so that different printed circuit boards from different manufacturers can plug in and work immediately. There are several competing standard bus structures on the microcomputer market, the most widely adopted of which is the S-100 bus. A standardized plug-in bus structure is called a <u>mother board</u> (also called a <u>cardcage</u> or <u>backplane</u>). The board contains slots into which you can plug printed circuit cards with various chips designed for specific purposes. There are boards or cards for virtually any purpose you can think of: interfaces, special graphics boards, voice recognition boards, language boards. Many of these come with their own central processing unit and/or ROM with some special programs on them. An S-100 mother board with circuit cards plugged in may be seen in the lower left hand quarter of the photograph of the inside of a computer shown on the following page.

S-100 motherboard with circuit cards plugged in inside a computer
Photo: Sharon A. Bazarian

COMMUNICATIONS
EQUIPMENT

Computer users can do a lot with wire: string it from building to building or even run it halfway across town to connect remote pieces of equipment together. Using wire in this fashion, you can connect terminals all over a building or campus to a central computer, or you can link several computers together in a network. But running your own wire at some point becomes impractical, and it begins to make sense to use that great network of wire that is already in place: the telephone system. The telephone system is set up to convert voice noises into electronic signals and then reassemble the audio signal at the other end. Thus, communication between computer devices through the telephone requires a special interface that will take the digital signals of the computer and convert them to audio tones before sending them on their way. And at the other end, the computer needs a box that will take the audio tones produced by the telephone and convert them back into digital signals recognizable by the computer device on the other end. Such a device is called a <u>modem</u> (<u>mo</u>dulator/<u>dem</u>odulator). There are two variations of modems: <u>direct-connect modems</u> and <u>acoustic</u>

couplers. Acoustic couplers such as the one pictured send and receive their signals directly through the mouthpiece and earpiece of the telephone, while direct-connect modems send and receive through wire connection to the telephone; otherwise they are identical in function.

Recall that interfaces between telephone lines and computer devices are serial in nature; that is, the bits of information or the tones representing them go through the phone line one at a time. Not only do the bits travel serially, but each group of eight bits (or each byte) is preceded by a start bit and ended by a stop bit. Thus it takes ten bits of information to transmit one character. The speed at which bits are transmitted and received becomes a real consideration for reasons of cost and efficiency. This rate is usually measured in bits per second and called the Baud rate. The commonly used Baud rates are 110, 300, 600, 1200, 2400, 4800, 9600, 19200. Currently, 1200 Baud (bits per second) or 120 characters per second (remember: transmission requires 10 bits per character) is the maximum rate attainable over ordinary public telephone voice lines with commonly available modems. Higher Baud rates require dedicated data lines and/or special and expensive modems. Even 1200 Baud is only available on relatively expensive modems. For those of us who cannot afford to have our data travel first class, 300 Baud is the standard rate.

There is lots more to hardware peripheral devices, but they all work on the same principles described above. They are either devices that allow you, the user, to make input to the computer or to obtain output from the computer, or they are peripheral storage devices that allow you to save programs and/or data between sessions.

Acoustic coupler
Photo: Texas Instruments, Inc.

SOFTWARE

But all this great hardware is worthless without software to run it. The classic error of neophyte computer buyers is to put all of their money into hardware and have none left for software. It is analogous to buying a record player without having any records available. In the horror stories that abound in the short history of computing, the one that seems to crop up over and over again is of the school system that bought a $50,000 computer, which then lay idle for two years for lack of software to run it. (Software, remember, is a collective name for those lists of instructions that tell the CPU what to do — whether to play chess or print the payroll.)

The process of acquiring a computer system should really start at the software end. The administrators who bought that computer should have first decided what use the school system wanted to make of the computer, then identified and priced the software necessary to perform those tasks, and only then chosen the hardware. Your purposes in acquiring a computer can be very general and educationally oriented, but unless you're interested in programming a computer at the binary code level, you will need software to fulfill those purposes.

There are two basic types of software: **applications software** and **systems software**. You have already been introduced to applications software: it is comprised of programs like the one to average numbers and the one to print the payroll checks. The effect of applications software is to insulate the user from the obscure and trivial operations down inside the CPU. A programmer has already figured out how to make the computer average numbers: the user doesn't need to deal with that side of the problem anymore. Applications software then is what makes the computer useful in doing the tasks we want it to do.

Systems software, on the other hand, is essentially applications software for programmers. It insulates them from the trivial and obscure operations down on the CPU level by making it much easier for them to write the programs to perform desired applications. It is systems software that makes it possible for one computer to be shared by several users at the same time, that provides for efficient management of files on the disk drives, and that allows the use of various computer languages.

Users only interested in specific applications and not intending to develop any applications programs on their own are prone to think that they need not care about systems software. Perhaps, but most applications packages eventually require modification and then the users will care. Further, if the systems software is poor and hard to use, then fewer good applications packages will be available for that system.

Systems software usually consists of an **operating system program**, several **utility programs**, and one or more **high-level language translators**. The distinction between these is somewhat blurred. Sometimes, for example, the operating system is made part of the language translator. Whether a particular function is included in the main operating system program, in a separate utility program, or in a language interpreter is the decision of the designers. How it is done is not terribly important, so long as the main functions are covered.

The operating system, generally speaking, allows the user to run programs and to control the movement of data to and from the computer memory and peripheral devices. A disk operating system (DOS) for example should allow you to name disk files, to obtain a list or directory of those names, and to copy files from the disk to another peripheral device. It should keep track of where all your files are on the disk — so you don't have to know or care.

Operating system utilities may include some sort of program to copy the entire contents of one disk onto another, a program to preformat new disks, some sort of text-editor to facilitate the typing in and changing of programs, and an assembler, which is a primitive language translator that makes giving instructions to the CPU a little easier. An assembler is just one step up from the binary codes that the CPU uses. Instead of giving the CPU a binary code meaning ADD, you can give the assembler a mnemonic instruction (perhaps ADD) and let the assembler translate that into binary code. Generally speaking, there is a direct one-to-one correspondence between an assembler instruction and a binary CPU-level instruction.

Assembler languages are sometimes referred to as low-level languages because of their close relationship to the actual operation of the CPU. High-level languages, such as FORTRAN, BASIC, COBOL, APL, and Logo are, in contrast, quite removed from the operation of the CPU. A single instruction in a high-level language may generate several CPU level instructions. The effect is to insulate you, the user, from the obscurity and triviality of the computer's operation at its most fundamental level. The trade-off is in efficiency. No one has yet written a language that performs as well as assembler: we pay for the insulation. But as the technology allows the speeds of these machines to increase and their prices to drop, it is a small cost to bear — and the benefits of high-level languages are many.

However appealing high-level languages may be to humans, they must be translated somehow into computer code for the CPU, since that is the only thing it understands. There are two types of translators: compilers and interpreters (an assembler is a special case of a compiler). Most high-level languages are compiled rather than interpreted. A language is usually one or the other, although BASIC is available in both compiled and interpreted versions.

A compiler works as follows: the user writes a program in a high-level language (such as FORTRAN, which is a compiled language) and stores that program in a file. The user then runs a FORTRAN compiler program, which translates the original program into machine code and stores that code in another file. Then the user tells the computer to load the machine code file into its memory and execute the instructions in it.

An interpreter works somewhat differently: the user loads a BASIC interpreter (for example) into memory, then gives the interpreter a BASIC program to run. The interpreter looks at the program one line at a time, translates and executes that line, and goes on to the next. Interpreters are easy to use and great for the "quick-and-dirty" program. But if a program is intended to be run often, it is better to write it in a compiled language, since an interpreter must repeat the translation process every time the program is run.

At the United Nations there are two kinds of human language translators: those who give a complete and uninterrupted translation when the speaker is done, and those who translate a speech line by line as it is being given. Compilers and interpreters are analogous to these two sorts of human translators. Clearly, each has a different function, though the general result is the same.

Most high-level languages were devised with a particular class of problems in mind. FORTRAN (Formula Translator) was designed to solve scientific and engineering problems easily and efficiently. COBOL (Common Business-Oriented Language) was designed for commercial data processing and reporting applications. BASIC was designed to be simple for nonscientists to learn and use in its rudimentary forms and yet to be very powerful in its full capability. Logo was designed to give children access to the full power of a computer as well as to be a powerful and elegant language for adults. Pascal was designed to combine the power of FORTRAN and COBOL with the more elegant logical structures of ALGOL (Algorithmic Language). Smalltalk is one of a class of artificial intelligence languages that insulate the user from the primitive operations of the computer even more than do the traditional high-level languages mentioned above. Instructing a computer with Smalltalk is much closer to instructing a person to do the same tasks.

In addition to being better or worse for certain classes of problems, high-level languages have a way of defining your computer environment, including the way you perceive your computer system and the way you use it. The situation is a little like the difference between hearing a play on the radio, seeing it on television, and attending it in person. The difference can be quite profound. Logo, for example, as described in Chapter 2 was specifically designed to create an environment in which children could experiment with and learn sophisticated mathematical concepts in a manner analogous to the way we learn our first spoken language. That a computer language can create an environment for exploring and experiencing mathland is a profound and extraordinary fact.

Yet another class of high-level languages is the author languages (see the Resources section: Author Languages for descriptions of several). These languages determine your programming needs from your responses to a series of questions. The author language program then produces a perfectly ordinary program in a high-level language, just as though you had written the program yourself. The effect is to allow you to write programs in a computer language without knowing much about the language.

Today there are literally hundreds of languages (and **dialects** of languages, which are different versions of the same mother tongue). Which ones you choose for your computer will depend on what purpose you would have it serve.

TIMESHARING AND NETWORKING

Timesharing

Timesharing is the use of one computer by several concurrent users. Typically, each user has a terminal that is connected to the shared computer. The connections can be made either through direct wires to ports on the computer or through modems and the telephone system.

Timesharing is based on the recognition that it is unusual for a single user sitting at a terminal to keep a central processing unit entirely occupied. By sharing the use of a Central Processing Unit among several users, the cost and power of one computer and its peripherals may be shared by many. However, you should note that the CPU can only do one thing at a time: it does not, as some think, actually process several user requests simultaneously. Rather the CPU will process one user's request for some small fraction of a second (called a **timeslice**), and then it will take up some other user's request. Timesharing operating systems are generally complex. The operating system must keep track of all the different users and where each user was last suspended while actually only servicing one user at a time. The timesharing system must also resolve contending requests for its services — not unlike a teacher in a crowded classroom with many students simultaneously clamoring for attention. Further, the computer activity of each user of a timesharing system must be insulated from every other user, so that one user's programs and data are not altered or lost by the interference of another user.

Timesharing usually requires fairly large and powerful hardware resources: a fast CPU, a great deal of memory, a large volume of hard disk space, a magnetic tape drive for back-up of information on the disks, sophisticated communications equipment, and a fast line printer. Although timesharing can work in a much less powerful environment, usually the constraints of such an environment make timesharing more trouble than it is worth. For example, although timesharing may be implemented on a system using only floppy disks for peripheral storage, this almost always results in a wrangle between the users over which disks will be on which drives. Nonetheless, in an appropriate environment, timesharing can result in a very cost-effective system on a per-user basis.

Networking

Networking is the communication between or the sharing of resources by two or more different computers. There are three broad categories of networks:

1. Resource-sharing networks.
2. Communications networks.
3. Distributed processing networks.

While timesharing is the sharing of one central computer among several users, resource sharing is the sharing of one or more peripheral devices among several computers. As single-user computer systems have increased in usefulness and decreased in price, the idea of sharing the more expensive peripherals has gained currency. For example, a school might wish to provide one printer for every four computer units. This printer could be shared by providing a rotary switch that controlled the actual connection between the printer and a single computer. In a more complex example, Corvus, Nestar, Intertec, and others manufacture intelligent hard disk systems designed to be shared by a great many computers (in the case of Intertec, you can attach up to 255 computers to one of their disk systems).

With the appropriate systems software to handle conflicting requests for the shared equipment, almost anything is possible. Any device that is not worth buying for every computer unit may potentially be shared by several units. Devices that have been effectively shared include high-speed printers, letter-quality printers, plotters, hard disk drives, and tape drives.

In communications networks the individual computers can send files or messages back and forth between the nodes (the computers) of the network. Communication networks can be particularly useful in education. Communication, after all, is a great deal of what education is about. Such networks can make possible a class of geographically separated students, can provide connections to large information systems (such as The Source), or simply provide a means of sharing ideas, programs, problems, and news, as for example, on a Computer Bulletin Board.

In distributed processing networks some data processing is done at remote computers and then transmitted to a central computer (uploaded) for more complex processing with results then sent back to the remote computers (downloaded) for review and more processing. In such a network, all communication is between the central computer and the units connected to it. Communication between the individual units, if any, is handled entirely by the central computer. Distributed processing is like timesharing with the terminals replaced by computers capable of doing some of their own processing.

Networking is only in its infancy at this time. It is an area in which we may expect great technological change and numerous creative applications over the next few years.

Choosing Your Computer System

Chapter

4

This chapter offers a general approach to the complex questions of choosing a computer system and some basic techniques for the slippery questions of hardware and software evaluation. Too many people are buying certain personal computers because it seems like the thing to do, or because they have been sold on a concept by an enthusiastic sales representative, or because their best friend just got one, or for some other less than rational reason. It is our hope that after reading this chapter you will buy whatever you buy as the result of a rational approach to computer system selection. There is still no guarantee that you will make the most appropriate choice, but your chances are considerably better.

In 1980 the business manager of a small company purchased a small IBM computer and some software packages to handle accounting functions and some other matters for the company. The combination of hardware and software worked adequately and met the needs of the company. A few months later IBM brought out a new and improved version of the same computer for several thousand dollars less. When asked if he did not now regret his decision, the manager replied that he did not, that so far as he was concerned the system was a success. The system met the need it had been purchased for, and its cost had already been justified at the time of purchase. That there was a price break just around the corner was not foreseeable at the time of purchase, and therefore not relevant to the decision.

About the same time, a mathematics teacher at an independent school persuaded her department to buy a small computer. She researched and purchased a very able microcomputer with some state-of-the-art features, but in her desire to get the best possible computer for the money allotted, she put all her money into the hardware and none into applications software. Her plan was to develop educational software in-house, mostly through her own programming. Just how the system was to be used was not clear to her colleagues, although hopes were high. The teacher, upon her return in the fall, plunged into learning all about the new computer system. She soon discovered that there was quite a lot to learn despite the generally superior instruction manuals for the system. The learning was time consuming. She also found that her full teaching load, her responsibilities in the dormitory, her coaching of a soccer team, her host of student advisees, and the several other demands of boarding school life allowed her no professional time whatever to spend on the computer. By the end of the first year, only a few students (who came to the school already having some knowledge of computers) and no faculty members other than herself had been exposed in any depth to the computer. Opinion of the system among the faculty was divided, but a large group had begun to feel that the computer had been a wasteful expenditure.

Both of these situations have elements of success and of failure in them, although by and large the first one was the more successful. The manager there had laid out very specific tasks for a computer system, located a combination of hardware, software, and service that could do those tasks, and decided that such a system was worth buying at its asking price. There were few, if any, surprises. The system performed the specified tasks within expectations.

In the second tale, the school and the teacher were not specific about the functions of the computer. As a result, no money was allocated to obtaining software nor was time allotted to any sort of organized program to expose students to the computer or to teach them rudimentary programming. Those interested in or responsible for the computer did not have the time to train others or expose them to this new educational resource. As a result, the computer languished, and unfavorable comment was heard in faculty meetings.

Yet, the situation at the school was not an unmitigated failure. The teacher had learned much about the new equipment — it worked and it was well documented. If the school were to allocate some money for software and some of the teacher's time to achieve some specific goals, the situation might still turn out very well indeed.

The problem is one of expectations. In the first case, they were met, which pleased the manager and his superiors, even though the expectations were really quite limited. In the second case, the expectations, even though they were vague, were not met and people were disappointed and bearish about further support. Human and political problems are sometimes much tougher than technical ones.

A RATIONAL APPROACH TO SYSTEM SELECTION

The purpose of the system selection process is to specify a computer system that will perform one or more specific functions for a price that seems worth it. The idea is for you and your colleagues to determine what the computer will do and how much that will cost. This gives the people who will eventually allocate funds for the computer a reasonable grasp of the decision they must make and creates a climate of reasonable expectations for the computer's performance. This approach should be taken whether you are a single teacher contemplating the acquisition of a single personal computer for your classroom or a committee charged with the selection of a far more powerful computer to serve many functions in the school. This approach should both increase your chances of adequate funding and increase the chance that your colleagues and others will regard this purchase as a success.

The central question is, "What uses do we intend to make of the computer now, and what further uses might we make of it in the future?" Those involved in the specification of a computer system should ask this question of every possible constituent group in the school. The answers will vary widely and will be constantly changing, but the question needs early and ongoing attention. The formulation of a catalog of desired computer applications is perhaps the single most important process you can undertake in evaluating and acquiring a computer system. It is essential, of course, that this "wish list" have some connection with the reality of both the technology and your budget. That this may be so, you may wish to use the worksheet in the Appendix that will assist you in matching desired applications with necessary components at a range of prices. But before using the worksheet, you need to know more about computer system components, both software and hardware, and how to evaluate them. This chapter is a guidebook to these somewhat mysterious regions.

LEARNING ABOUT COMPUTER SYSTEMS

You now need to gain a concrete, first-hand grasp of what a computer can and cannot do. Then you and your colleagues will be able to specify a cogent list of appropriate goals, based on your own knowledge and experience — especially experience. There is only so much that you can learn from books on this subject. Experience is critical. You need a "messing about" stage. That being the case, make gaining such experience in your school your first goal. Suggest to your potential funders that a small, inexpensive computer be purchased for the purpose of learning more about the state of the art and the art of the possible. Let the goals be to expose interested students and faculty to the system, to gain some knowledge and experience, and to see where you might go from there. Had these been the stated goals of the teacher in the second story above, the purchase of the computer might well have been a political success.

People are paid large amounts of money for specifying complex computer systems. Move within the range of your competence and experience. Do not try to implement a major installation of computer hardware and software unless you know what you are doing. Remember, the bigger the installation and commitment of funds, the larger the potential for disaster. And Murphy's Laws are very active in the computer field.

Having easy access to a computer is the best way to learn about computers, but it is not the only way. The classic approaches to learning about new fields apply to computer systems as well: read the literature and talk to those who have already acquired knowledge and experience. In addition to this book, there are a number of good, nontechnical publications to help you get started (see the Resources section: Periodicals and the Bibliography).

To find knowledgeable people, start with your local computer stores and dealers. It is most advisable to deal locally in any case, and people in such stores are usually quite helpful. The most useful of such stores are the independents, the ones not committed to any particular brand. But talk to them all; a good knowledge of local resources is essential to your acquisition decision. Find out what systems they are selling and why; tell them that you are a beginner in the field; solicit their advice and help. Be considerate of the proprietor's time: the retail computer business is highly competitive and profit margins are very narrow, so the salespeople are usually running behind schedule and are a little harassed. If you want to see the other end of the spectrum, go to a manufacturer of larger computers. They will give you all the personal attention of one of their sales reps for as long as you want it. Their profit margins are better.

Often, computer stores will have the equipment they sell set up for demonstration. Test drive it as much as you can. Borrow or buy the manuals and read them, particularly the manuals for beginners. There are two kinds of manuals: those that are intended to be instructional (like a text) and those that are intended to be used for reference (like a dictionary). Judge for yourself if the manuals are useful, readable, and complete. The collection of manuals for a computer system is called its **documentation**. Good documentation is hard to come by. When you find it, regard it as a strong indication of a well-engineered, carefully developed product.

EVALUATING SOFTWARE

If you are in need of one or more major software packages (a sophisticated record-keeping system for Basic Competencies, for example), you should parallel your search for a computer system with your evaluation of software. Depending on the relative importance of a specific package in the scheme of your needs, a choice of software package may dictate your choice of computer. Even though you might prefer computer X to computer Y, if a software package essential for your needs will not run on X, forget it. For example, if the computer language Logo is high on your list of software priorities, then, as of this writing, you must buy either an Apple, a TI-99/4, or a DEC minicomputer with graphics capabilities.

Here are some maxims to follow and traps to avoid when you are looking at important software. Software, of course, includes courseware, and these general rules are as applicable to courseware as they are to any complex and important piece of software. (Additional, specifically educational criteria for software selection will be taken up in the next chapter.) Applications software (including courseware) tends to be central to the question of what the computer is going to do, which is at the heart of our system selection process. Hence, many of these rules for software evaluation apply to hardware as well.

It is hard to make rules for evaluating software. It seems as though some of the best software works well despite violation of such rules. Be on the lookout for such exceptions. You may never find a piece of software that meets all the criteria; inevitably, you will have to compromise and weigh trade-offs. Advance awareness of the trade-offs is nonetheless very useful.

1. Look for Local Sales and Service.

No matter how well documented, every significant piece of software generates questions from its users. No matter how carefully designed and written, it probably has defects (bugs) in it. Someone familiar with the software on a technical level must be available to answer those questions and fix those bugs. Ideally, that person will be in your local calling area, will know you, your equipment, and your specific needs, and will have sold you the hardware, the software, and a maintenance contract. If this ideal is not available, your next best hope is telephone support from the group or company that produced the software. Research and test this long-distance option (even if local support is available). Some software companies are very helpful, some are not. In addition to software maintenance, you may need your local dealer for training. Even with good documentation and relatively experienced users, a short but intensive training session from a person already familiar with the software can save untold time and trouble.

2. Buy Software That Does What You Need It to Do.

Substantial differences in quality and performance are hidden under deceptively similar packaging. It is your task to break through the packaging to the operational substance of the software. Many vendors will try to reshape your needs to fit into their package, rather than providing a package with the flexibility to meet your needs. For example, you may find a grade-book management package that expects grades to be reported in numbers from 50 to 100. If your own system is based on letter grades or on some other method, this package may prove a poor choice. But approach the matter flexibly; a package may appear a poor fit because it does more than you wanted or because it is a better approach than the one you had thought out.

3. Obtain and Read the Documentation for the Software.

Read it before going to a demonstration or test to gain the most value from both the documentation and the demonstration. Recall the importance of good documentation as an indicator of a good-quality product.

4. Thoroughly Test the Software.

This should be done at an installation that already has the package up and running full steam. Many of the real drawbacks of a piece of software will not reveal themselves until it is fully laden with data and in constant use. Also, a full-dress demonstration of a package will suggest questions to you that you had not yet thought to ask. Make sure your test is "hands on."

5. Look for Good Error Checking.

If you enter a letter in response to a request for a number, does the program crash (that is, fail — perhaps losing all the work you've just entered), or does it merely indicate that your entry was unacceptable and ask you to try again? Well-designed software will trap all such errors internally, give you a plain-English statement of the problem, and send you back to correctly enter the response that caused the problem. With poorly designed software an unexpected response will often cause the program to fail or to provide incorrect results.

6. Demand Fast and Flexible Data Retrieval.

There is little that is more irritating than having information stored on a computer system that you cannot retrieve easily. Fast responses to queries are indications of sophisticated file design and handling. For example, if a school were to institute a basic competencies tracking system, qualified people ought to be able to display the record of a given student on request. Such a request ought to be fulfilled by the computer in a matter of a few seconds. If it takes more than that, the system is probably not worth your further consideration.

7. Buy Software That Makes the Computer Do the Work.

If you are constantly being asked by the programs to change disks or tapes or to enter the same information more than once, it could be a sign of inadequate hardware, inferior software, or both. In any case, continual shuffling of disks or tapes is more trouble than it is worth and should be avoided. Multiple entry of data is anathema.

8. Look for Software That Runs on Different Hardware.

Many users outgrow their first computer system very rapidly. Even if you do not, take it as given that someday you will replace your computer. When that day comes, it would be advantageous to be able to move your software packages to your new computer without an expensive conversion effort.

EVALUATING HARDWARE

Although we have separated the questions of hardware and software evaluation and implied that the software comes first, in actuality the evaluation of hardware and software must happen simultaneously. Identification of a wonderful software package is of little use to you if it only runs on computers that are practically unavailable to you.

The price revolution in computing has put much hardware and software within easy economic reach, but it has also led to a widespread belief that all computing is cheap. Not so. Some computing is very cheap, and some is very expensive. Large corporations pay hundreds of thousands of dollars for computer systems, while owners of small personal computers pay a few hundred. Do the corporations pay more because they want to? Is there any difference between the thousand-dollar system and the hundred-thousand-dollar system? Of course there is. It is the task of the would-be purchasers of computer services to discover if their intended applications for a computer system are in fact within their means.

General rules for buying hardware are at least as tricky as those for software. Nonetheless, we present the following ten rules for hardware evaluation. Take them as you would ten rules for a happy marriage: they won't guarantee success, but they might help.

1. Look for Local Sales and Service.

That this is also the first rule of software acquisition may indicate its importance. The rule is often hard to follow, even when local support is available, since most equipment can be obtained by mail at 20% less than retail. But computers, like everything else, break down, which is why you need local support. Make sure of your maintenance source before you purchase. A service contract, which normally will cost about 1% of the value of the equipment per month, is an essential item. Evaluate the quality of postsale service and support by calling several current customers of your potential service organization. If there is no locally available service, work out (and even test) the method by which you are going to move equipment back and forth. Figure out how long it will take and how long you can spare your most essential unit. Lack of adequate local resources for servicing is a serious enough drawback to consider delaying the idea of using computers in your school until such resources are available.

2. Beware of New Products.

Almost all hot new products go through a shakedown phase involving their hard use by consumers. This is called "letting your customers test your equipment." Unless you want to be part of testing the new product for the manufacturer or your need for its special features is overwhelming, you should wait until the company has learned its lessons and reflected them in new and much improved models.

3. Look for Durable Construction and Engineering.

If students are going to use it, it has to be rugged. Further, cheap construction or sloppy work anywhere should be regarded as a sign of poor quality work throughout. You cannot afford it.

4. Allow for Expansion.

It is practically a universal truth that most new users expand their computer use far more than anticipated in the first year or two. There are two strategies for coping with this problem. One is to try to anticipate the growth by purchasing hardware that is expandable or that is powerful enough at the outset to meet burgeoning demand. Alternatively, buy the minimal, nonexpandable system (usually much cheaper), but plan on going to some completely different configuration for your next phase. The route you choose will probably depend on your confidence and experience, but you should lean toward minimizing the cost of your "messing about" education phase.

5. Look for Good and Well-Documented Systems Software.

There are some very weak operating systems supplied with current hardware. In some cases they are functionally limited or unacceptably slow in performing their functions (e.g., it takes about fifteen minutes to make a copy of an 8-inch floppy disk under some personal computer disk operating systems); in some cases they are actually defective in their operation. Obtain a competent review from a consultant or computer magazine of any operating system you are considering that is more complex than a cassette-based system. You should get a similar review of the BASIC interpreter, (or indeed any prospective language translator which is supplied with a system) before purchasing. This is especially important if one of your major purposes in acquiring a computer is teaching programming. Not all BASIC dialects are created equal. There are some very poor interpreters on the market. If the one that comes with the system is not up to par, you may have to buy a different one. Your BASIC should handle decimal numbers as well as integers, and text character strings as well as numbers. BASIC was developed as a language that handled text more naturally and powerfully than its predecessors. Beware of stripped-down interpreters that lack these essential pieces.

6. Choose a System with More Than One Language Available.

BASIC is very good, but you may later find that some of your needs are better met by FORTRAN, Pascal, Logo, or COBOL. The point is that you cannot anticipate every need, but you can have a better chance of meeting most needs if you choose a computer with a variety of systems software support. Availability of languages for a computer is a good indication of such support.

7. Look for Systems with a Lot of Available Applications Software.

That others have written many programs for a computer is an indication of ease of programming, which in turn suggests quality in the operating system, language translators, keyboard, screen editing, and other components. Further, availability of packaged software may be essential in itself: many teachers do not have time to write all the programs they may want to use. It is nice to know that some of them have already been written by professionals.

8. Talk to Owners and Users of the Systems You Are Considering.

Bear in mind that it will be a little like talking to the proud owner of a new car. Most new owners will be quite pleased with their choice, whatever the objective merits of the case. Only a very few will admit to making amistake. Nonetheless, their reports of experiences with their systems will be very useful, especially if you have done your homework on the system so that you talk to them intelligently.

9. Don't Rush Anything.

Haste is a sure way to guarantee an unpleasant result. If everything takes three times as long as you expected, you are right on schedule. That's just the way it is in the world of computers.

10. Remember That All Rules Have Exceptions.

Use these rules, but do not be bound by them into doing something less than intelligent.

PRICE AND PERFORMANCE

Computers can be categorized almost endlessly. In this section we present our own breakdown with a discussion of available hardware systems in each of the following categories:

1. Hand-held computers.
2. Cassette based computers.
3. Floppy disk based computers.

4. Hard disk based computers.
5. Resource-sharing networks.

HAND-HELD COMPUTERS

Radio Shack (among others) makes a hand-held micro. The hand-held micro pictured retails for about $230.* It measures 11/16 x 6 7/8 x 2 3/4 inches, has a full 57-key keyboard for entry and a single 24-character display line. It accepts commands in a BASIC that is very similar to TRS-80 Level I BASIC. It comes with no provision for storage of programs or data, but Radio Shack will provide a cassette tape interface for about $50, a cassette recorder for about $80, or a

Hand-held microcomputer with audio cassette player/recorder
Photo: Sharon A. Bazarian

*All prices quoted in this book are based on information obtained just prior to publication. They are, of course, subject to change.

combination $6-column printer and cassette interface for about $150. Of course, once the interface and recorder are attached, you have lost the size and portability feature and have, instead, a small desk-top computer. Owning a hand-held computer is a bit like owning a calculator built into your wristwatch: you accept trade-offs in the form of loss of features for the convenience of compact-ness. The inconveniences you must accept in a hand-held computer are: a small, crowded keyboard; severely limited display (one line); limited provision for hardcopy output; limited language capability; lack of convenient mass storage; lack of graphics capability; and extremely slow operation.

The advantage is price. If a school bought one cassette recorder and one interface for every two hand-held computers, it would cost about $300 per unit. This could equip every student in a class of thirty for about $9,000. Although there is as yet little or no software available for hand-held computers, these units might be effectively used to teach rudimentary BASIC programming as part of a computer literacy component. Note, however, that the most inexpensive full-screen computers cost but little more than the hand-held computers and offer far more power and function.

CASSETTE BASED COMPUTERS

Cassette based micros were at the heart of the initial rapid growth of the home-computing and the school-computing markets in the late seventies. Here is where Apple, Radio Shack (TRS-80), Commodore (PET), Atari, Ohio Scientific, and other microcomputer manufacturers did most of their early business. All of these companies still offer micros with a cassette option, like the two pictured on the next page, although the majority of their sales are now in disk based micros. Casette based systems range widely in quality, features, and price; and it is often hard to make accurate comparisons from one vendor to another. One company will include a video monitor in its package, others will not. One company has a full-stroke key typewriter keyboard, another will offer a flat-panel membrane instead. One will offer easy expansion via plug-in boards, another will not be expandable — but much cheaper. Comparisons are tough.

By and large the cassette based micros are inexpensive. The Sinclair ZX81 starts at about $150 for the base machine, assembled, $100 in kit form. Other inexpensive units include the Commodore VIC-20, the M/A COM OSI Challenger I, the Texas Instruments TI99/4A, and the TRS-80 Color Computer. Cassette recorders are extra and so are the monitors. The theory is that people may already own a useable cassette recorder and a TV that they can convert to computer use. Schools may not own enough cassette recorders or TV sets to dedicate to the computers they buy. In that case, plan on spending about $150 for a black-and-white monitor or $400 for a color monitor, and $75 for a good-quality cassette recorder.

The products just mentioned are the bottom of the line for each vendor. This does not mean they are necessarily of poorer quality, but it does mean that they

Microcomputer with cassette option
Photo: Sharon A. Bazarian

Microcomputer with cassette option
Photo: Sharon A. Bazarian

will be the most stripped-down version of a computer that you can buy. (Now that you've bought this new automobile, wouldn't you like to buy some wheels to go with it?)

Near the other end of the cassette based micro price spectrum is the Apple, which runs about $1,250 for the Apple II—with 16K of memory (plus cost of cassette recorder, plus cost of color monitor). For this higher price, the Apple includes some very nice features, such as excellent color graphics and an eight-slot expansion bus. Still it does not offer everything you might want, such as lowercase letters, without which word processing can be tedious unless you purchase substantial amounts of additional hardware and software.

In the Appendix, there is a table listing a variety of cassette based micros and the features they offer. It will give you a good idea of what is available and at what price. The question of the quality of what you can buy is trickier and one that you will have to determine for yourself. Ford used to advertise that it built a quieter car than the Rolls Royce. Somehow, that does not quite translate to meaning that the two cars were of comparable quality, although both had many of the same features: tires, seats, and a trunk.

Cassette based microcomputers can't be beat for introducing people to computers and computing and for getting them started "messing about." Available for such micros are many games, demonstrations, calculation programs, graphics programs, some simulations, and some fairly powerful BASIC language interpreters, which are very good for teaching beginning BASIC to neophytes. There are even some quite powerful applications programs written for cassette based microcomputers, mostly in the engineering field, such as a program to calculate solar energy and insulation requirements for buildings in different latitudes and climates.

On the other hand, some disadvantages of a cassette based system are:

- It takes a relatively long time to load a program from a cassette into the computer or vice versa. An ordinary 16K program will take approximately ten minutes to load at 300 Baud (bits per second).
- Some of the cassette systems are unreliable. It is irritating to save a program that you have spent hours developing and then find at a later date that the computer won't accept the playback.
- Cassette systems are nearly useless for any application that requires the storage and retrieval of any significant amount of data. It can be done with great effort, but it is not worth it. For example, you can buy a word processing package that is cassette based, but the saving and retrieving of documents on cassette tapes is too slow and awkward to be of much use. If you recognize from the start that applications that process data files are beyond the scope of a cassette based system, you will have a much easier and more rewarding time with your system. Don't try to make a pick-up truck do the work of an eighteen-wheeler. Allow for the limitations of your tools.

The great advantage of the cassette based systems is that they are cheap, and a school can thus afford to provide sufficient units to work with a whole class. It is very frustrating to have too few units. For most classroom uses, one system for every four students is considered the maximum productive computer-to-student ratio.

FLOPPY DISK
BASED COMPUTERS

All of the manufacturers of cassette based microcomputers have provision for upgrading those units with floppy disk systems (see for example the top photograph of a floppy disk based computer). These vary in features, capacity, quality, and price (see the table in the Appendix). There are also some other manufacturers not in the cassette game, such as DEC, Xerox, Osborne, and Intertec, who make floppy disk based computers that are worth considering (see for example, the bottom photograph of a floppy disk based computer).

Floppy disk based computers vary even more in price than do the cassette based machines. They start at about $1,000 for the M/A COM OSI Challenger I and go as high as $5,000 for some of the more sophisticated systems. The price rises with increasing density of storage, reliability, speed of access, sophistication of operating system, and overall quality. There are many factors to consider in floppy disk based systems.

The great advantage of the floppy disk based computers is that they largely overcome all the disadvantages of the cassette based systems. Loading and saving programs is quick and painless, reliability is generally much higher than in cassette systems, and floppy disks allow you to make effective use of the computer for applications requiring storage and retrieval of data. The importance of this last point cannot be overstated. Historically, this is what computers have been all about. Even when they cost hundreds of times what they do now, schools used them for their capacity for storing, retrieving, and processing data. A computer system that cannot do so is, in some important sense, crippled.

Recall that computers cannot do anything that people can't. All computers do is perform certain repetitive tasks faster and, on the whole, more accurately than people. Thus, time is of the essence, and a computer that wastes five minutes of your time just loading up your instructions is not doing its job very well. Cassette based computers have their place, but virtually everyone who owns a cassette based machine yearns for a floppy disk system. If you start with cassettes, be sure to incorporate a better peripheral storage system into your plans for the future.

So what are the disadvantages of floppy disk based systems compared with cassette based systems? Complexity, for one. Controlling that floppy disk drive requires a much more sophisticated operating system than does a cassette

Floppy disk based computer
Photo: Sharon A. Bazarian

Floppy disk based computer
Photo: Sharon A. Bazarian

recorder. All of the features needed to handle the storage and retrieval of data require an operating system that will be much larger and more complex than will a cassette operating system. This means, in turn, that you must buy more memory. Further, since programs will now be easier to load and save, they will tend to become larger and more complex, and again require more memory. The choice of languages available will be much greater (about all you can get on cassette is BASIC); and the disk versions are much more powerful, again requiring more memory. Finally, the more powerful disk input/output routines in these other languages usually prove to be difficult for new users to master. The increased complexity may be bewildering to some users. It's harder to drive an eighteen-wheeler than it is a pick-up.

If your school intends to have a great many computer units, it may not be very cost effective to buy a floppy disk system for each of them. You may want to consider connecting several units to some sort of intelligent hard disk (see section on networking and resource sharing) or consider a timesharing system (see discussions below).

The following educational uses of the computer begin to make sense with a floppy disk based system.

1. **Word processing.**

   The ability to edit and rewrite papers with relative ease is nothing short of marvelous. The key to it is the ability to keep the manuscript on a floppy disk. Word processing is useful for teachers, for students, and for administrators.

2. **Classroom administration.**

   It now becomes possible to do sophisticated record keeping on the computer. There are systems that will track basic competencies, attendance, or any number of record-keeping functions.

3. **More complex tutorials, simulations, drill and practice sessions, or other CAI programs.**

   Any situation where it would be helpful to have the computer "remember" where you were when you left off last time can be handled by a floppy disk based system. Further, it is possible to tie all of these curriculum applications into record-keeping routines.

4. **Statistical analysis of raw data.**

   With a good statistical package you can collect data, store it on floppy disk, and then run analyses on it. This is great for teachers who like to put classes to work doing surveys, as well as for administrators who need to make pupil population projections.

5. Any application that requires the processing of data, provided the volumes of data are not too large.

   For example, a disk based computer in a science lab could track laboratory inventory as well as record data from actual experiments.

Timesharing with Floppy Disk Based Microcomputers

A timesharing configuration for floppy disk based microcomputers is possible but of dubious value. The reason for a timesharing system is to have the most expensive computer resources, such as the CPU, main memory, disk drives, and printers shared by several users, each of whom has his or her own computer terminal, usually a video display and keyboard. A timesharing system works by having the computer serve each user in turn. No matter how many users appear to be receiving simultaneous service, the computer is actually only working with one at a time. Therefore, the effectiveness of a timesharing computer depends on how many requests for processing it receives in a given time frame and how fast it can take care of those requests. The advantage of such a system is the per-user cost saving possible through such sharing. The compromises you make when you put together a timesharing system on a small floppy disk based computer are as follows:

- The 8-bit micro CPU chips are not designed to be fast and powerful enough to handle several users. For certain applications, several users can effectively share a single 8-bit CPU, but too often the demand for processing exceeds the power of the CPU, producing unacceptably slow response. For example, more than one person trying to use the same 8-bit CPU for word processing would almost certainly be a disaster.
- The operating system required for timesharing is much more complex than an operating system dedicated to a single user. It costs more and it consumes more computer memory (a limited commodity in most 8-bit systems).
- Given the small volumes of information that can be stored on floppy disks (relative to hard disks), the likelihood of competition for floppy disk drives is very great. That is, Tom can't put his floppy disk in the computer if Sally is working on hers. The only way that such sharing becomes possible is if the computer system is set up for several users working on the same application package at the same time. For example, if a series of drill and practice programs were all on the same floppy disk, then several users could be running such programs concurrently.

The last disadvantage given is by far the largest problem. It is usually impractical to configure a timesharing system without the larger capacities and higher speeds of a hard disk system. Unless your use of computers is unusually limited, such as in the example above, this is not a good alternative.

Suitable applications for timesharing floppy disk based systems include all of those listed for single user systems. However, recall that although all of those different applications are practical, they cannot all be available to all users simultaneously because of the limited amount of data that can be stored on a floppy disk. In the best of circumstances, a single, 8-bit CPU cannot be expected to serve more than four concurrent users.

HARD DISK BASED COMPUTERS

Hard disks are generally much faster, more reliable, and larger in capacity than floppy disks. The smallest hard disks hold about 5 megabytes (5 million characters) of information, which is 5 times the capacity of the largest floppy disks and over 50 times the capacity of the smaller ones. Much larger hard disks (from 10 to several hundred megabytes) are available for more money. Although hard disk drives cost more than floppy disk drives, the cost per unit of storage is much less than for floppy disk systems. The amount of storage available on a hard disk is more than a single user needs for most educational applications, so in schools the hard disk system is usually found in a multiple user computer system. This could be either a timesharing system or an intelligent hard disk (such as a Corvus) shared by several single-user computers.

Hard disks overcome the major drawback of the multiple user floppy disk system. With the significantly greater storage capacity of the hard disk, all program and data files of all users of the system can be available to the CPU at all times. The problem that Tom and Sally had with having information physically located on different floppy disks and the resulting competition for floppy disk drives just doesn't exist anymore.

Further, hard disks are much faster than floppy disk systems. That is, it takes less time for the CPU to get a chunk of information from a hard disk than from a floppy disk. For applications that require a great deal of input from and output to data files, this is an important consideration. Bear in mind that the requirements of a timesharing operating system often involve a lot of disk I/O in swapping users in and out of main memory. The speed of disk access is thus an important consideration.

Hard disks are much more reliable than floppy disks, which tend to take a terrible beating from users. Hard disks are contained in much more protective environments. The disk units are usually sealed so that there is much less chance of dirt or smoke fouling the recording surface or the heads.

With hard disks, timesharing with an 8-bit computer now becomes a better proposition. Once again, even with hard disks, an 8-bit CPU should not be used to serve more than four concurrent users, and even that load may be too much for some applications.

Timesharing with 16-Bit and Larger Computers

More powerful timesharing systems are available. These are based on 16-bit or larger CPU's, large and fast hard disks, and sophisticated operating systems. Such computer systems like the one pictured in use in a school are capable of supporting from 4 to 64 simultaneous users, depending upon the power and configuration of the machine. The evaluation, configuration, and acquisition of such a system requires careful study, expert consultation, and a lot of money.

Prices start at $20,000 and go up from there. Usually the acquisition of such a machine implies the employment of at least one full-time computer systems manager.

It is not that such systems perform any great tasks that the 8-bit CPU/hard disk combination cannot. Rather, such systems are simply capable of doing their tasks faster, handling a greater volume of data, and responding to a larger number of concurrent requests for processing. A large timesharing system might be capable of handling the academic and administrative computing for an entire school district; an 8-bit system is more appropriate for administrative use in a single school or instructional use in a single class.

Applications software for large timesharing computers tends to be qualitatively different from that available on the 8-bit machines. It is generally more sophisticated, often of an older generation of software development, and quite likely to be more cumbersome to use. The same critical judgments should be applied to these software packages as to any others. A high price tag is no guarantee of high quality.

The potential advantage of such large systems is cost per unit. A $50,000 system (including terminals) that will support 16 concurrent users costs about $3,000 per user, which is cheaper than some floppy disk based systems for single users. With the additional advantages of far greater range of power and sophistication, this is potentially a very attractive proposition. In addition, some of the vendors of large computers are open to negotiating substantial discounts for educational buyers.

However, the larger the system, the more potential there is for disaster. The planning and budgeting process for acquisition of a $50,000 system is obviously a

High school computer room
Photo: Sharon A. Bazarian

much weightier matter than the process of acquiring a $2,000 micro system. We have not provided a table of such systems in the Appendix, partly because of the difficulty of making a meaningful presentation of such varied and complex equipment, but also because the selection and acquisition of such computers is a matter that is ultimately better left to the experts.

RESOURCE-SHARING
NETWORKS

We have discussed timesharing as a means of controlling unit costs by sharing the more expensive elements of a computer system among several concurrent users. The basic problem with timesharing is that it seems that the saving gained by the sharing is often offset by the cost of increased requirements for CPU speed, main storage, and operating system complexity. Timesharing seems to make expensive a resource which at the single-user level is relatively cheap. Resource-sharing is a technique that avoids this dilemma.

The idea is to take an expensive piece of equipment, such as a hard disk or a printer that is not needed by every user at every moment and share it among several users, each of whom has his or her own computer. Commodore has a very simple way of doing this with a printer. The plugs for the cables carrying the data from the computers to the printer stack together, and the printer can be used by any one of the computers connected to it. The protocols for who uses it and when are largely a matter of verbal negotiation among the computer users ("O.K. if I use the printer now, Bob?" "Sure, just as soon as I get one more listing. . ."). It's primitive, but it's cheap, it works, and it's much better than only having the printer available to one of the computers.

A hard disk drive is potentially the most interesting and useful resource to share. Such a drive must be accompanied by its own "intelligent" controller to sort out, prioritize, and service conflicting requests for disk I/O's, but such controllers are not nearly as complex as a timesharing operating system. Such a system is known as an intelligent disk system, since it has its own CPU and limited operating system. As a nice side benefit, such a system will also allow you to share other devices such as printers or plotters. This works by having all requests for the printer go into a disk file called the **print queue**. These requests are then dealt with in order of arrival as the printer and disk have time.

This resource-sharing approach has only been around for a very few years, and its capacities and limits are not yet well understood. Intertec, one vendor of such systems, has a provision for attaching up to 255 of its Compustar computers to its intelligent disk systems. It is doubtful that the intelligent disk system could actually handle concurrent requests from 255 computers without becoming hopelessly mired. But it is clear that it can handle some large number of them. Much depends on the applications to be served.

Corvus, another manufacturer of intelligent disk systems, provides for attaching up to 64 computers to its disk systems. Corvus is, so far, the only vendor that allows different types of computers to be attached. That is, with Corvus you can have an Apple, a TRS-80 Model III, and an S-100 computer all accessing the same disk concurrently. Under Corvus's system each computer is given access to a separate physical area of the disk. Corvus sells special interfaces with its system in order to make the connection to each different computer.

Perhaps the key element in intelligent disk systems is the rate at which data is transferred between a computer and the disk system. The higher that rate, the better the disk system will be able to handle many concurrent requests for I/O.

COSTING OUT YOUR WISH LIST

Now that you know what configurations of computers are needed for what sort of applications under various circumstances, you are ready to develop a wish list that represents the perceived needs of you and your colleagues. Then, using vendor catalogs and the blank worksheet in the Appendix, you can cost out your various desired applications.

Suppose, for example, that you and your colleagues have decided on the following purposes or applications for a computer in your school.

- The English teachers would like to make word processing available to students for writing papers.
- The social studies teachers would like some simulations of various key situations in American politics (e.g., the Hayes/Tilden election). They would also like a statistics package that would be able to analyze survey data.
- The math teachers would like a series of tutorial and practice programs on math topics and the programming language APL.
- The art teacher wants a sophisticated graphics package and plotter.
- The assistant principal wants the beginnings of a school-wide computer literacy campaign with as many students as possible exposed to computers in a hands-on and unthreatening way. She would like students to begin learning to program a computer, but has no particular preference as to which language should be used.

Now you would duplicate and then fill out the blank worksheet supplied in the Appendix, using one or more pages for each application. It will take a lot of research and legwork to fill out the worksheets in full detail. When you are done, you will have a good idea of what products are available for your desired applications and what each one would cost if a computer system were solely dedicated to that application.

The next step is to look across the list of applications for pieces of the system that can be shared. Ideally, you will find a configuration of hardware that supports decent software packages for each of your applications. Practically, however, this will often involve compromise: the machine that supports most of your packages may not support all of your top priorities.

Now you need to factor in some general considerations for the system:

- How many people will use the system concurrently?
- Are you going to locate all the equipment in one place, distribute it to different locations, have it portable, or some combination of the above?

Now you are ready to cost out your entire system as:

- Several stand-alone micro systems.
- A timeshared system.
- A resource-shared system.

Typically, you will find that your original wish list far exceeds potential funding for this project, no matter how you configure the system. Now you must go back to the charts and look for the applications that are most expensive to implement. There is an old adage that states that 90 percent of computing is cheap; the other 10 percent is very expensive. If your desired applications are within the 90 percent range, you may be able to put together a very useful system for comparatively little money. It is almost axiomatic, however, that the most interesting applications fall into the 10 percent range. So it goes.

In your search for inexpensive ways to maximize the effectiveness of a computer, look for those applications that require the least computer time per student. For example, in some of the better simulations, one computer provides information to each of several groups using the simulation. The groups then go off and work independently of the computer, organizing their information and formulating their next set of decisions in the simulation. Typically, groups will finish at different times and thus their need to consult the computer will be staggered. On the other end of the scale, students using a word processor to type their papers may tie up computer units for hours, especially if they are just learning to type.

You may find that you have so exceeded your resources that you have to go back to square one and begin anew. Your time has not been wasted; at worst, you have a lot of knowledge and information that will be very useful in the future.

Charting out the applications is a very useful approach, but it does not tell you anything about quality. There is a substantial quality difference between a BASIC interpreter that will handle character strings and one that will not, or between a word processor that provides upper case and lower case letters and one that does not. You must determine for yourself the relative worthiness of the package.

Ultimately, you and your colleagues will have to establish priorities for your desired applications according to your sense of educational needs, technical considerations, and the political realities of your school. In order to do this, you may want to share the costed-out application list with members of the various constituent groups in the school to ask them for their priorities. Doing this maximizes participation of eventual computer users, although it also makes the decision-making process a bit more cumbersome.

Eventually, of course, you and your colleagues will have to make a proposal to those who allocate the money. If you have done your job, the proposal will ask for computer equipment for one or more carefully defined purposes. You will have spelled out the benefits and detailed the costs. You will have created a set of reasonable expectations in the event that the proposal is funded. Now it's up to the keepers of the treasury.

SUMMARY

Some last warnings:

1. **Don't try to do too much with too little computing power.**

   Do not, for example, expect an 8-bit CPU to support a major timesharing system of 16 terminals. Limit your initial expectations to tasks that are well within the capacity of the system you have budgeted. Avoid disappointment.

2. **Don't try to buy too much computing power for too little money.**

   There are manufacturers who have become price competitive by lowering the quality of their components rather than by technological breakthrough. Be especially careful to purchase top quality electromechanical devices (e.g., printers and disk drives), since these are more prone to failure than electronic components and are harder to fix.

3. **Listen very carefully but don't believe everything you hear.**

   Demand tests and demonstrations whenever possible. Be suspicious of claims.

So if you read the literature, evaluate your needs, follow all these rules, and avoid all the indicated traps, will you make the right choices of hardware and software? The answer is, "Not necessarily." It may be that there are no good choices for your particular need and budget. Or if there are good choices, they may not be locally available. Much depends on you and your own savvy. Be tough and thorough, but be flexible and open to new ideas at the same time. Learn as much as you can, but be aware that your information will never be complete and that there will always be much more for you to learn. Take heart in knowing that everyone, including the professionals, is in the same boat. There is simply no way of knowing all there is to know about computers.

Photo: Apple Computer, Inc.

Choosing Educational Software

Chapter

5

So far, in this book we have discussed procedures to help you select and purchase your computer system, including hardware, systems software, and general applications software such as text-editors, statistical packages, language interpreters, and accounting packages. Many schools would consider a system with these components to be perfectly adequate for all their classroom and administrative needs. With it, they could teach programming, do word processing and data processing, and develop their own instructional programs.

Other schools would find such a system to be totally lacking in the core element they feel they need: courseware, those packages of software and ancillary materials specifically designed for classroom instructional use. For such schools, computers are used primarily for Computer Assisted Instruction or Computer Managed Instruction, not for programming or as tools.

Although many schools use computers in a variety of ways, there do appear to be two competing philosophies of classroom use: one in which the student learns by using the computer for some purpose such as programming or word processing and one in which the teacher uses the computer in some way to instruct the student about something such as drill and practice of addition facts or simulation of the French Revolution.

Nevertheless, whether a school needs courseware or more general applications software, it is faced with the demanding task of selecting the materials appropriate for its educational purposes. What makes such educational software selection so difficult is the limited choice to be found among the vast quantity of software offered by a bewildering number of sources. Add to this combination of factors the consensus among educators that the quality of most educational software is low, and you have an unenviable task for teachers considering computer use in their classrooms.

In the following sections we discuss each of these obstacles to educational software selection and suggest some possible aids to teachers for overcoming them.

TOO MANY PROGRAMS FROM TOO MANY SOURCES

It seems that every day a new catalogue of educational software is published, a new software publishing house emerges from the woodwork, or a new software exchange springs up. The prospective software user is faced with making choices from among a vast number of educational programs from a large number and a wide variety of sources. These include major educational publishing houses, smaller software publishers, hardware manufacturers, computing magazines, independent software developers, educational product distributors, computer stores, software clearinghouses, software exchanges, user groups, friends, colleagues, and students. To help teachers cope with the proliferation of software and software sources, a number of organizations have published software directories that list and sometimes describe both (see the Resources section: Software for lists of software directories, catalogues, and clearinghouses).

Most computer educators agree that further steps need to be taken to provide teachers with a more systematic, comprehensive, and descriptive listing of available educational software. In the near future, we are thus likely to see on-line data bases, which teachers could access via computer, containing descriptions of available software. Each software listing would include descriptors such as subject area, application, grade level, instructional model, program style, and publisher, which would allow teachers to use their computers to sift through the morass of available materials to find those suited to their needs.

LIMITED CHOICE
OF EDUCATIONAL SOFTWARE

Despite the apparent wealth of available educational software, the range of choice for most teachers is rather limited, as we shall see.

Paucity of Available Languages and Tools for Classroom Use

Most available educational software is CAI. Teachers who are more interested in having students learn programming or in having them use computers as tools have a rather small number of programs from which to choose. They may select one or more of the few appropriate languages for student programming and one or more of the few available general applications packages such as text-editors, statistical packages, or accounting packages.

Unfortunately, for the most part even the languages and applications packages considered appropriate for schools are not really designed with classroom use in mind. Thus, teachers often must rewrite instructions so their students can use the programs and must create a curriculum, including ancillary materials, with which the programs may be used. While many teachers might welcome the degree of control over their curriculum this situation affords, others would cringe from the demands involved in such curriculum and materials development.

However, some hope appears to be on the horizon. During the last few years, research and development efforts have been directed toward creating languages and tools specifically for use by students in educational environments. Some of these were described in Chapter 2. So far only Logo has emerged as a language suitable for use by children. Numerous investigators are beginning to come out with word processing programs designed for particular uses with particular students in particular situations. Similarly, as described in Chapter 2 some programs that are hybrids of general applications software and courseware are beginning to appear, such as the Semantic Calculator. Teachers can probably look forward to more such educational computing tools in the future. Finally, also as discussed in Chapter 2, some computer educators are experimenting with piggybacking courseware onto general applications programs such as VisiCalc. Nevertheless, while the future looks bright for teachers intending to use computers as tools and for student programming, the present affords little in the way of choice.

Paucity of Available Simulation and Instructional Game Programs

Even for those teachers more interested in CAI, the choice of software is surprisingly limited. The vast majority of available CAI programs are the most pedagogically traditional ones: drill and practice (by far the most common), tutorial, and demonstration. Despite the obvious power of the computer to create simulations that can teach high-level thinking and problem-solving skills effectively, inexpensively, and engagingly, only a very few commercial software houses are publishing simulations. The same is true for instructional games, despite their great potential for learning, especially basic skills. It would appear that software publishers are playing it safe by providing computerized versions of traditional methods, on the assumption that since these are the methods that most teachers have used without computers, these will be the computer applications they are most likely to buy. In a way, the publishers cannot be faulted for this sound business strategy. The costs of developing more innovative CAI are high, the market for such programs is unknown but probably quite small, and most publishers are too inexperienced with this sort of curriculum to know what constitutes quality.

Teachers seeking innovative CAI have several rather limited options open to them. They can create their own simulations and instructional games — a very unlikely possibility, since these require a considerable degree of sophistication in both curriculum design and programming. They can scour the countryside for the few commercially available programs of this sort. And they can lobby the publishers, urging them to locate and support computer curriculum innovators, most of whom are working in the sanctuary of universities or major research organizations.

Machine Incompatability

Finally, the choices of software for all teachers — those seeking non-CAI applications, those seeking traditional CAI, and those seeking nontraditional CAI — are all further limited by the incompatability of the various makes of small computers. Most programs developed for one machine will not run on any other brand of machine. As a result, most publishers and individual software designers have developed educational programs for what they consider to be the top contenders for educational computer use: the Apple, TRS-80, and Commodore PET. Owners of other computers, thus, have far fewer programs to choose from. To make matters even more absurdly difficult, some programs designed for earlier versions of a given brand of machine won't run on later versions of the same brand and vice-versa.

Computer users would appear to be helpless in coping with this limitation, until the hardware manufacturers adopt a common microprocessor and operating system that would allow any software to be used on any machine. This is exactly what the recording industry has continually done, as each new innovation has emerged, such as high fidelity, long-playing records, stereo, cassette tapes, and quadrophonic sound. In fact, a number of microcomputer manufacturers have adopted a common operating system known as CP/M. However, computers using CP/M tend to be more expensive than were the popular cassette-based computers that originally stormed the schools, so that, as yet, little educational software has been developed for them. Nevertheless, some forward looking schools have opted for such machines because of the quality of language interpreters and general applications packages available for them and because now, and more importantly in the future, CP/M based machines are likely to be more versatile than machines with idiosyncratic operating systems.

Another way to approach a common operating system is to add to your microcomputer one or more additional microprocessors used in other brands of machine. Then software written for these machines may be run on yours, provided the diskettes are physically compatible. This is now possible with some computers and is likely to spread to others as companies produce so called **emulators** by modifying their machines to be able to accept microprocessors from others.

One other possible strategy for overcoming machine incompatibility is to use utility programs that permit software written for one machine to be converted into a form that could be used on another machine. At this time, such programs are just beginning to be commercially available and are limited in what they can do. For example, while such **cross-compilers** or **cross-assemblers** can easily convert a simple drill and practice program so that it may be used on a different computer than the one for which it was designed, so far they are unable to convert graphics features from one machine to another.

In sum, although there are developments that promise to widen the range of choice in educational software, the current situation contains surprisingly limited options amidst an apparent overabundance of products.

TOO LITTLE QUALITY IN EDUCATIONAL SOFTWARE

Observers of the current educational computing scene seem generally to agree that most available educational software, both commercially designed and teacher developed, is rather disappointing. Criticisms range from the trivial (programs have bugs that cause them to malfunction under various circumstances), to the very serious (many programs are unusable by students due to unclear instructions and incorrect assumptions about how children learn), to the profound (the majority of educational software consists of drill and practice and tutorial programs that limit the learning of children and endanger the future of educational computing).

While these criticisms do not apply to all educational software, there is widespread agreement that the state of the art of educational software development leaves much to be desired. Under such circumstances, it is important for educational computing advocates to develop strategies to protect teachers and students from poor software and to promote the development of good software.

Recognizing these needs, a number of educational organizations, computer users groups, computer magazines, software clearinghouses, and educational computing projects have attempted to develop systematic approaches to reviewing educational software and disseminating these reviews (see the Resources section: Software, for an extensive list of these sources of software reviews). In the future, the same on-line database that would list and describe programs might also include reviews of those programs by individuals and organizations. Unfortunately, for now, despite a growing number of software review mechanisms, the field remains a jungle filled with unreviewed, unknown software being hawked by the rapidly growing ranks of commercial vendors and being offered in trade by do-it-yourself teachers through software exchanges.

How are you, the beginning computer user, to know whether a program is worth buying, trading for, or using? Catalog descriptions should be regarded with utter scepticism. Reviews by others may help, if you trust their judgment. Thus you may wish to consult magazines, software reviewing organizations, and your colleagues. However, in the end, there is no substitute for trying the software out yourself and applying to it the kind of criteria most appropriate for you, your needs, and your teaching philosophy. In Chapter 4 we provided some guidelines for software evaluation in general. These we suggested you use when considering any software, including educational applications software. However, there are some additional procedures and questions you may wish to consider for the specific task of evaluating educational software.

PROCEDURES FOR EDUCATIONAL SOFTWARE EVALUATION

1. When you hear or read about a piece of educational software you think you might be interested in using, you should contact the publisher or other source to ask to preview the materials. Some software vendors will send materials "on approval" to be paid for or returned within a specified time, usually thirty days. Others will insist that materials be prepaid, but they have generous return policies. Still other vendors, aware that some users may copy the software and then seek to return it, insist upon prompt payment for materials received, with returns allowed only for defective materials. We would advise against dealing with this last group. (It has been suggested that an on-line data base for educational software might eventually permit users to access programs directly for previewing purposes. Such an extensive centralized resource of programs sounds rather futuristic at this point, given

the politics and economics of educational materials distribution, but the technology to do it does already exist.)

2. When you receive your materials, first read through the accompanying documentation to be sure you have the operating system, peripherals, and machine characteristics necessary to run the program. The documentation should also provide you with any directions needed for using the software that are not built into the program itself, such as loading instructions. You may wish at this time to make note of the authors' stated educational intentions for the materials.

3. You are now ready to run the program. We suggest doing this at least three times in three different ways. First, pretend you are a reasonably sharp student working through the program. Respond as you think such a student would. Make a note of any difficulties you encounter in running the program or in understanding the program content. Next, pretend that you are a difficult student. Try to crash the program. Make deliberate errors, both reasonable and unreasonable ones. Note how well the program withstands both types of errors. Finally, run through the program as a teacher, searching out every nook and cranny, at the same time as you thoroughly review the documentation and ancillary materials. As a further check, you might wish to ask some students to run through the program while you observe their level of interest and whatever difficulties they may encounter.

4. Now write up your assessment, perhaps using a form of your own design or one of the myriad checklists published by organizations and magazines. Such checklists may be useful both now and in the future. They can be presented to a principal or department chair as a rationale for the purchase or nonpurchase of a particular piece of software, and they can be used in the future by others considering purchase or use of the same materials. Even if you do not use a form in performing your assessment, you should consider some of the questions raised in the Guidelines for Educational Software Evaluation in the next section.

5. If you decide that the program is not worth purchasing, return it promptly to the vendor or individual developer. You may wish to send a copy of your evaluation along with the returned materials as a way of providing feedback to the vendors or developers. This is one way that educators may be able to influence the quality and type of software published.

6. If you decide to order the software, when it arrives be sure that a copy of your checklist becomes part of the school's annotated software catalogue so that other teachers may be helped in selecting programs for their classroom use.

GUIDELINES FOR EDUCATIONAL
SOFTWARE EDUCATION

Evaluating and choosing educational software is more complicated than checking off criteria on a list. Although most existing software evaluation guidelines closely resemble guidelines for evaluating traditional educational materials, such as textbooks and A-V materials, evaluation of computer materials also requires an understanding of the unique power of the computer to be more than a medium of instruction. Thus, for judging computer materials for classroom use, some new criteria have had to evolve, and because the form and function of some of the learning that is taking place are still largely unknown, it is not always useful to apply rigid standards to innovative computer uses.

Nevertheless, to any educational software package you can apply one universal standard for judgment by asking the question: "Does the package do what I want it to do?" Many schools are allocated a specific number of minutes a day to teach each subject and a limited amount of money to purchase instructional materials. To buy a $300 computer program, they may need assurance that they can get as much for their money as they can from buying five $60 sets of workbooks. Teachers know that they have been able to teach the multiplication tables to most of their students with workbooks. They need to be convinced that the computer can also do this, or they cannot devote class time or request the allocation of monetary resources to computer activities.

Yet the value of printed workbooks goes beyond their function as teaching materials. Assigning workbook pages to students as seatwork frees teachers to work with special needs students, correct papers, or prepare new lessons. If the computer programs can't provide the same freedom, then they may not be able to replace workbooks or any other instructional materials.

However, the potential of the computer is so great, both as an instructional medium and as an object to learn with, that it should probably not be placed in competition with workbooks or textbooks. The challenge for the educational community today is to define what students and teachers can do with computers that is better than or different from traditional ways of learning and teaching. Once that is accomplished, it is then incumbent upon educators to buy or create educational software that uses these unique capabilities of the computer in some way to achieve educational goals and objectives.

The search for quality educational software, as with most processes in life, is made up of a series of compromises. Nevertheless there are educational software packages that are better than others. Your task is to find those that will be best for you and your students. The guidelines discussed in the remainder of this chapter will provide some ways for you to do this. These guidelines have been divided into four broad areas of concern: program content, pedagogy, program operation, and student outcomes. In each area we raise a series of questions which are illustrated by vignettes based on real evaluation experience. These questions, the vignettes, and the comments that follow them are meant to be suggestive not comprehensive. They apply to some, but not all, educational software. You must exercise judgment in applying them.

Program Content

- Is the content of the materials suitable for your students?
- Does the content of the materials fit with your curricular goals?
- What values does the content convey?
- Is the content contained in the materials accurate?
- Is the content educationally significant?
- Are the goals and objectives of the materials explicitly or implicitly clear?

Steven Freed was caught in a dilemma. He wanted to use a simple computer program for reinforcing computational skills in his kindergarten class . Unfortunately, the school had chosen a K-8 program whose kindergarten level he doubted would be appropriate for his class. For example, the opening frame said:

WELCOME TO KINDERGARTEN.

There were no directions on the screen for how to proceed from there. In the manual, Steven found that he had to press the RETURN key. He realized that he would have to teach his students to recognize the opening words and to press the RETURN key when they wished to advance the screens.

The next screen presented a real puzzle, however. It had an empty box with an equal sign next to it. He went back to the manual, but there were no instructions. He started hitting keys at random, until the happy face came on when he hit the 0 key. The next screen presented the same box, but this time it had one dot in it. He typed 1 and the happy face came on again. Steven now knew what the program was trying to do, although the manual had not been clear about the program objectives. It was presenting the concept of numeration, identifying objects with the numbers. Unfortunately, it had started with zero, the most difficult number concept to teach. What was he to do?

Is the content of the materials suitable for your students?   Steven's dilemma is not an unusual one. Many educational programs being distributed have been developed by people who are experts in neither learning theory nor instructional design. The person who designed this particular program was evidently unaware of the inappropriateness of introducing the concept of zero to kindergarten students before they had mastered easier examples of numeration.

Another aspect of the program that was developmentally inappropriate was the written message WELCOME TO KINDERGARTEN, which virtually no kindergarten student could possibly read. However, Steven was probably correct in assuming that he could explain to his students which key they had to hit to advance the screens, and then they would be able to recognize what to do in subsequent sessions with the program. But, since the math sequencing was not developmentally appropriate for his students, either he had to abandon the program altogether or he had to explain the zero concept so that students would not become lost.

Two possible ways to determine whether a program is appropriate for a particular grade level or interest group are to run through the program and to read a scope and sequence chart or description of the program in the teacher's manual. However, it is not always easy to determine age suitability with computer materials. Many younger children can use programs that were written for older children, and some programs that appear very elementary are quite captivating to older students because of the novelty of the machine's presentation. Often appropriateness is determined by the type of graphics or animation used. Little animals jumping up and down may turn off older children no matter what the intended age level of the program.

In order to insure developmental appropriateness, some publishers and vendors are requiring that readability formulas be applied to programs and to their documentation. However, this is not always easy to do. The word "load" falls into the elementary word list because it is one syllable and readily understood. However, as you have discovered from reading this book, the word "load" has a far different meaning in the context of computers and therefore should not be counted in the formula in the same way. On the other hand, the words "Press" and "Return" would not fit into the first-grade curriculum, yet young children learn to recognize these words quickly in the command PRESS RETURN and can automatically perform the required action once they are shown how to do so.

Does the content of the materials fit with your curricular goals? Before deciding to use the program, Steven Freed also had to decide whether or not it fit his curricular goals. If he wanted his students to learn primarily without teacher intervention, these materials certainly weren't appropriate. On the other hand, the program could be used well enough as reinforcement for arithmetic concepts the children had already learned on their own. From the stated objectives in manuals that accompany software or from previewing the programs, teachers will usually be able to tell whether programs fit with their educational philosophy and goals. For example, if a school is teaching spelling through a sight method approach, teachers probably won't want a computer program that uses a phonics approach.

Sharon Jones was horrified. The simulation game she had just previewed stood for everything to which she was opposed. In it, settlers killed "hostile" Indians, women were portrayed as subservient to men, and the only blacks in the situation were in menial positions. Not only did the simulation reinforce stereotypes and glorify violence, but it provided a very misleading picture of the settling of the American West. As an American History major in college, Sharon had studied the important role of women settlers and free blacks in the movement to the West. Moreover, she knew only too well the shame of the white man's treatment of basically peace-loving Native Americans.

Sharon would certainly not use this simulation herself, and she wondered how it had ever been bought by her school. She decided to bring it up for discussion in her next department meeting.

What values does the content convey?   Some issues related to content that are often overlooked in courseware development have to do with social, psychological, and cultural values. As with other educational materials, you should carefully examine how programs deal with stereotypes. Computer programs can be sexist, racist, and violent in their presentation of materials. Most popular computer games, for example, foster a particular type of aggression and competition that may disturb many of us to see children engaging in. "Killing Klingons," and other space invaders type games should not be the only experience children have with computer programs. Instilling positive values is a goal of most education and should be reflected in the types of computer programs developed and selected for use in classrooms.

Is the content contained in the materials accurate?   Content accuracy is a perennial problem in educational materials of all kinds. Who is qualified and who has the time to check the accuracy of curricular materials? Presumably publishers assume this responsibility. However, publishers are staffed by fallible human beings, and small computer publishers are even more likely to be staffed by people who may be unfamiliar with program content. Moreover, many facts are socially constructed. To most Americans, reared on T.V. and movie westerns, it is a fact that Indians were brutal savages. Few Americans know the other side of the story.

Peter Smith was attending a workshop on teacher-designed computer programs. Phil DeLucca, the workshop leader, was demonstrating one of the programs he had created for his eighth-grade English class. It was a simple crossword puzzle on the computer screen that used vocabulary from the students' weekly vocabulary list. Peter was unimpressed. Next Phil put up on the screen a little program a junior high science teacher had developed in which students "guided" a rocketship to a safe landing on the moon. Peter became impatient. "What's the objective of that program?" he asked. Phil wasn't sure. He thought it had something to do with deceleration, but there was no documentation with the program to explain its objectives. Peter rolled his eyes to the ceiling and slipped out of the workshop as soon as he could do so unobtrusively.

Is the content educationally significant?   Every teacher has his or her own ideas of what is and what isn't educationally significant. Peter Smith apparently felt that reinforcing vocabulary words with a crossword puzzle was not educationally significant. You might feel differently. However, given limited computer resources, you will have to establish some priorities for computer use, and presumably you would want that use to be as educationally significant as possible. Thus, when considering educational software, you should ask yourself about the significance of what is being taught.

Are the goals and objectives of the materials explicitly or implicitly clear?   Peter Smith was also disturbed that the rocketship program had no clearly stated objectives. Perhaps Peter was a little impatient on this one. The designer of that program was a junior high science teacher who used the program in his own classes. He knew what his instructional objectives were. If he had intended the program to be used by others, he would have written up a little teacher's guide that stated these objectives.

Although stated objectives are often helpful, many teachers don't like the behaviorist assumptions behind them. They prefer to create learning environments in which unintended as well as hoped for learning may take place. Many simulations, computer languages like Logo, and tool programs like word processors may provide very rich learning environments without being accompanied by explicitly stated instructional objectives.

Pedagogy

- What is the nature of the feedback the program provides to students?
- What assumptions about learning and how children learn are built into the software?
- Does the software permit modification to meet individual student needs?
- Is the software package self-contained, or does it require teacher intervention?
- Can the program be used with various types of class arrangements (individual, small group, whole class)?
- Does the program tap a variety of learning modes (visual, aural, numerical, verbal)?

Jane stared at the algebra problem:

X + 5 = 7   X = ?

12.

NOT QUITE RIGHT.

Mr. Ramirez, the Computer Center director, looked over her shoulder and was amazed at the message being relayed by the computer. The answer is either right or wrong; nothing "quite" about it, he thought. Then he watched while Sam inserted the wrong answer in a different math series. The computer flashed a big red letter "X" across the screen. "That's awful," winced Mr. Ramirez.

He watched another program being used and saw an animation of a bird flapping its wings. Although it was a lovely graphic, it took several seconds and did not relate to the program. Then he saw two students playing a computer game, which was strictly against the rules of the Center. When he told them that, they explained that the game was their reward for having mastered their spelling words. It was part of the program. "What an interesting notion," he thought, and decided to buy more of this type of program for the Center.

What is the nature of the feedback the program provides to students?   One of the major strengths of computer programs is that they can provide immediate feedback to students. In the case of drill and practice or tutorial programs, this feedback provides reinforcement to shape student responses. Such reinforcement can take many forms. Generally, the best kind is related in some way to the content. For example, students may be rewarded for doing a set of problems correctly by being moved on automatically to a more advanced problem set.

There are generally three styles of reinforcement employed in CAI programs: passive, active, and interactive. Passive reinforcements include written statements such as "good" or "sorry, that's not quite right" whereas active reinforcements include animation such as a happy face and/or sound, like fireworks exploding in color and sound. The most interesting and rewarding reinforcement is interactive, such as that in the programs Mr. Ramirez ordered more of, in which students are rewarded by being allowed to play a game related to the content mastered.

All three types of reinforcement work and may be appropriate, depending upon the student and the situation. One caution: negative reinforcement for wrong answers should not be more engaging than positive reinforcement for correct answers. This is sometimes difficult. In some tutorial programs, it is more fun to get a wrong answer because an entertaining animated sequence follows that demonstrates the concept being taught. With such programs students who understand the concept will often deliberately give the wrong answer so they can watch the graphics. That is a tough problem to solve.

Several other considerations regarding reinforcement should also be mentioned. Programs should be flexible — if students don't want to watch an animation sequence put in for reinforcement, they should be able to <u>override</u> it. The statements used to reinforce should be appropriate to the age level, reflect positive values, and use constructive criticism when criticism is necessary. A big red "X" is probably not an appropriate response. Finally, learning theory suggests pretty clearly that intermittent reinforcement usually works better than continuous reinforcement, so a response after each answer is not necessary.

There are, of course, other forms of feedback besides reinforcement. You should use common sense and your knowledge of your students to decide the suitability of such feedback.

What assumptions about learning and how children learn are built into the software?   All curriculum has embedded in it assumptions about how children learn. Drill and practice programs, like the ones Mr. Ramirez was observing in use, assume a behaviorist model of learning. Most tutorials assume that students learn by being led logically to understand concepts. Many simulations are based on the assumption that affective learning reinforces cognitive learning. There is probably no correct view of learning. However, it is important that you know what learning theory is underlying any piece of curriculum you use, since the results of such use are often determined by the assumptions of the theory.

Mr. Ramirez walked away from the students doing drill-and-practice programs and turned to Dr. Ellis, the principal of a local junior high school, saying, "Drills have their place in education, I guess, but I get a lot more excited about learning when I see students working on projects like these." He walked over to a microcomputer that was being used by two fourteen-year-old girls. "Lisa and Susan are creating an animated picture of a horse, using Logo. They've been studying scientific photos of the way a horse moves. They've already gotten the horse to walk and trot on command. They came up to me in amazement last week to tell me that they had just discovered that in one phase of the gallop, all four of the horse's feet are off the ground at once."

The girl's heads were bent together over the <u>flowchart</u> they had created, as they tried to correct the rhythm of the horse's eyes while cantering. But they looked up, smiling at Mr. Ramirez. "Put Misty through her paces," he urged them. Proudly, the girls pushed the necessary buttons, and a good facsimile of a horse appeared on the screen. It walked, its head and tail bobbing in correct rhythm. Then, it trotted, its mane bouncing slightly up and down.

"Once we get all of the gaits the way we want them," said Lisa, her face alive with excitement, "we're going to make a farm field in the background for Misty to run around in."

Does the software permit modification to meet individual student needs?   One of the potentially most important uses of computers in education is for individualizing instruction. Programs that make this possible may be invaluable to teachers struggling to provide materials to students with a wide range of abilities and interests. Logo and various tool programs that are not designed with particular educational objectives in mind are likely to be most easily modified for different learners.

Teachers should be sceptical of tutorial or drill and practice programs that claim to individualize instruction. Both types usually accept only a single response, or at most a narrow range of predictable responses. Both are designed to lead students to predetermined ends. While such programs may have built into them instruction at several levels of difficulty, they are not easily modifiable to meet very different student needs.

Is the software package self-contained, or does it require teacher intervention?   While teachers may not always want programs to be self-contained, it is thrilling to see students like Lisa and Susan learning with a program entirely on their own. However, no programs are truly teacher-free. Mr. Ramirez helped the girls get started with Logo and directed them to the books they needed on motion. The issue is really whether students can work on a program without constant teacher supervision and direction. Most good programs make this possible by containing clear directions in the program itself and by making it easy for students to operate the program.

Regina Jones had her argument all ready for her department chair, Luisa Colon. She wanted her to order the simulation game LIFE. It would be perfect for her Family Living course. The game involved students first making life choices such as marriage, having children, going on for further education, and getting a job. Then, the students go through various life stages, from youth through old age, being affected by the initial choices they made, by chance, and by the new choices they make as a result of their new circumstances. Talk about lessons in fate control. This was it! And the beautiful thing about the program was that individual students could play it, small groups could play it, and the whole class could play it. That way, students who were frequently absent wouldn't miss out and yet, those who came regularly could have a valuable group experience. The only thing that worried Regina was that the program involved a lot of reading and had no graphics or sound. But she felt that the content of the reading would probably make up for this, since it consisted of real people living in urban neighborhoods like the ones in which her students lived.

Can the program be used with various types of class arrangements? Programs, like the simulation LIFE, that have been designed for use in a variety of classroom arrangements provide great flexibility to a teacher. Unfortunately, most CAI programs are drill and practice and tutorials, which are designed for individual use only. While some teachers have found ways to use such programs with small groups or the entire class, this is not their intended, nor their most effective, use.

Does the program tap a variety of learning modes? One of the strengths of computers for educational uses is their potential to tap multiple learning modes and thereby increase the likelihood of student learning. You should seek out programs that exploit the color, sound, graphics, numerical, and verbal capabilities of computers to enhance student learning. However, you should also beware of programs that are "full of sound and fury signifying nothing." Some software developers use sound, color, and graphics to disguise the essential vacuousness of their program. On the other hand, some programs, like the LIFE simulation may not require such enhancements to engage students in learning.

Program Operation

- Is the program free of bugs and breaks?
- How does the program handle user errors?
- How much control does the user have over the program operation?
- Are directions in the program itself clear and acceptable?
- Is there good clear documentation for the teacher?
- Is there good clear documentation for students?
- How well does the program use graphics, sound, and color capabilities?
- Are screen displays effective?

> Whiz! Clunk. Whiz! Clink. The game play of "Darts" was intensifying. Chuck and Gail were each trying to hit the next highest equivalent fraction. Their team mates watched eagerly. Suddenly, the game stopped as Chuck was aiming at 7/8. The screen froze, and an error message at the bottom of it signaled the problem: ERROR 220. Students started yelling at the machine, "You dummy! You did that yesterday. Everytime someone goes at the 7/8, you just stop. It's not fair!"

Is the program free of bugs and breaks? One of the most frustrating occurrences in using computer programs is getting stuck. For some reason, unknown to the users, they have done something that the program does not know how to handle and it becomes paralyzed. Good programmers can usually anticipate these kinds of situations and thus protect the program from such breaks.

Another way of partially resolving the problem is for programmers to create overrides — when a break is registered, the users can hit the RESET key and start over from where they left off, as though the program had a bookmark built into it. Creating these kinds of safeguards takes time, a lot of thought, and a lot of programming skill — all of which require extra development money. Publishers often don't want to put that additional money into the programs, and teachers who develop materials for software exchanges are often not sophisticated enough in their programming skills to be able to program out the bugs. However, eventually the field will mature enough so that programming routines to eliminate breaks will be familiar and inexpensive to apply.

How does the program handle user errors?   A second problem with breaks is the nature of the error messages themselves: often merely a line number and error code, which are completely meaningless to the student user. These error messages should be replaced with more informative and useful responses, which is relatively easy to do if programmers were just made more sensitive to the need to do so. For the time being, teachers may have to be patient. Creating educational programs is an emerging field with quite a long way to go before it achieves real quality. Nevertheless, programs with frequent breaks and useless error messages should probably be avoided.

Another kind of error occurs when students are asked to type in answers to questions. In many programs, incorrectly spelled responses are not recognized by the computer even if they are conceptually correct. When this occurs, programs should ask students to check their spelling. Then provision must be made in the program to allow students to correct their typing errors easily.

Lance was using a physics lab calculation program for the first time. A set of directions flashed on the screen. He read them carefully, pressed the RETURN key, and also read the next screen. Then he began to enter the data he had collected in the lab. After completing his data entry, he was following a calculation routine when the school fire alarm rang. He knew he was supposed to turn off the machine when that happened, but he didn't want to lose his data, so he left it on as he walked out of the building for the fire drill.

When he came back, the program was still there, but he couldn't remember whether to press RETURN or the space bar after completing a particular step in his calculations. The documentation for the program didn't say and he didn't know how to get the instructions except by starting the program over again, which meant that he had to reenter all of his data. Frustrated, he read the instructions, reentered the data, and had begun his calculations when the bell rang, ending the period. Lance looked at the clock, glowered, and put his program away.

How much control does the user have over the program operation? When students are told by a teacher to turn to the third lesson in a workbook, they can do so. When students are told by a teacher to turn to the third lesson in a computer program, they often have to rely on the good sense of the programmer/designer to have provided that option. This is usually achieved by using a table of contents called a <u>menu</u>, which provides a choice of where to go in any part of a program. Sometimes, a set of commands have been built into a program, so that if users need to move to different parts of the program, they can hit a certain sequence of keys that move them there. Such features mean that students no longer have to work through a predetermined sequence if it is not appropriate to their needs. They can now choose their own sequencing of content. Programs containing these options should be accompanied by documentation that describes them.

Another element of user control relates to rate and sequence. Whenever it is appropriate, students should be able to control how long materials stay on the screen so that they can read, process, and think through what they are being asked to do.

Are directions in the program itself clear and acceptable? One common problem in program design occurs when the program gives directions on the screen in sequential order, prior to actually beginning the required sequence. Then, if the directions are complicated, when they disappear from the screen they may be forgotten by the time the user is ready to start into the sequence. Teachers and students need access to the directions while they are using a program. This can be accomplished best by providing HELP keys or commands. Then, when users get stuck, they can hit a help key; it gives them directions. When they hit another key, they're back in the program where they left off. Another way to give directions is to place them in the documentation, but it is usually better to put them in the program in an accessible arrangement.

The accounting package Ira Bradshaw had been anxiously awaiting finally arrived. Knowing how complex computer programs are to operate, he read the users manual from cover to cover. Then he approached the micro with great trepidation. Would he erase the program? Could he break the machine? Following the directions with scrupulous attention to every detail, he inserted the diskette into the drive. Screen after screen appeared on the CRT just as the directions indicated that they would. At the tenth screen, he pressed "i" as directed in the manual, but the screen didn't change. Not only that, the screen wouldn't change no matter what he typed. So he began again. Three hours later, after rereading the manual dozens of times and trying various ways of getting that tenth screen to change, he called the software vendor to ask what he was doing wrong. After being passed from person to person for ten minutes, someone finally told him that the user manual had omitted an instruction and a screen. The corrected command was to press the control key and type "i." A bit agitated, Ira went to his keyboard, followed this advice, and advanced to the next screen with no difficulty. He knew now that this screen was not the one pictured in the book, but that if he typed in the next command he would be back in synchronization with the manual.

Is there good clear documentation for teachers? When you pick up a book, you open it and begin to read it. Sometimes the introduction explains how to read the book for various purposes and diverse audiences. When you buy slides, films, or other audiovisual programs, you need to know how to operate the projectors, but they operate consistently from program to program. However, unless a computer program is exceptionally simple, or all of the instructions are on the diskette or cassette, the quality of the users manual that accompanies it is exceedingly important.

The type of information that is needed in any users manual is determined by the level of complexity of the program and whether the user is a student or a teacher. At the very least a users manual for teachers should state what the computer requirements are for running the program. (For example, "You need an Apple II plus, with 48K and two floppy disk drives.") It also should tell you what operating system you need (e.g. DOS 3.3) or whether you can use the program with another operating system if you make some particular modification. In addition, the peripherals that are needed should be specified (e.g. game paddles, printer, or light pen). Then you are ready to begin to use the program with students.

Is there good clear documentation for students? A users manual for students should give the kind of information that they would get when they opened a book and skimmed it. Students should be able to tell how the program is organized and how they can run through it comfortably. A well-written program will have consistent commands for standard operating procedures such as advancing the program, correcting errors, and getting help in the middle of a lesson. These commands should be listed. If there are menus enabling students to select lessons or activities, the menus should be presented and explained as well. In addition, there should be a summary card that can lie flat next to the computer while the program is running to help students remember what the commands are and how to use them. Lance, in the previous vignette, would have been saved a lot of aggravation if he had had such a summary card.

Carmen Ruiz was at a computer store trying to choose a program for her first graders. As she typed the "A" key, the letter "A" danced across the screen and landed on an animated alligator. The word "ALLIGATOR" flashed on the screen. A little musical jingle played while the alligator continued to dance around, rewarding her for her correct answer. For the first few times she had been charmed, by the fifth she was bored and knew her students would be too.

The second program she examined was on color matching, but Carmen couldn't line up the colors correctly. Reds were being matched with purples — or so it appeared. The colors also bled into the text and, since the color was needed for the program content, it couldn't be turned off to make reading the text easier, even though it was very distracting.

The third program Carmen looked at had so much on the screen that she couldn't tell what to pay attention to. Everything was boxed by a flashing dotted line. Inside the box, sentences — all in capital letters — were lined up. In each sentence, a word was left out and a blank replaced it. Under the blank were three words as potential choices to use to complete the sentence. When the choice was typed in, it stayed at the bottom with either the word "CORRECT" or the word "INCORRECT" next to it. She quickly removed that program from the disk drive and gave it to the store manager with a thoroughly disapproving look.

Finally, Carmen got to the last program she was previewing. After watching it for a while, she breathed a sigh of relief. The pedagogical content of the program was enhanced by the use of graphics and color. The concept was regrouping in subtraction. The ones were in red and the tens were in blue. During a tutorial sequence, ten ones became one ten; they moved on the screen to the correct grouping circle and changed color. She decided that this program could really help students grasp the concept, so she wrote it down on a school purchase order to give to her principal for her approval.

How well does the program use graphics, sound, and color capabilities? Aesthetics in any medium is difficult to codify. However, one criterion that should be considered in assessing the aesthetics of computer programs is that the use of color, graphics, and sound play an integral role in the presentation of the content. If a story is being presented, then having an animated set of graphic images accompanying it may be aesthetically pleasing and motivating, thereby adding educational value. On the other hand, if the graphics don't relate to the lesson, they may become distracting, particularly with repeated use.

Are screen displays effective? Another aspect of computer aesthetics is the effectiveness of the screen displays. The third program that Carmen Ruiz examined was so busy, she didn't know what was going on. On the other hand, some programs may confuse students because they move needed information off the screen too quickly, simply to reduce the amount of information on the screen at any one time.

Student Outcomes

- How easy is the program for students to use?
- Is the program interesting to students?
- Does the program make appropriate use of limited computer resources?
- Do students enjoy using the programs?
- How well do students learn what the program is intended to teach?
- What, if any, unintended learning results from using the program?
- How effective is this program compared with noncomputer instruction in the same area?

Although these are questions best answered after students have actually used a program, teachers who know their students well can often predict how a program will fare with student use. In the final lengthy vignette below, a teacher reviews a simulation package and anticipates how her students will react to it. The vignette is offered, without commentary, as a summary to illustrate most of the issues previously discussed in this chapter.

There it sat — the Geography Search Program — all packaged direct from the publisher. Angela Palmieri ripped open the box and pulled out the pieces — a teacher's manual, student workbook, and the software program in its own little case with operating directions. Similar to most teachers, Angela quickly inserted the diskette into her computer without reading the directions — just to see what would happen.

With relief, she watched the program start operating automatically on her system. No problem with the operating system, she thought. Lots of animated graphics to watch in the title — that's a waste — but they're pretty.

From having talked with other teachers about the program before ordering it, Angela knew that in Geography Search her students would become the crew members of an ancient sailing ship looking for the new world. With the help of the computer, they would navigate the ship, using information about the position of the sun and stars, ocean depth, climate, and trade winds. Their goal would be to locate the new world and return safely home with riches that they would find there.

Angela pretended that she was one of her students, as she went through the program a few times, following each set of choices to see what the program would do. She made note of how easy it was to use, how well students could control the machine, and whether there were program breaks. However, she soon forgot about her software evaluation checklist and got really involved in the program. She was forced to read the student manual in order to understand how to interpret the charts on the screen that represented the baseline data for playing the simulation. Since the program was designed logically and consistently, Angela could get along well by using standard computer conventions for cursor movement without reading the manual—the sign of a well-designed program!

Once she was convinced that the program was operational, Angela went back and read the teacher's manual from cover to cover. She realized that she should have done this first. The manual was great. It gave her information about setting up her class record sheets to use in keeping track of student activities, suggestions for follow-up activities, and lots of help in anticipating student questions and problems. It did have some minor problems—the micros pictured had the wrong function keys: ENTER was pictured instead of RETURN. Since Angela knew what to do, it didn't matter, but she wondered why publishers or authors weren't more careful about such things that could really confuse beginners.

Angela discovered a crucial feature covered in the teachers manual: the assumptions that drove the model were listed. One such assumption was that students at sea could run out of food. But how long would it take them? Was this realistic? Could the students logically figure this out so they could plan appropriately? Could they try to ration food? In the program model, Angela found that the students could approximate how long their food would last, but they couldn't ration it. She realized she could discuss that in class. Another aspect of the model, the rules for following the stars, was totally accurate and could actually be transferred to a real sailing voyage. This was really powerful, she concluded, and returned to her review.

After several hours, Angela discovered that she was no longer just evaluating the operation and the content of the program. She was totally engrossed in the simulation itself. Observing her own obsession with a learning environment, she remembered a research report by Dr. Thomas Malone of Xerox that identified three components that made educational computer games fun for children: challenge, curiosity, and fantasy. Simulations and problem solving programs really seemed to offer so much more to students. She pictured her students playing with the Search Series. "Playing"—she laughed and corrected herself, "learning."

At that moment Paul Henson, the sixth grade teacher from next door, joined her. "So you're using Geography Search. My class is driving me crazy with Energy Search! They don't want to do anything else. So listen to what I've done. Students have to keep a log of their daily activities and thoughts. I've designed our grammar and spelling lessons around the logs. Not only that, but I find that if I use that setting for math problems, I can hold their interest better. Remember when we first decided to get the series—no one suspected how many unintended educational experiences we could structure around it."

"I even have a few kids who want to learn to program the computer to create their own simulation," added Paul. "They want to figure out how to set up the conditional statements to make it work. It's a little bit frightening because I'm not even sure if I understand how to do it correctly."

"Let it be a challenge to you," chuckled Angela. "Think of it as a joint problem solving activity requiring a team approach, with a project leader who may know less about each part than the team members. It's no different than life outside the classroom. You manage and let them create. Take a deep breath and go for it!"

Photo: Sharon A. Bazarian

Introducing Computers into the School

Chapter 6

Let us suppose, now, that you know something about computer systems and their educational potential, and that you would like to use computers in your school. What can you do to help bring this about? Request that money be earmarked for computers in next year's budget? Try to get the math department to share their computers with you? Ask your principal or director of instruction to look into buying computers for the school? Buy your own? All of these are among the myriad ways in which computer use in schools has been started or greatly expanded during the last several years.

However, there is much more to introducing computers into a school than simply borrowing, ordering, or buying them. There are crucial political, financial, and personal issues to be addressed. Who will be involved in the selection of computers? Where will the money come from to purchase them? Who will use them once they are in the school? Educators who wish to bring computers into their schools need to know how to address these questions.

THE POLITICS OF
COMPUTER ACQUISITION

Each history of educational computer acquisition is unique. However, for ease of discussion, we have identified three broad approaches to decision making from among the many stories of how computers have been introduced into schools.

The Centralized Approach

Large school systems and those with a strong central administration tend to handle all decision making in a centralized, usually top-down, fashion. Computer acquisition is no exception. Whether the school department is considering a district-wide timesharing system or micros within each school, the process of selecting machines, funding them, and placing them in schools is directed by the central administration. The logic for a centralized approach to administering a minicomputer timesharing system is clear. The expense of such a system and the number of people and amount of equipment involved require coordination, expertise, and accountability that only a central office of computing can provide.

The rationale for a centralized approach to administering microcomputer use in a school system may not seem quite so obvious. After all, don't most school building staffs manage their own audiovisual equipment and textbooks, from purchase through maintenance? Why not do the same for microcomputers and their software? The following vignette may shed some light on these questions.

The Office of Management Information Services (OMIS) of a large, western city school system that has taught programming as part of the mathematics curriculum since the sixties was considering switching from a timesharing system to stand-alone microcomputers. As a result of fifteen years of experience working with computers, the school system had a cohesive group of teachers, technical staff, and administrators who were able to work as a task force with OMIS to develop a well-thought-through plan for implementing this change. OMIS coordinated a three-phase process, beginning with a pilot project in which one microcomputer was used in one classroom. What was learned from this project, as well as from extensive teacher interviews within their system, enabled OMIS to write an extremely detailed Request for Proposal (RFP), which was sent out for bid to all microcomputer dealers in the metropolitan area. Based on the bids received, which included hardware, software, maintenance, and security information, one microcomputer system was chosen, and several units of this make were purchased. After a trial period with these machines, a second RFP was sent out, reflecting new lessons learned.

As a result, the school system bought thirty units of a different make that apparently was better suited to their needs. Currently, reports from that city indicate that teachers and students are very pleased with the switch from timesharing to micros and that the centralized planning and implementation strategy appears to have given the teachers information and the administrative support they felt they needed.

School systems, such as this one, that used timesharing systems for administrative purposes or for teaching programming prior to the recent wave of interest in computing brought on by the availability of microcomputers, are likely to handle the administration of micros just as they did timesharing. After all, the bureaucracy for computer management is in place, complete with procedures for equipment purchase and maintenance, project evaluation, and personnel accountability. Moreover, teachers and administrators in such school systems are accustomed to dealing with computer use through the central office. They rely upon the expertise and decision making of that office to relieve them of the burden of researching and selecting their own computer systems.

Even schools without a history of computer use may recognize advantages to centralized management of computers, such as:

- The financial advantage gained when a school system purchases a large number of micros on a bid basis, compared with each school purchasing several micros of different makes on their own.
- The increased potential for coordination of curricular uses of the computer so that, for example, students aren't taught the same things about and with computers in more than one grade.
- The availability of expertise for training teachers in computer use, answering technical and curricular questions, and screening software purchases.
- The procedures for hardware maintenance, which minimize the unavailability of machines when needed.
- A library of locally evaluated software, complete with locally developed teachers guides.

Of course, there are also problems entailed in a centralized approach to computer management, such as:

- Diminished teacher control of the curriculum.
- Teacher dependency on the judgment and decisions of others.
- Compromises necessitated by the use of one brand of micro, since no machine can handle all educational applications equally well.
- The possibility of less access to machines if system wide demand is great and other schools or programs are seen by the administration as having a higher priority.

- Teacher alienation due to their lack of involvement in planning for, purchasing, and determining use for computers.

Most school administrators, like the one in the following vignette, are sensitive to these problems, particularly the last one, and attempt to address them by the way they carry out their centralized approach to computer management.

Several years ago, Frank Jones, the Assistant Superintendent for Planning of a wealthy suburban school system, decided to introduce computer use into the elementary and middle schools in his district. Since the early sixties, programming had been taught in the high school as an elective, using timesharing on one of two small mainframe computers owned by the school system. Dr. Jones felt that it would be good politics to allow the high school to keep their system for themselves, so he decided to install terminals in the elementary and middle schools, which would connect to the mainframe used by the central school administration. He persuaded the various PTA's in the district to donate the money to buy the terminals and their time to monitor them.

Several problems arose almost immediately with using these terminals. First, they had to be located in rooms in the schools with outside telephone lines, often the main office or some out-of-the-way room. This made use by students and classes rather inconvenient. Second, the decision to bring computers into the lower schools had been made by the central administration without teacher involvement. As a result, many teachers were unsupportive of the new computer effort. Third, time on the central computer became less available to the schools because of increased administrative use.

It was around this period of time that relatively inexpensive microcomputers began to become more available. The decision was made, once again by the central administration, to acquire enough micros of various makes over a five-year period, roughly 1978–1983, to have one microcomputer for every two classrooms, K-12. However, by now Dr. Jones was well aware of the difficulties in getting widespread teacher and administrator involvement, so he developed a strategy to overcome this obstacle. He established a town advisory committee on school computing, formed largely to support his decisions. He proposed, and the committee endorsed, the creation of a program in which teachers with ideas for using computers in their curricular area applied to have a microcomputer for a specified project. Teachers whose plans were accepted agreed to have their "model" programs evaluated at the end of the year by Blanche Harris, the school system computer coordinator, and to revise the program based on that evaluation. They were also obliged to help other teachers implement similar programs in the following year. The "models" program was designed to encourage grass-roots teacher input and to provide administrative support for integrating computers into the curriculum, K-12. The program is currently proceeding, but slowly. Ms. Harris, who is assigned half-time as computer coordinator, is overwhelmed by demands for teacher training and support over and above her responsibility for the selection, evaluation, and cataloging of software, as well as the maintenance of equipment.

Centralized decision making with a veneer of teacher participation, as in the previous vignette, seems to be in vogue in school systems these days. Its effectiveness and appropriateness vary from system to system depending upon personalities, history, and situational factors too numerous to discuss. Sometimes, the degree of real teacher participation develops over time so that a shared decision making process, such as the one discussed last in this section, emerges from out of a centralized approach.

The Decentralized Approach

The small but growing subculture of elementary and secondary school computing is filled with stories of schools in which individual teachers or parents, sometimes acting alone, sometimes in conjunction with their colleagues, and sometimes in cooperation with the school principal, are responsible for introducing computers into the classroom. These cases have generally occurred in small school systems or in suburban areas where parents are very anxious to have their children use computers in schools, and school building administrators have considerable discretion over their budgets and curricula. The most common and exciting accounts tell of charismatic, inventive, brash computer buffs, like the teacher in the following vignette, who singlehandedly bring microcomputers into their school's curriculum.

George Russo, an elementary school teacher in a working-class suburb, became excited about the potential of the computer to help him keep track of student progress in his individualized approach to teaching basic skills. However, his enthusiasm was not shared by his principal or by most of his colleagues, none of whom addressed basic skills in a systematic fashion. So George approached the Gifted and Talented Committee for the school and persuaded them to include a microcomputer in their Title IV-B proposal for funding a Gifted and Talented gram. The program was funded and when the Apple microcomputer arrived, George volunteered to oversee its use. Since no one else in the school knew anything about computers, they were only too glad to take him up on his offer. So, George got a microcomputer in his room to use for his individualized program, as well as for the gifted and talented kids in other classes who came there in their elective periods.

Lone wolves, like George Russo, appear to be a disappearing breed, which may be just as well, since often the ending to the story is not quite so happy as the beginning. George, like many such educational computing entrepreneurs, left his school after a year, in his case to enter a graduate program in computer science. The barely tarnished Apple now sits on a shelf, since no other teacher in the school had developed any interest or expertise in working with it. The message seems clear: computer programs that depend on the energy, enthusiasm, and presence of one person are unlikely to survive. However, what appears to be happening, as more and more teachers become aware of the educational potential of microcomputers, is that two or more teachers join forces to bring computers into their school. As a result, we are beginning to see the birth of microcomputer subcultures in even small rural schools, like the one in the following vignette.

Sally Oakes, the junior high school science teacher at the Greenville School, a small rural K-12 school, and Libby Peterson, the school librarian, were turned on to microcomputers at a regional teacher center-sponsored workshop. But their school ran on a bare-bones budget and badly needed a new gym before investing in any newfangled educational gadgetry. The townspeople were very proud of their basketball teams, especially the girls' team, which had been state champion in its class for two years running. As a result, there was little inclination to spend money on anything other than a new gym. Nevertheless Sally and Libby were able to interest a number of their students in the prospect of having a microcomputer. Together, the women and the students raised nearly $500 through bake sales and car washes, and in an imaginative move, they revived the defunct Parent Teacher's Organization and got them to contribute $200 from their inactive treasury. They immediately bought a new TRS-80 and purchased some software for it through the regular library book budget. Within days the computer was in constant use by students in the library during unassigned periods, and Sally and Libby wondered where on earth they could get enough money to buy the three or four additional microcomputers they clearly needed.

However, even this cozy success story of cooperation has its dark side. Student expectations at Greenville ran high and consequently were almost fated to be shattered. First, one microcomputer was totally inadequate to meet student demand. Second, when that microcomputer broke down and was at the repair shop for two months, there were a lot of disappointed customers. Third, the repair bill ate up the entire library budget for the rest of the year. Fourth, neither Libby nor Sally knew enough about software evaluation to select good materials, so they wasted a lot of their meager budget on poor software. Fifth, and as a result of all of the above, students soon lost interest in the computer and Libby and Sally's colleagues thought they had wasted their time and the library budget.

Not all decentralized computer acquisitions have such dismal results. Many teachers who are computer enthusiasts succeed in interesting their colleagues in becoming involved. Many principals bring interested parents and teachers together to plan for computer use in the school. Many teachers have access to knowledgeable people who can advise them on software and hardware purchasing before they spend their limited funds. All of these conditions exist in the following vignette.

A parent who worked in the computer science department of a nearby major university approached John McKenna, the principal of Meadow-view Elementary School, with the proposition that a group of knowledge-able parents and enthusiastic teachers form a computer advisory committee to the school to make recommendations for computer use. Mr. McKenna agreed to the idea and soon found that among the parents in his school were nearly a dozen who worked directly with computers. Not only did ten of these parents agree to serve on such a committee, but through the companies in which they worked, the school was given three microcomputers of three different makes. These were kept in a newly created Computer Resource Room that was staffed throughout the day by parent volunteers with some knowledge of computers. Software for the computers was selected by the computer committee and paid for out of the school's instructional materials budget.

Despite the apparent success of this story, let us sound one word of caution to schools about accepting microcomputers as gifts. You could find such gifts to be Trojan horses. In accepting gift microcomputers, schools pretty much obligate themselves to using them with children which in turn requires the allocation of teacher time, the need for teacher training, the commitment of funds for software purchase and hardware maintenance, the scheduling of computer time during and after school, the possibility of needing to rewire rooms in the school, and many other unanticipated demands of a successfully run computer facility in a school. Who will give your school the money to do all these things?

Actually, by creating the conditions for such needs, gift microcomputers often end up seeding much larger and more systematic computer efforts in the schools. The presence of even one microcomputer in a school enables administrators to observe the interest of kids, teachers, and parents in educational computing and also to recognize the financial and administrative requirements entailed. The potential conflict between growing school community interest in computers and the costs involved may well set the stage for the last approach to introducing computers into the schools we will discuss: the shared planning approach. The rather tentative moral is: Perhaps you shouldn't look a gift horse in the mouth, even if it may be a Trojan horse.

The Shared Planning Approach

We have discussed school systems in which decisions about computing were made by the central administration and systems in which computers were slipped into the schools by the "back door," the result of individual teacher efforts or parents' donations. In both approaches, we identified potential problems that suggested the need for more broad-based planning involving teachers, parents, and administrators. In fact, such shared planning often emerges from other beginnings. Recall that Dr. Jones convened a town advisory committee on school computing to support his efforts. Although this committee began as a rubber stamp for his decisions, it does provide a potential forum for genuine sharing of ideas. Similarly, the parent-contributed microcomputers at Meadowview Elementary School created conditions that ultimately led the school system administration to establish a school computing task force to study future computer use.

Other school systems, like the one described in the following vignette, actually begin their efforts by creating a committee to study computing needs and goals.

Up until 1978, Hillsville, a wealthy suburb, had provided little computing experience for its students beyond several timesharing terminals at the high school that were the exclusive domain of the Computer Club. Then, cognizant of the growing importance of computers in our society, the Hillsville Board of Education appointed a citizens' committee to make recommendations on the future of computing in the Hillsville schools. The committee responded quickly and emphatically that computers should be used throughout the K-12 curriculum and that the Board should take all necessary steps to accomplish this. The Board did this. They appointed a computer steering committee composed of teachers and administrators and hired a university-based consultant to assist the committee in its decisions.

The computer steering committee also set to work quickly, planning a series of in-service workshops and purchasing ten microcomputers of three different makes for use in the workshops and in the schools by students and teachers interested in exploring their potential. Eight two-hour workshops were held that were attended by over one-third of the system's faculty, as well as by several principals and the superintendent of schools. At the same time, the steering committee set up a series of public meetings with parents, teachers, other citizens, and the press to develop community support for their efforts. As a result, when the school budget passed, it included a generous appropriation for computer materials and teacher training.

The steering committee has continued to guide the expanding computer presence in the Hillsville schools. They promoted several pilot projects, recommended the purchase of another twenty microcomputers, worked with the teacher-run staff development committee to plan further teacher workshops, and continued planning for further expansion. Because the steering committee enjoyed the confidence of teachers, parents, and the administration, they have been able to move swiftly and decisively.

The experience of Hillsville and other systems like it suggest several distinct advantages to a shared planning approach.

- A broad base of support for computing in the schools.
- A concentration of financial and human resources on designated projects.
- A range of expertise, point of view, and experience applied to issues of school computing.
- A forum for communication among various constituencies in the school system.

This should not suggest that a shared planning approach is without its potential problems. Committees can stifle action as readily as they can take action. One school system has had a committee studying computing for three years without any concrete decisions. In the meantime, several impatient teachers have obtained microcomputers for their classrooms, via various back-door methods.

A second problem with shared planning occurs when key decision makers are excluded from the committee and its proceedings. Great care must be taken in constituting the committee to include key department heads, influential teachers, and appropriate administrators. One school system computer committee made a serious error when it failed to involve the high school librarian and the director of vocational education in its deliberations. By doing so, it lost two valuable sources of ideas, internal funding, and political support. Later, the committee was forced to go, hat in hand, to these important people to ask for help. This belated request was not received kindly.

FUNDING COMPUTER
ACQUISITIONS
FOR THE SCHOOL

In these days of fiscal restraint, one of the most difficult tasks confronting a committee or group of educators who have decided to introduce computing into their school is finding the funds to purchase the necessary computer equipment and materials. The place to start looking for funds is at home, within the existing school budgetary apparatus at the department, school, and district levels. After these sources have been exhausted, you may wish to seek funds or equipment from outside the school system. Both of these routes are discussed below.

In most schools, departments or individual teachers submit annual budget requests for books, equipment, and other miscellaneous expenditures. Although each of these budgets is relatively small, by combining funds from several of them, a reasonable amount of money may be raised. Thus, one strategy is to fund the purchase of your first computer system, such as a single microcomputer, by persuading several departments or teachers to allocate some portion of their budget for that purpose. Such an approach is more likely to succeed if those from whom you are seeking help have been consulted during the planning phase of your efforts. Obviously those teachers and departments that see substantial applications in their courses will be most inclined to give up part of their budget for the purchase of a computer system.

Persuading a department or teachers to allocate part of their regular budget for computers is a political process, not unlike lobbying. It requires approaching key people in just the right way. You will need a strategy for approaching them. Who are the key people with whom to talk? Department chairs? Senior members of the school faculty? What approach will appeal most to them? Labor saving arguments? Curricular rationales? Considerations of school politics? Personal approaches? You will, at least, need to make clear "what is in it for them" to those whom you need to persuade.

Most school building budgets contain discretionary funds controlled by the principal, as well as "fat" built in for emergencies. By developing a strategic plan, you can enlist support to persuade the principal to allocate some of these monies toward the purchase of a computer system. How should you approach the principal? What sort of financial support should you ask for? What sort of results can you promise the principal if a computer system is purchased?

The allocation of monies within a school or a department for a special interest is bound to arouse resentment among those who do not share that special interest, or who question its wisdom. It is important that you anticipate this and develop a dialogue with these potential antagonists. Perhaps they can be shown that the computer will assist them in their priority area. You and the other pro-computer people might offer to support them in the future in seeking funds for their special interest. Maybe they can be persuaded that the computer will benefit the kids and the school in general and thus indirectly will help them in their efforts. However, it is probably realistic to anticipate that there will always be some members of the staff who are antagonistic, or at least sceptical about computers, perhaps for very good reasons, and who may resent the allocation of funds for them. A continuing effort is needed to communicate with these colleagues about computing in the school, their concerns about it, and their ideas about educational innovation.

Some schools and departments may lack sufficient flexibility in their budgets to find enough money to implement the kind of computer system desired. While one possible response might be to settle for a more modest system, this could have serious costs. In the short run, it could result in the loss of allies as their desired applications are eliminated or curtailed. In the long run, buying too little computing power at the outset may necessitate trading in the entire system for an adequate one later, at considerable additional expense, financially and politically. So, if possible, seek monies adequate to fund the system deemed desirable as a result of your planning and research.

The most likely source of such monies is the local education budget. Even in times of fiscal restraint, funds are allocated for purchase of equipment and supplies. Thus, you may be able to persuade the principal to increase the school's request for equipment and supplies to include the purchase of a computer system. However, if the desired system is an expensive one, in the context of the overall school budget, the principal may need to make a special request for its purchase to the Board of Education. In such a case, groundwork and public relations are best done by a planning committee such as those discussed earlier. The board of education is more likely to approve a large expenditure for computers if it feels it has voter support and that the entire school system will benefit. Of course, a district or town-wide computer system may need to be much more elaborate and expensive than the system you had originally envisioned. Herein lies one of the Catch-22s of computer acquisition. The more extensive the system, the more allies one has for obtaining it; but also the more expensive it is, the more difficult it may be to fund it. This catch has led many individual teachers to go it alone in obtaining one or two relatively inexpensive microcomputers for their own classrooms. There is little doubt that this is the easiest route to acquisition, and it may well be a necessary first step. However, if computers are to make a major impact on education in schools, larger expenditures for bigger systems or more microcomputers will be needed, and this will require a broad base of support and participation from teachers and citizens in the town or district.

External Sources of Funding, Equipment, and/or Services

In the unlikely case that your school has failed to locate any money for computers from within the system, or in the more likely case that you have succeeded but would like to increase the resources available to you, pursuing external sources of funding is the next logical step to take. In the recent past, individual teachers and small groups of teachers have often taken this approach as their first step rather than pursuing the search for internal sources as discussed above. However, with the decline in federal and state support for education, it is likely to become more and more difficult for small-scale projects to find such financial support, particularly if they have not first checked out their own system's resources. The chance of receiving most government funding is greatly improved if it can be demonstrated that the local system has already made a financial commitment to computers. In fact, federal, state, and foundation support often require that funds requested from them be matched by funds or in-kind services from local sources. Conversely, most local sources of assistance such as citizen groups, corporations, and institutions of higher education are more likely to respond to a desperate plea from teachers whose town has not provided funding for computers, particularly if these contributions may act as a seed to encourage the schools to support computers eventually. In both cases, it is essential to pursue internal sources of funding first.

Aside from foundation support, which in many ways is more like federal and state funding, most private assistance is likely to come in the form of donated equipment or services, rather than money. Parents' groups, local businesses, and civic organizations are all potential donors or lenders of computer equipment, as well as potential teachers, consultants, or volunteer aides for a school computer program.

The possibilities of finding local computer resources are practically endless, largely because we are rapidly becoming a computer-based society. Any reasonably thorough survey of a sizable community should uncover numerous individuals, businesses, and organizations who are involved with computers.

Large corporations with local plants are particularly appropriate targets for requests of assistance. These are the employers of the parents of your students. They have a stake in the economic well-being and stability of the area. School people can approach such corporations with a variety of reasons for their making a contribution to a computer progam in the schools: simple public relations, corporate social responsibility, training future employees, and, in the case of a computer-related corporation, building future markets. In fact as the computer industry grows, more and more communities will find themselves in proximity to corporations dealing directly with computers. These corporations and the many individuals who work for them and live in the community are fair game for a dedicated group of educational computer advocates to approach for all the help they can get, including the (tax-deductible) donation of time and equipment.

Another major source of expertise and access to computer time are institutions of higher education, both private and public. Those communities fortunate enough to have a local college, university, or technical school have one of the best, most accessible computer resources available. Most such institutions consider themselves to have a special obligation to the communities in which they are located. Institutions of higher education are usually a tax drain upon a community since they are tax exempt. Often they try to pay back the community by providing cultural, technical, and other services. If the college has a time-sharing computer facility (as many colleges do), they can lend the local schools a small number of terminals and give them a reasonable amount of "free" computer time, at a relatively small cost to the college. In addition, college students with an interest in computing are quite easily enticed to come to the local schools to help elementary and secondary school teachers and students learn how to use the computer.

Dartmouth College in Hanover, New Hampshire has an extensive timesharing system that includes some 600 terminals distributed all across campus. As part of its community services, the college allows local community members free access to designated terminals at certain hours (the computer runs from 7 AM until 3 AM). At one time, local children had access to any terminal on campus on a lowest-priority basis (that is, any college student could kick them off at any time, though most of the college students were reluctant to exercise this right); now most local students must use the terminals in their own schools. Access to the college's computers unquestionably encouraged many schools in its vicinity to use computers; and today, as a measure of the success of this policy, many of those schools have their own computer facilities.

Although few colleges have the financial means of Dartmouth, or a time-sharing system as extensive, most have sufficient computer resources and a large enough sense of civic responsibility to provide local schools and their students with a reasonable amount of assistance and access to computer time. These are resources well worth pursuing.

Let us turn finally to state and federal funding, which was at one time the brightest hope for educational innovation, in general, and for infusion of computers into the curriculum, in particular. Today, such funding seems unlikely as a result of massive cuts in the federal budget, cutbacks in state funding of education in numerous states, as well as local taxpayer revolts and statewide ceilings on local spending (such as Massachusetts' Proposition 2½ and California's Proposition 13). Indeed, we are observing serious reductions in educational programs we have long taken for granted such as art, music, athletic teams, and guidance services, as well as massive layoffs of tenured teachers, shutting down of underutilized buildings, greatly increased class size, and a hard line on limiting teacher salaries and benefits. It would hardly appear the opportune time to be seeking funds from state or federal agencies to purchase computers, which might seem to many to be a fad or a frill.

But there are still reasons to hope for funding from these sources. First, there are hundreds of federal and state programs which were established by law, such as Title I, Title IVB, and Title IVC of the Elementary and Secondary Education Act (ESEA), as well as Public Law 94-142 and various state laws governing education of the handicapped, state laws directed at the gifted and talented, and state and federal laws dealing with bilingual/bicultural education. One viable strategy for obtaining government funding for computers in the school is to think of ways computers can be used to promote the objectives of the programs for which funding still exists. Most of these educational programs require considerable record keeping, involve highly individualized instruction, and are directed toward students not being adequately served by the schools. All of these characteristics suggest that computers would be very useful tools in pursuing the program objectives.

It goes without saying that once computers or software or personnel time have been obtained under the sponsorship of a program grant, care must be taken that the target group for which the grant was received is indeed served. However, it is legitimate and inevitable that some of the equipment and materials obtained will also be useful to the general school population and that external funds for budgeting these special program areas may allow the school to divert other funds to the computer program.

Another ray of hope in the external funding arena is a bit paradoxical. Precisely because there is much less money available for educational innovation from agencies such as the Department of Education, the National Institutute of Education, and the National Science Foundation, computers may stand a good chance of getting a large chunk of that limited pie. With a smaller funding budget, agencies will be forced to establish priorities for their funded projects. Computers present what may be a very attractive priority area. They can provide concrete, measurable, and dramatic results. They are inherently innovative, carrying little potential for reinventing the wheel. They are energy efficient. They may be cost effective, if properly utilized. They are good for business, and what's good for business is good for the economy — and what is good for the economy may eventually relieve the tight budget situation. They carry the potential for real invention, innovation, and change, beyond what even the current grantees may envision. If the choice were between a proposal for yet another curriculum development project on the one hand, and a proposal which would provide a school with a computer system to be used by hundreds of students and dozens of teachers in virtually every subject area and every grade level for years to come, there would seem to be a very good argument for choosing the latter. Thus, in hard times, computers in schools, like discount department stores, used car lots, and local tag sales, may be more financially successful than they would be in times of plenty.

For more information on funding computer systems, see the Resources section: Funding.

PREPARING TEACHERS AND ADMINISTRATORS FOR COMPUTERS IN THE SCHOOL

Having considered the political and financial requirements for obtaining computers for your school, you are now ready to deal with some tricky personal issues. Even if you follow the shared planning approach and have a cross-section of townspeople and school people working with you, there will still be many people in your school who do not look forward to the arrival of the computers. Despite the widespread and varied use of computers in society and the growing number of personal or home computers, many people still view computers with a great deal of suspicion.

For teachers this suspicion may be magnified by some of the ways in which a computer culture conflicts with a school classroom culture. For example, unlike most classroom problem-solving situations, computer-based problem solving often involves no right or wrong answer, but instead a choice of the most appropriate or elegant or efficient solution. Teachers may not be comfortable with such a view of problem solving, since they are generally used to problems with single answers: answers, moreover, that they know. Further, when working at a computer, the student or teacher is constantly facing what might be described as really tough problems. People who use computers learn to jump right into such problems, to try out approaches, to learn from their own mistakes, and not to get discouraged quickly. This way of working is much less systematic than most textbook-based problem solving, which generally lays out a particular procedure and then asks the student to apply that procedure to a set of similar problems. Teachers who are used to textbooks and a more prescriptive approach to problem solving may find the looser, empirical approach used with computers inconsistent with their teaching philosophy.

Another potential conflict between the computer and classroom cultures is the time it takes to complete an exercise or understand a procedure with computers. Computer-related assignments are rarely as discrete as: "Read the chapter and answer the questions at the end." Assignments are more often some sort of challenge where the student and teacher must adjust to the longer amounts of time required both for the total problem solution and for each session at the computer. This time issue is particularly frustrating for novice students and teachers, given the organization of most schools into periods of certain lengths with fairly rigid scheduling of student time.

Perhaps the most frequently discussed conflict between computer and classroom cultures revolves about the issue of teacher authority. We often hear how quickly students learn to use the computer, far surpassing the knowledge of untrained adults. In a school setting where the superior knowledge of teachers is closely linked to their authority over students, this state of affairs can threaten the social order of the classroom. Many teachers worry that they will be unable to answer student questions about computers and, thus, lose the respect of students whom they must instruct in other areas of knowledge. Such fears do not appear to be altogether unfounded.

Some educators feel that teacher discomfort with the computer culture will change as school computer use increases. "Interest will develop naturally. Teachers always want to be on the bandwagon." Others do not see teacher suspicion of computers as a problem in the first place. "Those that want to use the computer seek out the computer resources; those that don't, don't." However, if using the computer as an effective tool in the curriculum is your goal, you need to give some thought to preparing your colleagues for the arrival of a computer culture in your school. In the following sections we will discuss both informal and formal ways to do this.

Exploring Computer Applications

Your first job as a computer change agent is to get your colleagues interested in the possibilities of using computers in their classrooms. Such an interest can go a long way toward overcoming teacher wariness of computers. This was certainly our strategy in this book when we described a range of classroom computer applications in Chapter 2. You might be able to do the same sort of thing, only more effectively. Instead of just telling about computer applications as we did, you can actually demonstrate the applications and let your colleagues "mess about" with them.

Start by identifying computer applications that could address what you know to be needs and concerns of your school staff. Then arrange to buy, borrow, or preview a variety of software that would appeal to different members of your faculty. Establish times and comfortable settings in which to demonstrate these various applications and provide the opportunity for your colleagues to explore these uses at their leisure. Some examples of possibly attractive computer applications are discussed below.

Word processing can be an exciting computer application for the whole school. Try putting a computer with word processing software and a set of simplified instructions in the teachers' room and watch what happens.

Anything that makes uninteresting tasks easier appeals to most people, and teachers are no exceptions. Software packages for word processing are available on just about every make of computer. Pedagogically, word processing is one of several appropriate introductions to computers because the skills learned, such as entering and manipulating information, are skills required for many other computer applications. Of course, one potential problem in teaching word processing to a large number of people is the large amount of computer time such an application demands. However, this demand may also help people see the need for more computer facilities!

A similar and even simpler application that might encourage teachers to mess about with the computer is an electronic message system, enabling teachers, students and even parents to send, receive, and answer messages effortlessly. This message capability can be centered at one location, but has a great deal more utility if part of a network.

The head of the computer center at Stanford University chose the electric message system to "hook" her faculty on computer use. She began by providing the president of the university and other university V.I.P.s with an electronic message system and small portable terminals. They were then as close as the nearest telephone to a way of receiving and being able to respond directly and instantly to messages, memos, meeting requests, and the like from anyone on or off campus. The increased ease in carrying on everyday business from any part of the country persuaded these busy V.I.P.s, who were often off campus, of the utility of the computer. Their requests and those of others in the university community for computer services have continued to grow, along with the budget for the computer center and the influence of its director.

At the high school level, teachers or students often set up electronic "bulletin boards" on which people can leave messages for anyone who calls up the computer.

Another attractive application, especially for teachers who work with special needs children or slow learners, are quality drill-and-practice programs or CMI packages. You might arrange with a sales representative to demonstrate one or more of these commercially available packages and leave them in a resource room in your school to try out for a short period of time.

Many elementary school teachers who must teach math never become comfortable with the subject and find it difficult to provide interesting and challenging mathematics work for their better students. Try turning them on to Logo. Set up a computer with Logo in a classroom and invite your colleagues to come and observe the children using it. Then invite them back to use it themselves after school. The excitement and accessibility of Logo virtually guarantee success with students and teachers alike.

Finding computer applications that will appeal to high school social studies teachers may prove to be the most difficult task. Most are former history majors who do not view themselves as quantitative social scientists and hence see little use for computers, which they identify with math. Even the professional social studies teachers' organizations at the regional and national levels have been quite slow to introduce sessions relating to computers, and exhibitors at such meetings rarely bring computer-related books or computer instructional materials with them.

However, some of the most exciting uses of the computer are to be found in social studies. Easy-to-use statistical packages can aid students in carrying out simple research projects. Teachers and students can access large bodies of up-to-date information on almost any conceivable topic from information networks such as the Source. Word processing programs can turn the nightmare of the student research paper into a dream for student and teacher alike. And finally, using high quality simulation programs, or better yet, curricula that teach students to build their own models and simulate them with the aid of the computer, may be just the sort of activity to excite the innovative social studies teacher. Perhaps you could arrange with the social studies department of the high school to run an in-service workshop for them in which you demonstrate some of these applications.

There are similarly exciting and powerful computer applications in the science and math areas, particularly demonstrations, simulations, and the use of computers as laboratory tools to collect and analyze data as is done in scientific laboratories. In general, science and math teachers are quite open to computer use, so that you might be able to give one or two such teachers a quick lesson in using such applications and then have them show their colleagues what to do. This approach, known as "each one, teach one," is quite effective with groups who are inclined to learn what you wish to teach and is an important element in the staff development approach discussed below.

Beginning Staff Development in Educational Computing

After a school staff has experienced a positive introduction to computers, staff members need further exposure to and training with computers if they are to be able to use them effectively in their classrooms. Despite this, most schools are spending large amounts of money on both hardware and software and negligible amounts on teacher training. Instead, they rely on outside agencies, such as teacher centers or state staff development centers, to provide workshops. Unfortunately, there are usually too few sessions in these workshops for teachers to gain expertise or confidence in being able to use computers and often little or no follow up.

A very fine suburban school system may serve as a stunning example of this problem.

Livermore, a well-known progressive school system, hired an outside consultant to provide the elementary teachers in one of its schools with a one-day workshop on computers. At the end of the day, the school was given a computer and some software, and the teachers were asked to experiment with using the computer in their classes. The results were less than promising. Norma Bragg, a fourth-grade teacher, perhaps typifies the teachers' response to this experience. She is intimidated by the machine and feels that the children are far more comfortable with it than she is. So she lets the kids play with the packaged software. They love it, it keeps them busy, and she is fulfilling the request that the computer be used. Beyond that, it is doubtful that Norma has gained much from the experience in either knowledge or confidence.

Although outside agencies or highly paid consultants may be able to provide a better experience than the Livermore elementary teachers had, it is doubtful that any single workshop or even a several-session workshop is adequate. What is needed for effective staff development in educational computing is an on-going in-service program, for which we offer the following suggestions.

- Seriously consider having your own school system "experts" run the workshops so that they are available for follow-up questions or problems.
- Hands-on experience at the computer is critical. At a minimum, guarantee that half the training time is at the keyboard.
- Be sure that initial exposure includes a strong dose of non-math experiences, such as word processing.
- A feeling of teacher control over the machine is crucial. Use of Logo or an author language like PILOT provides teachers with almost instant success in simple programming.
- After awhile, expose teachers to a variety of computer languages to promote an understanding of the flexibilities of languages and the different methods of thinking about problems that each stimulates.
- Promote a positive attitude of working together, of expecting to need help, and of seeking help.
- Encourage experimentation at all times.

A lack of time is always the biggest obstacle to staff development. This problem is even worse for computer training. The time needed to provide teachers with a usable set of computer skills is greater than for most other educational training. The constraints of teachers' normally heavy schedules are often exacerbated by the limited amount of computer equipment available. The fewer computers or terminals, the less machine time for teachers. To alleviate this problem somewhat, many schools encourage teachers to take microcomputers home for weekends and vacation periods. Some schools allow teachers to audit high school computer science courses, and still others have other teachers or parents available as consultants to teachers in their study efforts.

Training Computer Change Agents

A more in-depth approach to teacher education is needed for those teachers wanting to be local computer resource persons. Such training may be obtained through full-term courses at local universities when available. But here, too, there are problems, mostly associated with the nature of the departments that offer the courses. If a course is offered by the computer science department, two constraints exist for most teachers: either such courses require that students have an undergraduate major in mathematics, science, or engineering or, even if there are no stated prerequisites, such courses often suppose a technical background, so that a person lacking one may quickly become lost.

Graduate courses in computers in education, designed especially for people without a mathematics or science background, are just beginning to appear at some universities, and very few undergraduate teacher education programs as yet offer courses in the use of computers in education. Where appropriate courses do exist at universities, some school systems underwrite their teachers' costs for enrolling in them. Larger school systems may even arrange to have graduate courses taught at their own schools, for interested staff members, providing them to their teachers free or at a reduced rate.

These and other approaches to staff development in ed-ucational computing need to be expanded if computers are to achieve their potential in schools. The training of teachers to use computers effectively for educational purposes stands as one of the biggest problem areas in educational computing today.

CONCLUSIONS

Teachers across the country, including both those who have been computer users for some time and relatively new computer users, are reporting that the introduction of computers into schools is happening relatively smoothly. Some teachers are now using computers in their classrooms, and many more are likely to become interested in learning about computers in the near future. Some teachers are going to great personal lengths to get information and training about computers in education.

It is clear, too, from reports from all over, that most preadolescent students can be easily taught about computers and how to use them. Schools are reporting strong student interest. For both students and teachers, the major element to successful computer use seems to be time. As noted by one library director, "The crucial factor with utilization of the microcomputer, and by inference any computer, is that there is no way one can bypass the time, that is, hands-on time, it takes. One cannot read about it and learn it."

Integrating Computers into the School

Chapter

7

Your computers have arrived. They are sitting in an assortment of boxes filling half the main office. It is time to answer some necessary questions. Where will they be located in the school? Who will have access to them? Who will coordinate their use? How will they be kept in working condition? How will they be protected from damage or theft?

These questions must actually be considered well in advance of the arrival of the computers. They deal with crucial issues that can make or break a computer program in a school. The location of computers and decisions about access may determine how thoroughly computers are utilized by members of the school staff. Provisions for maintenance, safety, security, and service may determine how available computers will be to students and teachers when they need them.

This chapter provides you with some possible answers to the questions above based on a survey we conducted during the preparation of this book. We wrote to hundreds of schools using computers for instruction and asked them these same questions.

LOCATION OF THE
COMPUTER FACILITY

The location of computers in a school can have great impact on their utilization and acceptance by a school staff. Possible locations will differ widely from school to school, but a common set of factors will influence your decisions about placement, including: the type and amount of equipment available, current long- and short-term instructional plans, the physical layout of the school and constraints imposed by networking, available personnel, and security/maintenance considerations.

Ease of access should be one of the main goals in deciding where to place computers. If most of the computers are going to be centrally housed, a location is needed that is within the general traffic pattern of the school, such as the library or media center. The location must be able to remain open for the longest possible number of hours. A library works well because of its continuous adult supervision and because of its tradition and procedures for storing and retrieving information. Some schools have terminals and software available for checking out from the library in the same manner as books. Some typical locations that do not lend themselves to widespread access are a corner of the school basement, a large empty closet or storage room, a mathematics room, or the nurse's office.

Whether or not all the computers are centrally located, there needs to be some area designated as the computer center, where computers can be housed when not in use elsewhere and where computer-related materials can be kept and used. The space chosen must be big enough to hold all the manuals, books, and magazines that would contribute to use of the computers in the school. It should also be located as near as possible to someone with some expertise in computing. Of course, a full time computer coordinator to oversee the center is ideal. However, the room should be free enough from a feeling of supervision to encourage experimentation among the computer users. A computer laboratory, supervised by a teacher designated as computer director and whose office or classroom adjoins the computer room, is an arrangement that often works well.

If the teachers in general feel comfortable with computers, there may be such a large demand for the use of computers in the classroom that centralized housing of computers is impractical, except after school hours. In this case, the equipment requirements for each course or class should be considered. Some examples of computer locations for certain types of courses follow.

1. For a computer science or business course, a traditional classroom setting is probably appropriate, with one computer or terminal per student as the ideal, as well as a large screen projection unit connected to a computer for large-group instruction and demonstrations.
2. If computers are going to be used in the school for remedial work and/or basic skills reinforcement, a constantly supervised resource room is the best

arrangement. No matter how good the CAI program is, it is still just a program and cannot anticipate all individual questions and needs. A person is needed to aid students in obtaining greatest advantage from such programs. This person might be the resource room teacher, a parent volunteer, a student volunteer, or a teacher's aide.

3. Some elementary school teachers and some secondary math or science teachers use computers in units designed to introduce students to computers. Such units may run anywhere from two weeks of classes every day to sixteen weeks of classes once a week. They often include information on the history of computing, how the machines work, and an introduction to computer programming. Students studying such units are generally expected to put in some time using the computer. Since several classes might be studying this unit at about the same time, it would be helpful if the computers were on portable carts containing additional extention cords and outlets as might be needed, so they can be moved easily from room to room.

Usually there are far fewer computers than students in such classes, so some students use the computer while the rest of the class is involved with other school work. In these situations, teachers and students may find computers in use in the same room to be a distraction. Placing the computers in an adjoining room visible to the teacher from the classroom may solve this problem.

4. If computer use is totally integrated into the science, social studies, English, or mathematics curriculum, there will be a great demand for computers. In such cases, one computer or terminal located permanently in each classroom or laboratory in departments making heavy use of computers is an absolute minimum. In addition, there should be sufficient computers or terminals available to these classrooms to allow for no more than four students per station. To accomplish this, it may be best to assign a class set of computers (10-15) to each department with heavy demand and have the department work out the distribution of access among its members.

5. For use in vocational education courses, a laboratory setting with electronic equipment, including computers, is required. An introduction to computer electronics could be beneficial to any student in the school. In fact, computers can sometimes help bridge what is often a social class barrier between vocational education students and college preparatory students. For example, in one school, a notoriously tough vocational education student impressed a physics class with a demonstration of the computer-controlled lathe he had designed and built.

6. For computer use in a self-contained elementary classroom, the ideal situation would be one computer for every one to three students. One computer for the entire classroom is a more realistic arrangement, given budgetary constraints. In this case, the computer should be placed in a spot in the room where one to three students can work at it without distracting

the rest of the class. The computer screen should be located so as to minimize glare from windows or overhead lights. It would be helpful if the teacher could connect the computer to a larger video display unit for total class instruction. The computer should be placed away from the chalkboard since it must be kept dust free, and it should probably be locked up when not in use.

7. A terminal or microcomputer linked to a database of information relating to students, staff, and school system resources might be very appropriate in a central teachers' meeting room, the central office, or the guidance office. This could provide a simple way to demonstrate the computer as a useful tool to sceptical staff, as well as give those who have never used a computer the ability to watch it being used. Appropriate software such as word processing should also be available at such locations, along with the necessary instruction manuals.

ACCESS TO THE
COMPUTER FACILITY

A crucial question to address in the integration of computers into a school is who will have access to the computer facilities? The answer can be quite simple: anyone who has the time. On the other hand, some feel that student access to limited computer resources should be determined by such factors as enrollment in courses using computers; generally high academic achievement; selection by the mathematics teacher, programming teacher, or guidance counselor; or participation in a targeted program like "gifted and talented" or "learning disabled." Schools seem to be divided between allowing anyone to use the computers and having an established procedure that limits access in some way. In one school, at first only people who had taken the introductory course in computers could use them, but later with an "each one teach one" staff development policy, use spread quickly so that there are now no restrictions on access. In another school, students must have an audiovisual license to use the computer. To acquire such a license, students must demonstrate knowledge of how to run the computer. Generally it appears that schools new to computing and inner city schools, with their special security concerns, have the most restrictions on access, but that as school people become more comfortable with the computer facility, access is handled as it is in most library/media centers: availability to the total school population, with an imposition of only those rules needed to maintain order and equipment security.

A more subtle issue of access is that of creating a computer environment equally appealing to female and male students. There is accumulating evidence that computer courses, like math and science courses, are experiencing a high percentage of female dropout beyond the introductory level. This dropout seems to occur even earlier when computers are housed in a central location rather than in classrooms. A "boy's club" atmosphere tends to pervade the computer room, even in elementary schools. One teacher in an affluent, K-8, suburban school was very disheartened by this, commenting, "The director of our computer program and 90 percent of our teachers are female, yet there is clearly a feeling that the computer room (located within the general library area) is male territory."

Another question related to computer access is how access to administrative information, such as pupil and personnel records, will be limited. Most schools have clear guidelines regarding student and teacher rights to their own files and regarding the limits on access to these files by others. These rules may be harder to enforce when such files are placed on the computer. Students are adept at cracking protective codes, so that real consideration should be given to using a different, and physically protected, computer system for records requiring any degree of confidentiality.

To a great extent, access to computing facilities depends on the amount and kind of time students and teachers have available to them during the day. In some schools computer access is allowed only during class. Others allow computer use anytime but only during the regular school day, while other schools provide free access only after school since computers are used for classes during school time. One suburban high school gives Computer Club members keys to

Photo: Sharon A. Bazarian

the school so they can use the computer at any time, day or night. Several schools allow students to sign out microcomputers to take home at night and on weekends. Regarding this approach, one school administrator commented that while anyone may borrow microcomputers, only a few actually exercise this privilege. In other school systems there are waiting lists to borrow computers to take home.

Several considerations are important when developing access rules. First, doing work on a computer often requires blocks of time much greater than for most other educational tasks. To spend two or three hours or even all night working through a problem is not uncommon. Even though there are times when it is appropriate to encourage students to do their thinking away from the computer, given unlimited computing facilities, it is often more productive for students to have terminals available for receiving feedback to their ideas. This is even truer for teachers who are developing computer-related curriculum.

Another crucial question regarding access arises when a school decides to make its computer facilities available for as many hours as possible: who will staff such a facility? There are many options here, primarily determined by the perception of the need for supervision and by budgetary considerations. Several schools that have required supervision at all times have been very successful in supplementing staff with community volunteers, either parents or retired townspeople. Other schools assign older students as computer room aides. This problem is not unlike staffing school libraries, except that a person with some knowledge of computers can increase considerably the usefulness of the facility.

BASIC INFORMATION NEEDED IN A COMPUTER FACILITY

With any computer there is a minimum set of information needed by people to use it: how to turn on the computer, how to handle disks or cassettes properly, how to access the particular program needed, what to do if the computer malfunctions, how to shut off the computer, and where to put away materials. However, there are many ways to communicate this information, depending on the physical location of the computer. For example, if computers are set up for public access, as they usually are in museums and libraries, the computer is always on, and the user merely answers questions on the terminal to select a program from a listing (menu) presented by the computer. At the other end of the continuum is the computer that must be <u>booted</u> (loading the operating system into memory and starting its operation) by each user. In this case, a user must know the exact procedure to boot the particular computer being used. This may involve loading disks, toggling switches, setting Baud rates, and typing responses to the computer's inquiries, using a predetermined sequence of letters, numbers, and other symbols. In between the above two extremes, and found most commonly on timesharing systems, is a <u>log-in</u> procedure requiring the user to turn on the terminal, give an account number and password, request the computer to run a certain program, or look at a catalog or directory of programs available, and then choose one to run. But even the timesharing procedure can vary depending on whether the user is following the computer's operating system or the procedure of a particular language or other type of software.

Whatever the procedure, directions must be clearly posted, so that anyone without computer experience may read or be read them and so be able to use the computer. Information about idiosyncracies of particular computer units or terminals should be available to all users. Simple suggestions such as, "If this computer does not boot the first time, try twice more, then use another disk," can be very comforting for novices who will tend to believe problems to be all their fault. Other kinds of information might best be noted right on the disk, such as "Boot the machine with the 3.2 Disk Operating System (DOS) master disk to run programs from this disk." (Do not write directly on the disk; write on a gummed label and then affix it to the disk.) In addition to posted information, demonstration sessions should be offered on a regularly scheduled basis, and the schedule for these sessions should be made known to all persons in the school.

A minimum set of written materials should be available wherever there is a computer or terminal. This includes copies of all manuals that accompany the computer, books relating to the languages available on the computer, and pamphlets that accompany any software available to be run on the computer. This is inevitably a great deal of written material, so that it is often very helpful to provide a summary guide. Rewriting the most used manual and removing the jargon may help novices follow it more easily.

In addition to the above materials, a computer center containing a variety of computer newsletters, magazines, and books is a great asset. The wide array of written materials now inundating the market can provide enough reading and computer challenges to keep students of all ages involved for quite a long time.

A means for distributing information about new software purchases or changes in hardware should also be provided to all present and prospective users. This can be done through a traditional bulletin board in a computer center or through a computerized bulletin board, in which a "hello" program automatically gives important news of this sort when a user logs on to the computer.

As we discussed earlier, many communities have people working in computer or related industries who have expertise in areas useful to computer novices. These people are often quite willing to give time and advice to their local schools. If there is a college in the area, faculty in pertinent fields can be excellent resources. Members of education departments at colleges and universities who have some expertise in computers for educational purposes may be able to direct teachers toward well-designed educational materials for computers. (See the Resources section: Continuing Education for a partial list of colleges and universities offering degrees in educational computing).

State education departments are also potential sources of knowledge about computers in education, although as with universities, the degree and quality of that knowledge may vary widely from place to place. If nothing else, departments of education may be able to put teachers in touch with other schools who are using computers, and they may even be helpful in identifying potential state and federal funding sources for buying computers.

The most obvious source of information are other teachers and students within the same system who have acquired a degree of computer expertise. One example may be the local vocational technical school where both teachers and students have a knowledge of electronics. They could help others understand some of the technical writing that accompanies peripherals such as printers, or they might help maintain the computer equipment.

Many other people can be important sources of information about computers. For example, there are local, regional, and national educational users groups for just about every brand of computer. Information about these groups can be found in computer newsletters and magazines. For a partial list of people resources, see the Resources section: User Groups and Computer Clubs, Resource Centers, Projects, Computer Learning Places, and Associations.

REASONABLE RULES
AND GUIDELINES
FOR THE COMPUTER

The usefulness and continued existence of computers in a school require that there be a set of reasonable rules and guidelines for fair and appropriate use. These guidelines should address such issues as:

- Length of time allowed for one person to sit at a station when there is a demand from others.
- Priority of usage such as administrative programs versus instructional programs, time-consuming programs like word processing versus time-efficient drill-and-practice programs, and classroom assignments versus games as entertainment.
- Number of students per station, as it affects the noise level and general atmosphere of the room;
- Maintenance of order in the computer room.

The length of time appropriate for one sitting is task dependent. One problem encountered by teachers who are developing computer-related curriculum is determining what is a reasonable assignment for a traditional-length class period. There never seems to be enough hands-on time.

At the Prairie School, a small rural school in Minnesota, where there is a high demand on the computer facility, time is alloted to each elementary student for basic skills aid by requiring each student to have a signed pass from the teacher for entrance to the computer room. The pass has the following information on it: a) area to be drilled in, b) software and hardware to be used, c) the class the student came from, d) the time the student left the room, and e) the length of time the student may stay. With this information, a management aide loads the programs in the microcomputers for the students and gets them started.

One way to cut down on student time at the computer facility is to forbid game playing. At a private school in Delaware, students may not play Star Wars-type games. They must have written the programs they use themselves. When a similar rule was invoked at a middle school in Massachusetts, the students immediately began writing their own game programs. Some teachers are firmly opposed to this kind of rule. Two computer teachers in two different high schools also in Massachusetts have found that game playing is an excellent way to motivate apathetic students to become interested in school. In their view, being in the computer room playing games is better than hanging around the parking lot all day. They find that some of these students even learn to program.

Noise level is often a difficult issue in a central computer room, or even in a classroom with one terminal, because the atmosphere of working together, asking for help, and sharing ideas is so important in computer projects. How else can a contagious excitement be created? However, limits are always needed. A number of high schools are coping with this problem by having their computer users society determine and enforce all rules relating to the computer and computer room. One rule recently established at a western high school was to lock the door to the computer room twenty minutes after the start of each period to help control the general commotion. The computer users society at that school also determines how much disk space is allocated to each person and what software is available to whom.

MAINTENANCE AND SERVICE
OF THE COMPUTER SYSTEM

Computer maintenance is rarely seen as a problem by people responsible for computer facilities. That does not mean that maintenance is not necessary. It is as much needed for computers as for any other piece of school equipment, and is generally handled in the same manner. Most school systems negotiate maintenance contracts for their equipment. With the computers used up to the mid-seventies, a maintenance contract was standard. However, when the personal computers appeared, often sold through stores rather than by sales representatives, maintenance contracts became more of an option.

Repairs

Repairs on smaller computers are much less expensive. Most micros are portable enough to be brought or sent to the repair shop. This is certainly not the case for the larger computers, whose repairs require visits by fairly expensive technicians. Further, some of the personal computers are designed to allow a degree of in-house maintenance. Computer stores even sell such things as diskette cleaning kits. However, do-it yourself computer repair persons should exercise care, since fooling with the electronics of a computer may void some parts of the manufacturer's warranty. Some computer stores themselves are not equipped to provide service; they merely ship broken computers back to the manufacturer. School systems across the country handle their need for repairs in a wide variety of ways. An independent school in New Hampshire keeps a service contract on their DEC PDP-11 system and on their Apples. On the average, the DEC terminals have required service once per year, while the micros have required service only in the rare cases when there has been inadvertent student abuse of them. A mathematics instructor from a school system in North Dakota calls a farmer in the area, who has an electronics background, when something goes wrong with the school's TRS-80. If he doesn't have the answer, he sends the equipment to the Radio Shack repair center.

Distance to the repair shop is often the major problem in maintenance. Some schools can get 24-hour service from the local shop, while other schools report having to drive anywhere from seven miles to the local United Parcel Service office in order to generate a four-day turnaround, up to 250 miles to a computer repair center. The situation in Alaska is perhaps extreme, where the isolation of many schools magnifies the maintenance problem. Most maintenance in Alaska is done under a depot arrangement with in-state vendors. One school in a rural town in Vermont has the policy, "They who break, take." Compounding the problem of distance is the occasionally unreasonable length of time taken for repairs. One high school science teacher from a city in Oregon had to wait one month each for the repair of a microcomputer and cassette deck. In contrast to this, the computer coordinator from an elementary school in Indiana negotiated an agreement with the dealer to repair within 24 hours or provide a loaner to the school.

Cost of maintenance of computers varies as much as the computers being served. The monthly maintenance (parts and labor) charged by DEC for a contract on one of its smallest machines, the PDP-11 V03, is approximately $250, while the monthly maintenance agreement arranged by one school with a local computer store for service calls and labor on six Apples is $25. A junior high school in Colorado estimates the maintenance cost for its Apples at about $30 per machine per year, and similarly a high school in Rhode Island budgets $300 per year for the maintenance of its nine TRS-80s. It is important that the cost of maintenance be included as a budget item, so that you won't have to beg the principal for money if your computer breaks down. Including the maintenance costs as part of the bid specifications for purchasing computers, as is done by several larger school districts, might be worth considering. Maintenance should be budgeted at 10-12 percent of the cost of your equipment per year. Service contracts are usually written on this basis.

Many schools choose to do their own repairs on their microcomputers. A school district in Arizona paid for its AV technician to have two days of training by a Commodore PET technician. Another school reported that their basic PET repair kit was a Phillips screwdriver. A middle school teacher in Texas with an electronics background purchased test equipment with Title IV-C funds and does his own repairs.

One maintenance strategy is to buy equipment that is fairly easy to disassemble and to purchase an extra unit for every so many working units. When a working unit breaks down, it can be repaired with parts cannibalized from the back-up unit. Then the parts for the back-up unit are replaced via mail or UPS.

Prevention

Whether repairs are done in-house or sent out, some preventative steps can be taken and some minor checkups can be done on-site. The physical environment of the computer might affect its performance. Keep these points in mind.

1. **Dust is damaging to both the computer and the disks.**

    Chalkboards create large amounts of dust. White boards — boards written on with colored markers — are a fine substitute for chalkboards. If this is not possible, keep the machine covered when it is not in use, or install an electrostatic air cleaner in the computer room. Keep the doors to the disk drives closed, again to keep out dust. Store the disks upright in envelopes to keep them dust free. Of course, do not allow smoking in the computer room by anyone, even teachers and the principal.

2. **Computers tend to be sensitive to static electricity.**

    The computer room should not be carpeted or have plastic furniture. If there is a carpet, it is possible to install an antistatic mat ($50-$200 each) under the computer. Putting a humidifier in the computer room will also help control static electricity.

3. **Computers are also sensitive to power spurts.**

    A high school in Montana was experiencing five or six surges per day before they bought surge suppressors for about $60 each. The power company couldn't handle the power demands of their rapidly growing valley.

4. **Several schools have had problems with computers' on-off switches.**

   A cure for this is to plug the computers into a power strip, leave the computer switch always on, and turn power on and off by the strip switch, which is much easier to repair. Microcomputers use very little electricity, therefore turning them off frequently is unnecessary.

5. **Sometimes computers are sensitive to heat.**

   This problem increases with the size of the computer. However, all computers should have reasonable ventilation. Do not choose an inside room without a fan. Disks are sensitive to both heat and radiation emitted by video monitors, thus disks should not be left very near an operating TV or monitor.

6. **The mechanical parts of the computer, such as disk drives and printers, can be damaged by jarring.**

   However, many people transport computers hundreds of miles without experiencing any problems. Saving original cartons might aid in this process.

When something goes wrong with the computer, several do-it-yourself steps should be taken before you bring it in for repair.

- Read the manual.
- Check all connections.
- Make sure the problem is not a software problem rather than a hardware one. Try another tape or diskette. Jiggle the diskette a little to make sure it is centered properly in its jacket. Diskettes wear out. Normal shelf life of most diskettes is about four years, but with frequent use, many will wear out within half a year, and there are many poor quality ones on the market that wear out much sooner or are defective when purchased.
- Push down the chips of the main board, which might have become loose. **Before doing this, make sure the computer power is off.**
- Clean the gold-plated copper contacts of input device boards, such as the disk controller card, by wiping them off with cotton saturated with denatured ethyl alcohol or an equivalent.
- Be careful not to conduct static electricity. Touching the power unit before touching any chips will safely remove static electricity. Also be very careful not to touch any of the insides of the computer with metal jewelry.
- Invest in a disk-cleaning kit and use it.

As a means of preventing lengthy disruption of the whole computer system, have at least two of everything: two computers, two disk drives, two monitors, and so forth. Even more important, back-up copies of all software should be stored away and checked every now and then to make sure they are working properly. Students should be taught to make back-up copies of their own projects, if losing them would cause a hardship. One easy way to create back-ups of programs under development is to retain the most recent version and the one just previous on the same disk but under different file names, deleting only older versions. In addition, back-up copies of entire disks should be made regularly and kept in different locations from the originals.

Commercially produced software is usually protected by copyright, and unauthorized duplication of it is illegal. Some, but not all, software vendors will permit you to make back-up copies of their cassettes or diskettes for your own use or will sell you back-up copies at a sharply reduced price. You may want to take a closer look before purchasing any software for which you can neither make, nor inexpensively obtain, legal back-up copies.

This matter of copyright, copying, and back-ups is one of many unresolved issues that is bound to plague educational computing for some years to come. Ultimately, computer-using educators, publishers, and authors will need to resolve this issue fairly for all concerned.

From a management point of view, the most efficient way to maintain a computer facility is to have at least one full-time person in charge. This is perhaps more important for centers with larger computers, where maintaining an up-to-date operating system and up-to-date manuals can be extremely time consuming. However, even in locations using just microcomputers, having one person responsible for hearing complaints about equipment and responding to the problems is very helpful. This person is then able to build up a degree of expertise which is possible only over time. Assigning part of a teacher's time to computer room supervision is one way for schools to begin budgeting for the eventual hiring of a full-time person.

Security

One final area of concern in maintaining computers in a student environment is the issue of security, both of the hardware itself and of the information stored on the computer. Although many computer-using educators do not regard security as a serious problem, others are extremely concerned about it. All schools seem, at least, to take security precautions.

Several different approaches are taken to minimize the likelihood of abuse to the machinery. In many instances, one central computer room is chosen as the physical arrangement for ease of security. Then all the equipment is protected by locking the room when it is not supervised. A high school in Minnesota has had no security problems as a result of allowing its students to use equipment from 7:30 A.M. to 4:45 P.M. and then locking the computer room door. In a high school on the west coast, the doors of the computer room are always kept locked. Students who have been admitted allow others to enter. When the teacher leaves, the room is emptied and locked. In addition to locking rooms, in several schools the computers are bolted down to tables. Other schools have security alarm and guard systems. In general, security problems are eliminated by having supervision, either by adults or by reliable older students.

Schools without one central computer room generally have computers returned each night to a central location that can be locked. Schools that have experienced problems use double locks, or as is done in one middle school in a Connecticut city, all computer units are transported to a lockable storage closet in a locked classroom in an inaccessible part of the building. In a New England private school, computers are kept in individually locked cabinets and signed out through the mathematics teacher in charge of the computer program. One way that schools eliminate all this need to lock up equipment is to allow computers to be checked out day, night, and weekends by individuals who are then responsible for their safety.

Data security is a very different kind of issue, because it usually involves students acting on rather different motives. Breaking through a data security system and stealing information or computer time is seen by some computer zealots as an intellectual challenge, while stealing hardware usually occurs for other reasons. Nevertheless, in both cases illegal acts are committed and both offenders are criminals, although the intellectual crimes are often treated very differently.

Here again, many educators do not appear to be worried about data security. A boarding school in New Hampshire simply changes the passwords for the privileged accounts occasionally. Similarly, a high school in Nevada uses a security system that limits the students to a certain set of commands, only allowing them into certain areas of the computer. The school also uses a password system that is changed sporadically. One computer teacher has found that students who are tempted to break security codes usually stop at that and do not tamper with stored information. However, over the years some frightening stories of what high school students have done to computer security systems suggest that student computer crimes can be very destructive of databases and programs. For example, in one school, students broke the administrative codes and altered grades on student permanent records.

When an abuse of computer equipment or files does occur, the steps taken in most places seem comparable. In one public school, the Computer Coordinator talks to the offenders, appealing to concerns for individual rights and the inconvenience of others. If the abuse continues, then disciplinary action is taken. Similarly, in another school system, the Director of Instructional Technology tracks down students who steal IDs and places them on restriction; that is, no access to computers for three days or more depending on the student's involvement and the problems caused. Perhaps more effective is the preventative philosophy followed in most computer environments that encourages sharing, minimizes secrecy in programming classes, and establishes an atmosphere of respect and trust.

CONCLUSION

Although computers have been in a few schools in some manner for over twenty years, the sudden explosion of educational computing brought about by the development of microcomputers has resulted in hundreds of thousands of computers in thousands of schools. If you are considering the use of computers in your school, there is much you can learn from the experiences of others. In this chapter, we have shared with you the collective wisdom of several hundred computer using educators on some of the most practical matters you will face as you seek to integrate computers into your school.

Photo: J.D. Sloane

Issues and Choices in Educational Computing

Chapter
8

LOOKING BACKWARD

The history of the use of computers in education goes back almost twenty years. During the sixties, a major effort was launched to harness the educational potential of computers. Involving government agencies, university researchers, and computer manufacturers, it ended up costing many millions of dollars. With much fanfare, an "educational revolution" was declared, although its actual realization always seemed "just around the corner." Today, with the advent of microcomputers, there has been a renewal of this optimism in the minds of some educators who see these powerful machines as a source of the revitalization that our educational system so sorely needs. As we consider the real potential for computers in education for the future, it will be useful to learn what we can from the past.

The sixties can be thought of as a period of heavy investment in research and development in educational technology. Although the investment may yet pay off, the effort is generally thought of as having been a failure. Despite a rather extensive publicity campaign carried on in educational circles by the government, the computer manufacturers, and advocates of computer assisted instruction, none of this research had much immediate impact on mass education. Among the most publicized early projects were:

- The "Talking Typewriter" of Yale University's O. K. Moore, which was supposed to effectively teach reading and writing to two- and three-year-olds. The cost per learner, however, was astronomical.
- I.P.I., the "Individually Prescribed Instruction" project, which created a "complete" set of elementary school learning objectives and programmed a computer to provide daily tests and lesson assignments for all the students in a Pittsburgh elementary school. The intent was to free teachers from the burden of record keeping as well as from the process of making daily decisions about what and how students should learn. It was assumed that machines would be better at those tasks than teachers. Teachers would function as tutors, helping the children maximize the learning from their computer-prescribed lessons. The project made a point of including no learning objectives that were not readily measurable. Grammar was included in the curriculum. Creative writing was not.
- The activities of Patrick Suppes at Stanford University, who predicted that in the foreseeable future every child could have the same advantage that Alexander the Great had — a personal tutor as brilliant, patient, and creative as Aristotle. He began to "build" such a tutor by breaking down the learning of arithmetic into its most minute objectives. Suppes' work, as we shall discuss later, has survived into the present, albeit in a somewhat modified form.

Despite successful evaluations of these and many other pilot projects, computer assisted instruction, as these activities came to be called, did not become a significant ongoing part of many school programs in the sixties or even in the early seventies. A study carried out by the Educational Testing Service in 1972 (see Bibliography) concluded that these approaches had not been more widely adopted for a range of reasons. Among these were:

- The cost of the hardware needed to reach masses of students and the cost of developing quality educational software were much too high. It turned out that producing effective computer tutorials required very high-priced experts in the psychology of learning and computer programming, working for much longer than had been anticipated.
- Teachers were afraid of technology. They didn't learn to use CAI systems easily and got quickly discouraged when parts of the systems malfunctioned (as many computers do from time to time). The common rhetoric about computers being better teachers than humans was offensive, especially when compared with the actual quality of most of the instructional programs available. Finally, teachers feared the loss of their jobs — not a totally unfounded fear, since many of the proponents of CAI claimed that teachers

could be replaced by technicians who would help run the machines and tutorial aides who could help students with their lessons.

- Inadequate provisions had been made for teacher training. No organization seemed to be taking responsibility for this aspect of introducing computer materials into schools. Teachers could not use materials and equipment that they didn't understand.
- The claims of CAI proponents about the effectiveness of their systems had been greatly exaggerated. CAI, as developed in the sixties, simply could not do as much as had been claimed for it. Mostly, it was used as a way of helping students learn rote skills by providing reasonably flexible drill and practice. While this was certainly a useful function, it was hardly a re-creation of Aristotle, or even effective competition for the average teacher.
- Fundamentally, schools are conservative social systems. They do not adopt new methods easily. Proponents of CAI had not paid enough attention to the issues involved in implementing their innovations in school settings.

The ETS study made a number of recommendations, none of which questioned the educational soundness of CAI in general, but rather addressed issues of development, support, and implementation. It suggested that major efforts— to be funded mainly by the government—be directed towards developing new and better materials, training teachers, evaluating the effectiveness of CAI, and promoting it heavily among parents and educators.

During the seventies several major federally funded research, development, and evaluation projects were undertaken, primarily with the support of the National Science Foundation and the United States Office of Education.

- The Huntington I and II Projects led by Ludwig Braun at the State University of New York at Stonybrook developed a number of computer simulation activities that could be used to enrich instruction in high school and junior high school science and social studies.
- Thomas Dwyer's Solo Project at the University of Pittsburgh produced activities and materials that used computer programming activities to teach elements of standard high school mathematics.
- Alfred Bork at the University of California at Irvine established an Educational Technology Center where he and colleagues developed approaches to designing and authoring CAI modules in the form of tutorial dialogues. Most of the projects of the Center have related to college-level science courses, but recent efforts include materials for junior high school courses and tutorials to facilitate science learning in public libraries.
- The PLATO project at the University of Illinois created a large body of CAI materials and a system by which users were linked to a large timesharing computer that could be used as a communications network as well as for instruction. PLATO is now a commercial project of the Control Data Corporation. It is used primarily for industrial training programs at present and is still too expensive for many schools to consider.

- A state-funded project, the Minnesota Educational Computing Consortium (MECC), pooled resources at the state level to provide computer access, teacher training, and curriculum development for all the schools in Minnesota. MECC (pronounced "MECK") has also carried out a number of federally funded projects, notably in the area of computer literacy.

These were just a few of the activities that received federal government support during the seventies (see the Resources section: Projects and Research and Development for descriptions of some other projects). Although they were originally developed for large timesharing systems, most of them have been, or are being, redesigned for microcomputers. They may thus eventually enjoy a much larger impact than the original projects did, since many more students will have access to microcomputers.

To make our discussion of the past a little more concrete and to clarify some of the issues raised by the efforts of the sixties and seventies, we will briefly consider the ideas and careers of three pioneers in the field. Patrick Suppes, Arthur Luehrmann, and Seymour Papert have all been active in computer education since the sixties. The different directions they have chosen for their work illustrate three different trends that continue to be important as we attempt to understand the choices available to us in the eighties and nineties.

Patrick Suppes

Patrick Suppes of the Institute for Mathematical Studies in the Social Sciences (IMSS) at Stanford University might almost be considered "the father of computer assisted instruction." Having begun with the lofty goal of turning a computer into an individualized tutor for everyone, his accomplishments have been more modest. Suppes has been relatively successful at creating a reasonably large body of less comprehensive computer programs. Each of his projects centers on a particular course or subject. His approach is to begin with a rigorous logical analysis of the subject matter, combined with a careful study of possible learning strategies. The results of these investigations are then implemented through well-structured systems of programmed instruction that provide immediate feedback to the learner, branch to the appropriate next lesson, and keep meticulous records of student progress.

The huge effort needed to devise and program such systems has led Suppes and his coworkers to direct their efforts toward specific populations of learners who they feel have the greatest need for specialized supplementary or individualized learning experiences. Low-achieving students who need drill and reinforcement in basic skills, handicapped students, college students taking courses in subjects with low enrollment at a particular college, and gifted high school students who could not be adequately served by their own schools have been among the target populations served by Suppes' efforts.

Many of Suppes' projects have received positive evaluations. Following successful reports from one study in which all the students in the elementary schools of McComb, Mississippi practiced their basic skills using computer terminals connected by telephone to a host computer at Stanford, Suppes helped to found the Computer Curriculum Corporation. CCC has since marketed the same type of educational materials to school districts with high proportions of "educationally disadvantaged" students. These services are usually paid for with federally funded Title I grants.

Arthur Luehrmann

Arthur Luehrmann has been an outspoken advocate of computer literacy, by which he means allowing the public increased access to computers as powerful tools and to the skills necessary for controlling (programming) them. Formerly with Dartmouth College's Kiewit Computation Center and later director of the Lawrence Hall of Science computer science programs, he has spoken and written extensively to support his goal and to oppose trends that are in conflict with it. In an influential article that has often been reprinted since its original publication in 1972, "Should the Computer Teach the Student, or Vice-Versa?" (see Bibliography), Luehrmann strongly argued that computer programming skills were basic skills for citizens of a computer-based society, as important as reading and writing skills for a print-based society. By limiting educational use of computers mainly to CAI, he argued, we were shortchanging our students — effectively training people to be second-class citizens of a society in which jobs, social status, and influence would increasingly go to those who could understand and control computers.

Recently Luehrmann has initiated a personal campaign to promote the idea that computer literacy — primarily meaning the skills associated with programming computers and using them as vehicles for personal expression — should be considered a fundamental goal of our educational systems at all levels. He has been critical of those who have defined computer literacy to mean primarily a body of information about computers, rather than the skills needed to control them. He contends that advocates of such a limited definition of computer literacy are diverting attention from the more fundamental goal of helping students develop the basic skills they will need to succeed in our society.

In 1981, Luehrmann founded his own company, Computer Literacy, Inc., an organization devoted to promoting computer literacy by means of curriculum development, seminars, lectures, and consulting. One of the first major efforts of the company has been to develop a curriculum intended to teach all students at the seventh- or eighth-grade level to program computers using BASIC. Luehrmann reasons that every school system can afford to train one teacher and set up one computer laboratory (containing a minimum of eight microcomputers) to provide students with a minimal introduction to computer programming.

Seymour Papert

Seymour Papert, director of the MIT Logo Group, part of the Artificial Intelligence Laboratory at the Massachusetts Institute of Technology, has been largely responsible for a radically different approch to the educational use of computers. Rather than being concerned with preparing people for jobs in a computer-based society, or with using computers to replace instruction by teachers, Papert's work has centered on the use of computers and computer programming to create entirely new types of learning environments for children. Dissatisfied with the educational potential of the computers and computer languages available to schools when he began his work in the late sixties, Papert set out to create his own explicitly educational computer language. His efforts, partially described in the discussion of programming in Chapter 2, and discussed more fully in his recent book, *Mindstorms* (see Bibliography), have resulted in the creation of the computer language, Logo, and a wide variety of related computer programming activities for students.

Working with colleagues at MIT and at Bolt, Beranek, and Newman, a Cambridge, Massachusetts consulting firm, Papert based the Logo language and related activities on his prior research in the psychology of learning (six years spent working directly with Jean Piaget in Geneva, Switzerland) as well as on programming concepts from the field of Artificial Intelligence (a branch of computer science which has the aim of developing machines capable of carrying out "intelligent" behaviors). Logo is designed to have "no threshhold, no ceiling." It can be used by children to create meaningful computer programs in their first computer sessions, as well as by sophisticated programmers developing complex computer applications such as adventure games, "intelligent" conversational programs, or business and scientific applications.

Critics of Papert suggest that his approaches cannot be successfully implemented in conventional schools because of the way in which he has down played the importance of teachers and conventional curricula. However, Papert's "natural learning environments" seem to depend on teachers — in fact, on those who are rather sophisticated in their knowledge of both the specific subject matter being studied and the ways that students develop their own understandings of that subject matter. The problems involved in training such teachers and developing materials to support new forms of teaching and learning become critical ones if Papert's vision of the computer as a learning tool is to be widely and effectively shared.

Like Luehrmann, Papert is an advocate of educating people to control computers, rather than having people taught by computers. Indeed, the Logo language and activities are seen by many educators as ideal vehicles for developing computer literacy. However, Papert's primary interest is in promoting the development of human intelligence, rather than in producing programmers who can take jobs in industry. While Papert believes that Logo experiences will indeed develop better programmers, he is much more concerned that they help to develop more articulate, self-aware, confident learners. In this emphasis, he is often a critic of those advocates of computer literacy who tend to focus primarily on the development of computer skills rather than on the intellectual development involved in computer programming.

To conclude our brief historical overview of computer education, we should look at what was happening in schools during the late seventies just before the large-scale introduction of microcomputers. CAI, as has been mentioned, was not a major factor in many school systems, although a number of Title I programs around the country used their funds to lease the hardware and software needed for Patrick Suppes' CCC materials. The number of schools using computers for programming instruction at the high school level, usually as part of a math or business education course, was more significant. Such schools often integrated simple programming activities into existing courses, such as programming a computer to calculate the roots of quadratic equations in a basic algebra course, or programming a computer to do some simple data processing in a bookkeeping course. Thus, students could learn a little about programming (in BASIC) while reinforcing their mathematics or bookkeeping knowledge. A much smaller number of schools had computer programming courses, as such, and these were usually given as electives, also in the mathematics or business education departments. Relatively few schools had electives in computer science or programming languages other than BASIC. Those that did have such courses tended to be in more affluent suburban areas, or vocational schools, or schools close to universities with strong computer science programs. Thus, despite a good deal of publicly and privately supported research and the efforts of pioneers such as Suppes, Luerhmann, Papert, and a number of others, computers had very little impact on precollege education before the advent of microcomputers.

EDUCATIONAL COMPUTING IN TRANSITION

Microcomputers have made a dramatic impact on both the potential and the reality of educational uses of computers. Since the introduction in 1977 of the Commodore PET, followed closely by the TRS-80 and the Apple, educators have begun to think differently about computers. As we have discussed at various points in this book, there are several reasons for this:

1. The reduced cost, portability, reliability, and "friendliness" of microcomputer systems has overcome many of the objections that were fatal to educational computing in the sixties and seventies.
2. The expanding use of computers in society, combined with increased public awareness of their importance, has put pressure on schools to introduce

computer literacy programs, teaching students about computers' importance to society, as well as training them to use and program computers.

3. Unlike many of the educational innovations of the sixties, use of computers in schools seems to have strong grass-roots support among teachers, as well as administrative and community backing. Enthusiasm for computers among educators probably comes from their newness, the intellectual challenge and sense of innovation they present, and their potential for making dramatic progress in certain areas. But it may also arise from the opportunity for teachers to pick up a salable skill at a time of financial hardship and job cutbacks in education.

4. An entirely new educational role, that of computer change agent or advocate, has been developing within many schools. Many individual teachers have been responsible for the introduction of computers into their schools. Some teachers bring their own computers to school. Others convince school administrators or parent organizations to purchase computers with discretionary funds. And even when computers are introduced through administrative decisions, individual teacher enthusiasts play a major role as advocates and developers of their uses within a school. Some teachers have even learned enough programming to develop simple computer-based learning activities for their own classes or to teach programming to their students.

5. A number of computer magazines, educational periodicals, curriculum publishers, universities, and teacher organizations (see the Resources section: Associations, Periodicals, and Continuing Education for a selected annotated list of some of these) have begun to promote educational computer uses very heavily, raising again the vision of the "computer revolution in education" we were promised in the sixties.

6. These and other causes are combining to produce a bandwagon effect. No school system wants to be last, although few seem clear about where they are going with the microcomputers they buy.

A survey conducted in the spring of 1981 by the National Center for Educational Statistics (NCES) of the U.S. Department of Education (see Bibliography), indicated that "about one-half of the nation's school districts provide students with access to at least one microcomputer or computer terminal." Eighty-seven percent of these schools had at least one computer or terminal at the secondary level, and 29 percent had at least one in an elementary school. Further, 18 percent of the districts that reported having no computers had definite plans to acquire them during the next three years. The actual percent acquiring computers could well be higher, since many districts without computers reported that their future plans were "indefinite."

However, amidst this new enthusiasm for computers in education, we should remember similar enthusiasm in the early sixties and recall the corresponding disillusionment that resulted when computers failed to produce anticipated educational breakthroughs. Although the situation now may well be different, the lessons of the past should not be ignored by those who seek to influence the use of computers in schools during the eighties. Looking at past experiences and at current practices, there are a number of important potential problem areas that we have touched upon in this book and that need to be considered carefully by those concerned with educational computing.

Where Will High-Quality Educational Software Come From?   As we have said numerous times in this book, most of the educational software available today is not of high enough quality to make significant differences in students' learning experiences. Although the cost of computer hardware is declining dramatically (and seems bound to continue to do so), there is no indication that the cost of software development will decline. In fact, the kinds of pedagogical, psychological, and programming expertise needed to create high-quality educational software, as well as the time needed for its development, practically guarantee that high-quality software products will be greatly outnumbered by poor ones.

Educational publishers, also experiencing a bandwagon effect, have been rushing to test the market and establish a position in the educational software field, even though they are not yet able to develop or deliver much in the way of quality products. An informal survey of the thousands of commercially available educational software packages now on sale suggests that the majority offer minor variations of the same basic type of program: drill and practice and occasionally programmed tutorials, primarily in mathematics, followed by spelling, grammar, and phonics. More sophisticated packages, offered as "systems" by some of the larger publishers, merely add some kind of management or record-keeping capability. Remarkably few commercial packages make use of other approaches — simulations, high-resolution graphics demonstrations, or the use of computers as instructional learning tools, for example.

Over a period of time, selective purchasing may improve the quality and variety of educational software products. Currently, many software producers are claiming that they are offering what their customers want. However, it is doubtful that educators have had much real impact on software product offerings. They have been buying what is available, often sight unseen. This is hardly surprising, since most teachers using educational software have not been trained to evaluate it. Nor have most school systems yet undertaken any systematic evaluation of the effectiveness of the software they are introducing. And the manufacturers have done little to encourage or even make possible such assessments.

As discussed in Chapter 5, one major difficulty with currently available educational software and the documentation that accompanies it lies in its lack of pedagogical sophistication. A software package designed to foster individualized learning is unlikely to be equally effective with students of very diverse learning styles. In promoting packages for use with all students, software producers often neglect to emphasize this. What is the learning theory embedded in a particular piece of educational software? How can it best connect with other modes of learning available to the student? Software producers generally offer little help with such questions, and teachers are left to figure this out on their own or to go ahead and use a program with little knowledge of its real effects — planned for or unintended.

How will teachers get the training they need?   As indicated in Chapter 6, schools investing tens of thousands of dollars each year for computer hardware seem to be spending much less on teacher training. Part of the problem is that money for hardware may come from corners of the budget involving a great deal of administrative discretion. On the other hand, teacher training money usually comes out of the area of the budget earmarked for staff development, which is already highly constrained by other demands. Half of the school systems responding to the previously cited NCES study listed teacher training as one of their most critcal needs. Informal discussions with many school district officials reinforce this finding and also indicate that many school people are hoping that outside sources will be found to provide and fund such training.

Is currently available computer hardware really reliable and easy to use?   As discussed in Chapter 4 some of the same factors that tend to produce poor-quality software are operating to influence the production, distribution, and maintenance of computer hardware as well. Today's microcomputers are really a new type of product, with many "kinks" to be ironed out over the next few years. Products are sometimes put on the market with known problems. Those who sell them cannot always repair them or give intelligent advice about their use. Today's microcomputers are subject to many potential breakdowns due to a variety of factors, including: mishandling of equipment, disks, or cassettes; loose connections; malfunctioning hardware elements; static electricity and power surges; and heat or humidity. These problems may tax the patience of even the most dedicated educators who, after all, have much more important tasks before them than the care and feeding of recalcitrant microcomputers.

Introduced into schools too soon, with poor quality hardware and software and with too little provision for teacher training, microcomputers could easily wind up on the shelf and in closets, joining other past technological wonders such as educational TV, 8-mm film loop projectors, slide-tape systems, and language labs.

What kinds of social problems are being introduced into schools along with microcomputers?   Any technological innovation carries with it problems associated with societal transitions. One such problem in the educational domain may arise from the disparity in computer-related knowledge between some students and their teachers. In almost every school, some students (at all age levels) know more about computers and how to use them than their teachers do. This may raise serious problems for many teachers, especially at a period in our history when teachers feel their authority to be declining. As computers become more important in schools and in society, such disparities could become more significant.

Societal innovations also often exacerbate existing social problems. Thus, for example, there may be social class and sex-role biases that are being reinforced by differential student access to computers. Preliminary information indicates that students from higher socioeconomic levels are more involved with computers, in and out of school, than those from less advantaged backgrounds. Boys seem more involved with computers than girls in many schools. Will school computer use reinforce the effects of sex-role stereotyping in our society? How are schools taking this kind of issue into account in their planning?

What are appropriate educational goals and curriculum materials for computer literacy?   Schools that want to teach computer literacy have a problem. There is no general agreement about what that term should mean, let alone any recognized or tested curriculum materials in the area. Since the concept of computer literacy is itself undergoing major changes, it is unrealistic to expect consensus on goals for teaching computer literacy at this time.

During the next few years there will undoubtedly appear a number of books and curriculum materials claiming to teach computer literacy. Educators should examine these materials carefully. Do they teach students to use and program computers by means of real experiences? Or are they limited primarily to teaching about computers? Are they overwhelmingly laudatory and optimistic about the impact of computers on society? Or do they provide a balanced presentation, including many of the real issues and problems that today's students will face as tomorrow's citizens in a computerized society?

How can educators begin to make use of the genuinely new learning potential of computers?   This is one of the most difficult problems. Considering all that may be possible to do educationally with computers someday, it is likely that the realization of this potential will require significant changes in patterns of teaching and learning. If computer-based learning is forced to fit older patterns of education, we run the risk of being like Cinderella's stepsisters, who tried to force their large feet into a tiny glass slipper. If new ways of learning are to be explored, educators and citizens will need to allow for periods of experimentation and exploration and a suspension of judgment while the necessarily slow process of creating new curricular materials and systems for educational management takes place.

Logo is a case in point. Students using Logo activities learn mathematics in a very different way than they do in the traditional mathematics curriculum. Currently, it is considered reasonable to adapt these activities to serve as "enrichment" in the existing math curriculum. However, to take real advantage of the new learning possibilities inherent in Logo will require a major reorganization of goals and objectives, scope and sequence, and teaching strategies for mathematics education. Is there any reason to be optimistic that our educational systems will undergo such changes? Past experiences with educational reform have shown, sometimes with painful consequences, that significant and lasting reforms do not occur unless there is a broad consensus favoring new educational goals, not only among educators, but also among the public at large.

Educators are looking for help with these problems. In the recent past, the federal government could be expected to provide major support for educational innovation. Given the present political climate, federal assistance seems unlikely. State governments, local high-tech industries, computer manufacturers, and interested parents are all possible sources of support. Knowledgeable students may also play a major role in helping the development of educational computing programs within their own schools.

Ultimately, the responsibility for the future use of computers in education lies with each local school district. Without a clear, well-thought-out, well-planned, well-funded and well-supported local effort, no amount of support from the outside can be effective in the long run. Schools will have to do a great deal of learning during the next few years in order to meet the challenge of providing the sort of education people will need for living in the eighties and beyond. Whether schools will meet that challenge effectively will be decided in each district by its own staff and school board. There is simply no way to pass the buck!

LOOKING AHEAD

We conclude this book with a look at the future of computers in education. Temporarily bypassing the transitions that we know must occur during the next decade, we will suggest some alternative visions of what education might be like in the nineties. The decisions that must be made during the next five years will be better informed if we have a map showing where we might be going. Although much of what happens in the future will be determined by forces beyond our control, present decisions can have an important influence on the future. Given the diverse nature of American educational institutions and the life and work habits of Americans, any real future is likely to be more complex than any of the future scenarios we describe. While one of these visions might prevail to the exclusion of all others, our fuzzy crystal ball suggests the likelihood of a blend.

Future #1: *Educational Computing Turns Out to Be Another Passing Fad.*

We have seen the appearance of a number of pervasive technological innovations in this century. Many of these, such as the telephone, television, the automobile, and the airplane, have had profound influences on all of our social institutions, including schools. However, it is difficult to pinpoint many direct influences of these technological innovations on the way teaching and learning are carried out in schools. Many educational observers and innovators had expected film and television technologies to lead to major changes in the structure and content of school programs. While it is true that these media have been used widely in the schools, it would be hard to argue that education would be significantly altered if they were totally removed. The failure of educational uses of television in schools to approach the effectiveness originally predicted has been particularly striking, especially in light of its influence on our culture and learning through home viewing.

The influence of computers on education may follow the same path. As computers continue to increase in importance in society at large, their indirect influence on the content and practice of education are likely to be significant. Direct influence is another matter. Once the present wave of intense interest in educational computing has passed and computers have become generally accepted as part of the cultural scenery, we may find that they have made little real change in our educational institutions. They may find their own niches as tutorial machines for remedial use, or as record-keeping devices, making school enrollment and attendance figures more accessible to adminstrators. But, fundamentally, the process of teaching and learning may continue to occur in pretty much the same way as it does today, under the direction of a teacher who can call on various kinds of teaching materials such as film strips, cassette tape recorders, overhead projectors, or computers. CAI may continue to be of limited importance. Computer literacy may be absorbed into the general culture and not need any special courses in school. Professional and technical training of workers for computer-related industries could take place in vocational schools, universities, and on the job. And the new learning possibilities contained in computers may filter into homes a lot faster than into conservative institutions like schools.

Those who prefer this vision of the future might just want to ignore and deemphasize the current wave of interest in computers and suport those teachers who continue to teach without computers. They might accept a computer presence in the school, on a limited basis, but only when it is proven that computers can be helpful in teaching a particular concept or performing a specific service. A slogan for this view of the future of educational computing might be, "This, too, shall pass!"

Future #2: *Education Becomes More Centralized and Systematic Through Use of Computers.*

With computers continuing to decrease in cost and increase in power, the nineties may see the realization of the dreams (or the nightmares) of some of the visionaries of the early sixties. Advances in computer science, as well as in the psychology of learning, may lead to the development of "intelligent" tutorial systems — able to teach, test, prescribe, and keep records of each student's educational program in a systematic way. Curriculum developers, psychologists, and programmers may then become more important than teachers in terms of influencing how and what students learn. Whether a student learns at school, at home, or at some type of learning center, may become irrelevant.

This type of scenario may be viewed positively or negatively, depending on your perspective and your optimism about the future. In such a future, central planners in the government or in quasi-governmental agencies, staffed by highly trained psychologists, would become more important than local decision makers in determining the course of education in all communities. While this may seem abhorrent to those who value the diversity and individuality of present systems, there are others who would see in this approach the potential for improving the learning of those whose education is now substandard.

A major concern about this type of system would be the ease with which everyone's thought and expression could be centrally manipulated and monitored. This is the nightmare of George Orwell's *1984*, with Big Brother watching us all. Yet, certainly such a result is not inevitable. Nevertheless, whether one is optimistic or pessimistic about the learning potential and the possible threat a centralized educational system poses to human freedom, it should be clear that with such a system, vigilance by educators and citizens will be needed.

Those who favor some form of this future vision and its potential benefits might support the commitment of large financial and human resources to research and development of large-scale learning systems, while at the same time being extremely cautious about the introduction of the present generation of personal computers and CAI packages into the schools. Sophisticated computer assisted instruction is unlikely to be possible with today's personal computers. Widespread use of these limited machines at this time might lead to disappointments that could prejudice future developments.

Those who oppose this vision of the future are also likely to be extremely critical of the present generation of CAI packages. If large-scale systematic teaching and learning is thought to be harmful, it should not be allowed to get a foot in the door. Already some future-oriented school administrators are looking forward to using computers to take on some of the work previously done by teachers recently laid off due to budget cuts. If microcomputers can be used to permit class sizes to increase, with little or no loss of measureable student achievement, this could give impetus to large scale computerization of education.

An interesting dilemma is posed by a version of this scenario in which systematic computer assisted instruction is used primarily to enhance the learning of those students whose education is now considered to be substandard. An argument is often made that instruction delivered by computer could hardly be worse than, and might easily be superior to, the education presently available to students in economically depressed rural or urban school systems. However, critics of the use of CAI to instruct the "educationally disadvantaged" point out that such graduates of computerized learning systems may become used to dociley following instructions given by computers, while more affluent, suburban students learn to program computers and thereby control them. This may result in the latter developing the skills needed for better jobs and higher status in an increasingly computer-based society, while relegating poorer students to membership in a permanent under class. Thus, a well-meaning attempt to improve the education of the disadvantaged could lead to wider socioeconomic gaps than now exist. The foundation for this scenario is currently being laid in numerous urban school systems where microcomputers are being used to provide basic skills instruction to low-achieving (often minority) students and in suburban and more affluent school districts where computer literacy is a major educational goal.

Future #3: *Schools Themselves Become Irrelevant.*

Some futurists argue that we are presently involved in a transition from an industrial to a postindustrial civilization and are thus already experiencing major changes in many of our social institutions. Schools and mass educational systems are cited by such futurists as examples of institutions particularly suited to an industrial society, but ill-suited to survival in a postindustrial one. In this vision of the future, computers and communication networks are seen as a major cause of the shift to a postindustrial society and as providing the technological framework for the institutions that will develop in such a society.

This future includes extensive use of computer/communications systems in every home. Commuting to centralized places for work and learning will be replaced by offices and classrooms in the home, primarily to save energy. It is possible to imagine students doing at least part of their learning at home, being taught by their parents and/or communicating with teachers and other students via computer networks. Working and learning at home would not mean elimination of social contacts now associated with work or school. Since time saved by not commuting could well be spent in more contact with people in the immediate neighborhood.

Such a scenario distinguishes between the educational potential of computers and their current use in formal educational institutions. Already, more people may be learning with and about computers in nontraditional educational settings than in conventional schools. Computer stores, computer clubs and users groups, business and vocational schools, and computer bulletin boards accessible to owners of home computers are among the many mechanisms currently available for such learning (see the Resources section). In addition, a number of corporations have begun to create or buy computer-based instructional modules for employee training.

Through computers, education may take place anywhere. More and more people may use this fact to resolve their concerns about the costs and effectiveness of the schools. They may remove their children from the schools and cease supporting schools financially and politically. In this "deschooled" vision of the future, Seymour Papert's notion of a computer as a personal learning device may take on great importance. Although relatively few parents have, as yet, removed their children from schools in order to offer them a home/computer education, the potential for providing at least some of a child's learning at home, both with and about computers, may soon accelerate what is now only a small trend.

Perhaps there is little that educators can do about this scenario one way or the other, except to prepare for it. After all, learning that takes place outside of school is not synonymous with learning without teachers. There will still be roles for educators in a "demassified" society, although their social roles may be very different when the instructional and custodial functions of educational institutions are separated. An educator in a postindustrial society is more likely to look like an independent consultant than like what we think of today as a teacher. Some educators may have a great deal more status, flexibility, and social rewards than our present society offers. Those educators who have bought their own computers and have begun to develop educational materials, of whatever kind, for sale to others may be preparing themselves to function effectively in this particular culture.

Future #4: *The Computer Literate School.*

Let's suppose that none of the extremes described above come to pass during the next ten years and that whatever trends occur are at least somewhat "mixed." In such a scenario we might see schools surviving and learning to make use of computers in a variety of educational modes. The computer literate school could become one of many settings in which people learn both with and about computers.

Teachers in computer literate schools would use computers in a variety of ways, just as they now use language in a variety of ways: to teach, to motivate, to stimulate, to entertain, and to explain. Although not all teachers and not all teaching would necessarily involve computers, teaching with and about computers could encompass all the ideas of Suppes, Luehrmann, and Papert, as well as those of many others. By the nineties, access to computers may no longer be an issue, at least in this country, and we will have had more than a decade of experience using them for many different educational purposes.

Educators who prefer this vision and who want to work toward making it a reality face a paradox and a dramatic challenge living in a period of transition. If our children are to grow up computer literate, they must have a computer literate society to grow up into and in particular a computer literate school in which to learn. Our problem is to create computer literate learning environments for our children now, when we are not yet computer literate ourselves.

Both the need and the opportunity are now present. Children in school today need to grow up computer literate. While we don't yet know the precise qualities of the computer literate school, the pioneers have at least shown us a few of its elements: well-designed CAI to aid in the learning and reinforcement of certain skills, many opportunities to do programming and use computer tools, and the creation of computer-based learning environments to provide entirely new approaches to learning. Unknown pioneers now in our midst are beginning to show us other elements of the computer literate school. Perhaps some of these pioneers are our students.

The major problem we face is educating ourselves. Despite all the limitations, the lack of funds, the lack of support for innovation, very primitive hardware and software, all the conservatism of schools as institutions, educators who prefer the vision of the computer literate school must start educating themselves.

As authors of this book, this is the vision we see ourselves working towards. A familar set of questions seems a relevant way to close.

If not now, when should we give our students the education they need?

If not here in our own schools, where do we think it will happen?

If not ourselves, as educators with a vision toward which we are working, then who will begin?

Appendix

INTRODUCTION
TO COMPUTER
COMPARISON CHARTS

True comparison of computer systems is not possible. Computers vary so much in features and design that inevitably you will find yourself comparing apples and oranges. Further, tables such as the ones following represent but a subset of the information about these computers and these tables are scarcely the computers themselves. To understand the computers one must experience them. It is our hope that these tables may provide a guide to such experiences.

We have listed here some (though not all) of the inexpensive cassette based and diskette based computers. Beyond these categories computers become far more diverse and complex. Summarizing them in tables is difficult and often misleading. Such systems are very worth your attention, however, for when you are faced with the prospect of providing computing for large numbers of people, these larger systems may well be more economical than the personal computers described here.

Explanation of the Information Categories in the Tables

Manufacturer: the company that makes or contracts for the manufacture of the computer.

Model: the designation or name given this computer by the manufacturer.

Base Price: the minimum suggested retail price for this computer. Often equivalent to the price of a car without wheels. Does not take into account discounting practices. These prices are subject to change.

Operational Price: includes the wheels. The amount you must pay to have the computer equipped with a monitor for video display and a cassette recorder or pair of diskette drives for peripheral storage. Where these items are offered by the manufacturer, we have used those prices. These prices, too, are subject to change. Otherwise, we have allotted $400 for a color monitor, $150 for a black-and-white monitor, and $75 for a cassette recorder. Where color is a feature of the computer, we have specified the color monitor, otherwise the black-and-white, indicted thus: (BW). The operational price also includes any additional equipment necessary to bring the cassette based computer to 16 kilobytes of user RAM (random access memory) and the diskette based computer to 48K of user RAM. This policy has resulted in a dramatic price increase for some computers, notably the Commodore VIC-20, for which one must buy an expansion board before bringing the memory to 16K.

CPU Chip/Clock Speed/Word Size: the name or number of the microprocessor being used, the speed in mega-Hertz at which that chip is driven, and the word size in bits directly addressed and processed by the chip. Comparisons of speed are only applicable between similar chips, although a low speed may be an indication that the manufacturer has deliberately set the clock speed slow to use less expensive electronic components in manufacture.

User Memory: the amount of RAM in kilobytes available to the user. The first figure is the amount that is supplied with the base price machine. The second figure is the upper limit to expansion.

Additional Memory: the cost per unit of memory expansion. In some cases this is accomplished by removing the original RAM supplied with the computer and substituting a larger block of RAM. We have indicated this situation by the word 'to.' E.g. 'to 16K/$100.'

System ROM: the amount of ROM (read only memory) supplied with the computer containing the operating system and language (if suppled, usually BASIC).

BASIC in ROM: indicates whether or not BASIC is supplied with the system ROM.

User ROM: indicates whether or not the user is able to plug ROM packs (or cartridges or modules) containing packaged programs into the computer. Where available we have indicated the upper limit in kilobytes of such modules.

Expansion Bus: indicates whether or not there is a connection to the bus structure of the computer by which the capacity and function of the computer can be extended. For example, the Apple II is suppled with an expansion board into which up to eight additional printed circuit cards may be inserted, providing more memory of different languages, or lower-case letter capability.

Monitor: indicates whether or not a monitor for video display is included in the base price model computer.

RF Modulator: indicates whether or not this device, which permits using an ordinary TV for a monitor, is included. It should be noted that the quality of resolution of even a good TV is generally inferior to that of a monitor.

Screen Display: The number of rows by the number of columns of characters which may be displayed on the monitor screen.

Graphics Resolution: the number of rows by the number of columns of dots which may be displayed on the monitor screen.

Color: the number of colors available. In the Apple II and the IBM Personal Computer, there is a trade off between fineness of resolution and number of colors. The finer the resolution, the fewer colors you have available.

Keyboard Type: full stroke, half stroke or flat panel. The full stroke is similar to a quality electric typewriter keyboard, the flat panel is a touch sensitive membrane (the keys are painted on), and the half stroke is a cheaper version of the full stroke. We also give the total number of keys supplied on the board.

Lowercase: included, not included or not available. For example, the Apple II does not come with support for lowercase letters; however, one may purchase a plug-in board to add this feature. Hence, not included.

Numeric Keypad: included, not included or not available.

RS-232 Serial Port: indicates whether this industry standard interface is included, not included or not available.

Parallel Printer Port: included, not included or not available.

Other Interfaces: indicates the presence of other I/O ports such as for game paddles. The presence of a connection for the video display is assumed and therefore not listed.

Cassette Recorder: included or not included. Price supplied if available from manufacturer.

Motor Controls: indicates whether or not the controls of the cassette recorder are under the command of the computer or whether they must be operated manually by the user.

Transfer Rate: the rate at which information is passed between the computer and the recorder or the diskette, in bits per second. 10 bits is needed to transmit one character.

1st Diskette Drive: Capacity and Price: Capacity in kilobytes (KB). Attaching the first drive often requires paying for a controller for the drive and for additions or upgrades to the operating system and languages. Hence the first drive is often more expensive than subsequent drives.

Additional Diskette Drive: Capacity & Price: Capacity in KB; price in dollars.

Average Seek Time: the average time, in milliseconds (msec), that it takes to access any given sector on the diskette. One of several measures of drive performance.

Operating System: Diskette drives need a disk operating system to function with a computer. This field lists the operating system normally supplied by the manufacturer or vendor.

Notes: an attempt to mention interesting or awkward features which elude description in the above categories.

CASSETTE BASED COMPUTERS

Manufacturer	Apple Computer Co.	Tandy-Radio Shack
Model	**Apple II+**	**TRS-80 Color Computer**
Base Price[1]	$1330	$399
Operational Price[1]	$1805	$957[1]
CPU + Memory		
CPU/Speed/Word Size	6502/1MHz/8 Bits	M6809E/.894 MHz/8 Bits
User Memory	16K/48K	4K/32K
Additional Memory	16K/$120	To 16K/$99, to 32K/$149[1]
System ROM	14K	8K
BASIC-in-ROM	12K Applesoft BASIC	8K (16K ADV BASIC $99)
User ROM	Via Expansion Cards	Up to 16K in ROM Paks
Expansion Bus	8 Expansion Card Slots	Not available
Video		
Monitor	Not included	Not included ($399)
RF Modulator	Not included	Included
Display Size	24 × 40	16 × 32
Graphics Resolution	Lo 40×48, Hi 192 × 280	192 × 256
Color	15 in Lo-Res, 6 in Hi-Res	8 colors
Keyboard		
Type/# Keys	Full stroke/52 Keys	Half stroke/53 Keys
Lowercase	Not included	Not available
Numeric Keypad	Not included	Not available
I/O		
RS-232 Serial Port	Not included	Included
Parallel Printer Port	Not included	Not available
Other Ports	Game I/O Connector	Game I/O Connector
Other Ports		
Cassette I/O		
Recorder	Not included	Not included ($60)
Transfer Rate	1500 Bits/Sec	1500 Bits/Sec
Motor Controls	Not available	Not available

Notes:

[1]All prices subject to change

—Includes 2 game controls

—Cassette interface regarded as unreliable
—Logo Available

—Can connect up to 4 diskette drives using special ROM PAC

[1]plus installation fee

CASSETTE BASED COMPUTERS

Tandy-Radio Shack	IBM	Atari
TRS-80 Model III	**IBM Personal Computer**	**Atari 800**
$999	$1265	$899
$1059 (BW)	$2040	$1449
Z-80/2.03 MHz/8 Bits	8088/4.77 MHz/8 Bits[1]	6502/1.8MHz/8 Bits
16K/48K	16K/64K[2]	16K/48K
16K/$99[1]	16K/$90	16K/$100
14K	40K	10K
14K BASIC	MBASIC (extended $40)	8K BASIC Cartridge
Not available	8 K socket included	Up to 16K in Cartridges
Not available	5 Expansion Card Slots	Atari 850 ($220)
BW built in	Not included	Not included
Not applicable	Not included	Included
16 × 64	25 × 80	24 × 40
48 × 128	100 × 160, 200 × 320, and 640	192 × 320
Not available	16 in Lo, 4 in Med, 2 in Hi	16 colors, 8 intensities
Full stroke/65 Keys	Full stroke/83 Keys	Full stroke/61 Keys
Included	Included	Included
Included	Included	Not available
Not included ($99[1])	Not included ($150)	Included
Included	Not included ($150)	Not included
		Game I/O Connector
Not included ($60)	Not included	Not included ($100)
500/1500 Bits/Sec	1000/2000 Bits/Sec	600 Bits/Sec
Not available	Yes	Included
—Provision for 2 internal and 2 external 5¼″ diskette drives	—Performance not appreciably faster than Apple or TRS-III	—External Power Supply —Monitor Cable not included ($50)
[1]plus installation fee	[1]8 bits external 16 internal [2]expandable to 256K via extra boards	

CASSETTE BASED COMPUTERS

Manufacturer	Commodore	Commodore
Model	VIC 20	PET 4000
Base Price[1]	$299	$995
Operational Price[1]	$1016[1]	$1070(BW)
CPU + Memory		
CPU/Speed/Word Size	6502/1.2MHz/8 Bits	6502/1.2MHz/8 Bits
User Memory	5K/32K	16K/32K
Additional Memory	3K/$40, to 32K/$360	16K/$300
System ROM	16K	18K
BASIC-in-ROM	Included	Included
User ROM	Up to 64K in Cartridge	2 ROM Slots-4K each
Expansion Bus	Available ($100)	
Video		
Monitor	Not included	12″ Green phosphor built in
RF Modulator	Included	Not necessary
Display Size	23 × 22	25 × 40
Graphics Resolution	161 × 132	200 × 160
Color	16 colors	Not available
Keyboard		
Type/# Keys	Full stroke/66 Keys	Full stroke/72 Keys
Lowercase	Included	Included
Numeric Keypad	Not available	Included
I/O		
RS-232 Serial Port	Not included	Included
Parallel Printer Port	Not included	Included
Other Ports	Game I/O Connector	8 Bit User Port [1]
Other Ports	8 Bit User Port[2]	
Cassette I/O		
Recorder	Not included ($75)	Not included ($75)
Transfer Rate	300 Bits/Sec	300 Bits/Sec
Motor Controls	Included	Included
Notes: [1]All prices subject to change	—External power supply —Very reliable, but slow cassette interface [1]Includes expansion board [2]User programmable can be serial or parallel	—Very reliable, but slow cassette interface [1]User programmable can be serial or parallel

CASSETTE BASED COMPUTERS

Commodore	Sinclair Research, Ltd.	Atari
CBM 8000	ZX81	Atari 400
$1495[1]	$150	$399
$1570 (BW)	$475 (BW)	$949
6502/1.2MHz/8 Bits	Z-80A/3.25MHz/8 Bits	6502/1.8MHz/8 Bits
32K/96K	1K/16K	16K
64K/$500	To 16K/$100	Not available
18K	8K	10K
Included	Included	8K BASIC Cartridge
2 ROM Slots-4K each	Not available	Up to 16K in Cartridges
	Included	Atari 850 ($220)
12″ Green phosphor built in	Not included	Not included
Not necessary	Included	Included
25 × 80	24 × 32	24 × 40
200 × 320	44 × 64	192 × 320
Not available	Not available	16 colors, 8 intensities
Full stroke/72 Keys	Flat panel/40 Keys	Flat panel/61 Keys
Included	Not available	Included
Included	Not available	Not available
Included	Not available	Included
Included	Not available	Not included
8 Bit User Port [1]	I/O via Bus Connector	Game I/O Connector
Not included ($75)	Not included	Not included ($100)
300 Bits/Sec	Not available	600 Bits/Sec
Included	Not included	Included
—Very reliable, but slow cassette interface	—Sophisticated BASIC —Compact dimensions 6.5″x8.5″x1.5″ —Weight: 12 oz.	—External Power Supply —Monitor Cable not included ($50)

[1]Includes 32K RAM

[2]User programmable can be serial or parallel

CASSETTE BASED COMPUTERS

Manufacturer	M/A-COM OSI	M/A-COM OSI
Model	**C1P Series 2**	**C4P Series**
Base Price[1]	$549	$995
Operational Price[1]	$1072 (BW)	$1628
CPU + Memory		
CPU/Speed/Word Size	6502/1MHz/8 Bits	6502/2MHz/8 Bits
User Memory	8K/32K	8K/32K
Additional Memory	4K/$79[1]	
System ROM	10K	10K
BASIC-in-ROM	Included	Included
User ROM	Not available	Not available
Expansion Bus	630 Expansion Unit ($240)	4 Card Slots
Video		
Monitor	Not included	Not included
RF Modulator	Not included ($39)	Not included ($39)
Display Size	24 × 24	32 × 64
Graphics Resolution	256 × 256	256 × 512
Color	Not included	16 Colors
Keyboard		
Type/# Keys	Full stroke/53 Keys	Full stroke/53 Keys
Lowercase	Included	Included
Numeric Keypad	Not included	Not included
I/O		
RS-232 Serial Port	Included	Included
Parallel Printer Port	Included	Included
Other Ports		Game I/O Connector
Other Ports		2 Keypad, Modem Interfaces
Cassette I/O		
Recorder	Not included	Not included
Transfer Rate	300 Bits/Sec	300 Bits/Sec
Motor Controls	Not included	Not included
Notes: [1]All prices subject to change	[1]Requires 610 Board ($298). 610 Board includes 8K	—Many extra features included —Very fast operation —Good upward expansion capability

CASSETTE BASED COMPUTERS

Hewlett Packard	Texas Instruments
HP-85A	**TI-99/4A**
$2750	$525
$2750 (BW)	$1125
HP/NA/8 Bits	TI/NA/16 Bits
16K/32K	16KB/72KB
16K/$195	32KB/$400
32K	26KB
Included	Included
Up to 48K in Cartridges[1]	Up to 30KB in Modules
IEEE-488 Interface	Included
5″ Monitor built in (BW)	Not included ($400)
Not necessary	Not included ($50)
16 × 32	24 × 32
192 × 256	192 × 256
Not available	16 colors
Full stroke/92 Keys	Half stroke
Included	Not available
Included	Not available
Not included	Included
Not included	Not included
4 HP Peripheral Plugs	Game I/O Connector
Built in	Not included[1]
6500 Bits/Sec	600 Bits/Sec
Yes	
—40 Column printer built in	
[1]Requires ROM Drawer ($45)	[1]Requires Cassette cable ($15)

DISKETTE BASED COMPUTERS

Manufacturer	Atari	Atari
Model	**400**	**800 (48K)**
Base Price[1]	$399	$1099
Operational Price[1]	$2099[1]	$2699
CPU + Memory		
CPU/Speed/Word Size	6502/1.8MHz/ 8 Bits	6502/1.8MHz/8 Bits
User Memory	16K[1]	48K[1]
Additional Memory	Not available	Not available
System ROM	10K	10K
BASIC-in-ROM	8K BASIC Cartridge	8K BASIC in ROM Cartridge
User ROM	Up to 16K in Cartridges	Up to 16K in Cartridges
Expansion Bus	Atari 850 ($220)	Atari 850
Video		
Monitor	Not included	Not included
RF Modulator	Included	Included
Display Size	24 × 40	24 × 40
Graphics Resolution	192 × 320	192 × 320
Color	16 Colors, 8 Intensities	16 Colors, 8 Intensities
Keyboard		
Type/# Keys	Full Panel/61 Keys	Full stroke/61 Keys
Lowercase	Included	Included
Numeric Keypad	Not available	Not available
I/O		
RS-232 Serial Port	Included	Available w/850
Parallel Printer Port	Not included	Not included
Other Ports	Game I/O Connector	Game I/O Connector
Other Ports		Atari Serial Port
Diskette I/O		
1st Drive Capacity/Price[1]	163K[1]/$600	163K[1]/$600
Addt'l. Drives Capacity/Price[1]	163K/$600	163K/$600
Transfer Rate		
Average Seek Time		
Operating System	Atari Disk OS	Atari Disk OS

Notes:

[1]All prices subject
to change

[1]System software will
absorb some space

[1]System software will
absorb some space

DISKETTE BASED COMPUTERS

M/A-COM OSI	M/A-COM OSI	Hewlett-Packard
C1P MF Series 2 (32K)	**C4P MF Series**	**HP-83**
$1499	$2300	$2250
$2374	$3175	$5330 (32K)
6502/1MHz/8 Bits	6502/2MHz/8 Bits	HP/NA/8 Bits
32K	48K	16K/32K
Not available	Not available	16K/$195
1K	1K	32K
Not available	Not available	Included
Not available	ROM card may be added	Up to 68K Modules
630 Expansion Unit ($240)	Expansion Bus	IEEE-488
Not included	Not included	5″ BW monitor built-in
Not included ($39)	Not included ($39)	Not necessary
24 × 24	32 × 64	16 × 32
256 × 256	256 × 512	192 × 256
Not included	16 Colors	Not available
Full stroke/53 Keys	Full Stroke/53 Keys	Full stroke/92 Keys
Included	Included	Included
Not included	Not included	Included
Included	Included	Not included
Included	Included	Not included
	Game I/O Connector	4HP Peripheral Plugs
	2 Key Pad, Modem Interface	
90K/Included	90K/Included	270K/$2200
90K/$475	90K/$475	270K/Included
125 Bits/Sec	125 Bits/Sec	250K Bits/Sec
		187 msec
Pico DOS and OS-65D	OS-65D	HPOS

—Many extra features
—Very fast operation
—Good upward expansion
   capability

DISKETTE BASED COMPUTERS

Manufacturer	Apple Computer Co.	Osborne Comp. Corp.
Model	**Apple II +**	**Osborne I**
Base Price[1]	$1330	$1795
Operational Price[1]	$3130	$1795 (BW)
CPU + Memory		
CPU/Speed/Word Size	6502/1MHz/8 Bits	Z-80A/2MHz/8 Bits
User Memory	16K/48K	60K[1]
Additional Memory	16K/$120	Not available
System ROM	14K	
BASIC-in-ROM	12K Applesoft BASIC	None
User ROM	via Expansion Cards	None
Expansion Bus	8 Expansion Card Slots	IEEE-488 Connector
Video		
Monitor	Not included	5″ Monitor (BW) built in
RF Modulator	Not included	Not applicable
Display Size	24 × 40	24 × 52
Graphics Resolution	Lo 40×48, Hi 192×280	
Color	15 in Lo-Res, 6 in Hi-Res	Not available
8Keyboard		
Type/# Keys	Full stroke/52 Keys	Full stroke/66 Keys
Lowercase	Not included	Included
Numeric Keypad	Not included	Included
I/O		
RS-232 Serial Port	Not included	Included
Parallel Printer Port	Not included	Not available
Other Ports	Game I/O Connector	Modem Interface
Other Ports		Ext. Monitor Connector
Diskette I/O		
1st Drive Capacity/Price[1]	116 K/$645	100 K[1]/included
Addt'l Drives Capacity/Price[1]	116 K/$525	100 K/included
Transfer Rate	156 K Bits/Sec	
Average Seek Time	200 msec	
Operating System	Apple DOS	CP/M
Notes: [1]All prices subject to change	—Includes 2 Game controls —Logo available	—Includes MBASIC, CBASIC, WORDSTAR MAILMERGE, SUPERCALC —200 K Drives Available —Portable: Fits into its own briefcase [1]System software will absorb some of this space

DISKETTE BASED COMPUTERS

IBM	Texas Instruments	Intertec
IBM Personal Computer	TI-99/4A	**Superbrain D D**
$2235	$525 (16K)	$3250
$3545	$2625 (32K)	$3250
8088/4.77MHz/8 Bits[1]	TI-9900/NA/16 Bits	Z80A/4MHz/8 Bits
48K/64K[2]	16KB/72KB	64K[1]
16K/$90	32KB/$400	Not available
40K	26KB	IPL Only
M BASIC (ext. $40)	Yes	Not available
8K socket included	Up to 30K in Modules	Not available
5 Expansion Card Slots	Yes	Not available
Not included	Not included ($400)	12″ green built in
Not included	Not included ($50)	Not necessary
25 × 80	24 × 32	25 × 80
100 × 160, 200 × 320, and 640	192 × 256	Not available
16 in Lo, 4 in Med, 2 in Hi	16 Colors	Not available
Full stroke/83 Keys	Half stroke/41 Keys	Full stroke/80 Keys
Included	Not available	Included
Included	Not available	Included
Not included	Included	2 Included
Not included		Not included ($150)
	Game I/O Connector	
160 K/$790	90 K/$800	188K/Included
160 K/$570	90 K/$500	188K/Included
250K Bits/Sec		256K Bits/Sec
IBM PC DOS		CP/M (included)
[1]8088 has both (8 bit and 16 bit characteristics) [2]Expandable to 256K using expansion cards	—Logo available	[1]Assume that 20-30K RAM will be absorbed by operating system and language interpreter

DISKETTE BASED COMPUTERS

Manufacturer	Commodore	Commodore
Model	VIC 20 (32K)	PET 4000 (32K)
Base Price[1]	$659[1]	$2590[1]
Operational Price[1]	$2257	$2590
CPU + Memory		
CPU/Speed/Word Size	6502/1.2MHz/8 Bits	6502/1.2MHz/8 Bits
User Memory	32K	32K
Additional Memory	Not available	Not available
System ROM	16K	18K
BASIC-in-ROM	Included	Included
User ROM	Up to 64K in Cartridges	2 ROM Slots/4K each
Expansion Bus		
Video		
Monitor	Not included	12″ Green built in
RF Modulator	Included	Not necessary
Display Size	23 × 22	25 × 40
Graphics Resolution	161 × 132	200 × 160
Color	16 Colors	Not available
Keyboard		
Type/# Keys	Full Stroke/66 Keys	Full stroke/72 Keys
Lowercase	Included	Included
Numeric Keypad	Not available	Included
I/O		
RS-232 Serial Port	Not included	Included
Parallel Printer Port	Not included	Included
Other Ports	Game I/O Connector	8 Bit User Port
Other Ports	8 Bit User Port	IEEE-488
Diskette I/O		
1st Drive Capacity/Price[1]	170K/$599	170K/Included
Addt'l. Drives Capacity/Price[1]	170K/$599	170K/Included
Transfer Rate		
Average Seek Time		
Operating System		

Notes:

[1]All prices subject   [1]Includes 32 K of RAM   [1]Includes CBM 4040
                                                            Diskette Drives

DISKETTE BASED COMPUTERS

Commodore	Commodore	Heath/Zenith
CBM 8000	**Super PET**	**H/Z-89-91**
$2790[1]	$3290[1]	$2895[1]
$2790	$3290	$3640[1]
6502/1.2 MHz/8 Bits	6502 & M6809/1.2MHz/8 Bits	Z80/2.05MHz/8 Bits
32K/96K	96K	48K[1]/64K
64K/$500	Not available	16K/$150
18K	36K	8K
Included	Included in 8032 Model	Not available
2 ROM Slots/4K each	2 ROM Slots/4K each	Not available
12″ Green built in	12″ Green built in	11″ green built in
Not necessary	Not necessary	Not necessary
25 × 80	25 × 80	25 × 80
200 × 320	200 × 320	250 × 640
Not available	Not available	Not available
Full stroke/72 Keys	Full stroke/72 Keys	Full stroke/60 Keys
Included	Included	Included
Included	Included	Included
Included	Included	3 Included
Included	Included	Not included
8 Bit User Port	8 Bit User Port	
IEEE-488	IEEE-488	
170K/Included	170K/Included	100K/Included
170K/included	170K Included	100K/$625[3]
		CP/M
	—includes 2-BASICS, PASCAL, FORTRAN, APL,	[1]Assembled and tested kits available for less
[1]Includes CBM 4040 Diskette Drives	Assembler(6809) [1]Includes CMB 4040 Diskette Drives	[2]16K used by system [3]requires H-88-1 controller ($120)

DISKETTE BASED COMPUTERS

Manufacturer	Tandy-Radio Shack	Tandy-Radio Shack
Model	**32K Color Computer**	**TRS-80 Model II (64K)**
Base Price[1]	$749	$3899
Operational Price[1]	$2147	$5049
CPU + Memory		
CPU/Speed/Word Size	M6809E/.894MHz/8 Bits	Z80A/4MHz/8 Bits
User Memory	32K	64K
Additional Memory	Not available	Not availalbe
System ROM	16K	IPL only
BASIC-in-ROM	Extended BASIC included	Not available
User ROM	Up to 16K in ROM Paks	Not available
Expansion Bus	Not available	4 Expansion Card Slots
Video		
Monitor	Not included	12″ BW built in
RF Modulator	Included	Not necessary
Display Size	16 × 32	24 × 80
Graphics Resolution	192 × 256	Not available
Color	8 Colors	Not available
Keyboard		
Type/# Keys	Half stroke/53 Keys	Full stroke/76 Keys
Lowercase	Not available	Included
Numeric Keypad	Not available	Included
I/O		
RS-232 Serial Port	Included	2 Included
Parallel Printer Port	Not available	Included
Other Ports	Game I/O Connector	External Disk Port
Other Ports		
Diskette I/O		
1st Drive Capacity/Price[1]	156K/$599	416K/Included
Addt'l Drives Capacity/Price[1]	156K/$399	486K/$1150
Transfer Rate	250K Bits/Sec	500K Bits/Sec
Average Seek Time	Not available	260 msec
Operating System	Color Disk OS[2]	TRSDOS

Notes:

[1]All prices subject
  to change

[1]Only 32K RAM
[2]OS is in ROM Pak
  really an extention
  of BASIC

DISKETTE BASED COMPUTERS

Tandy-Radio Shack	Cromemco
TRS-80 Model III (48K)	System One
$2495	$3995
$2495	$4995[2]
Z-80/2.03 MHz/8 Bits	Z80A/4MHz/8 Bits
48K	64K[1]
Not available	Via S-100 cards
14K	IPL only
Included	Not available
Not available	Through expansion cards
Not available	8-S100 Card Slots
12″ BW built in	Not included[2]
Not necessary	Not necessary
16 × 64	25 × 80
48 × 128	via S-100 cards
Not available	via S-100 cards
Full stroke/65 Keys	Not included[2]
Included	
Included	
Included	2 Included
Not included	
	via S-100 cards
131K/Included	390K/Included
175K/Included	390K/Included
	512K Bits/Sec
TRSDOS	CDOS
	—High quality equipment S-100 bus provides broad capability for additional features and expansion
	[1]system software may absorb 20-30K
	[2]Terminal required ($1000)

DESIGN WORKSHEET

Application: _____

Page: _____

System Components	Vendor or Manufacturer	Local Sales and Service	Remote Service	Remarks	Price
PKG I WORDSTAR	Micropro 1299 4th St. San Rafael, CA. 94901 (415) 457-8990	The Computer Place 101 Broadway (Art)	Micropro provides manuals, updates, etc.	One of the better software packages	$ 500
CP/M Operating System	Digital Research P.O. Box 579 Pacific Grove CA. 93950 (408) 649-3896	"	Digital Research	required for WORD-STAR; much other software available	$ 150
Intertec Superbrain w/a 280 K Diskette Drives + 64 K RAM	Intertec 2300 BroadRidge Rd. Columbia, S.C. 29210 (803) 798-9100	"	Intertec	includes keyboard + monitor; commercial quality 24 x 80 screen	$ 3000
IDS 560 printer cables, interfaces, installation	Integral Data Systems Milford, N.H. (603) 973-9100	"	IDS	dotmatrix, but has "correspondence quality" overprint	$ 1400
Total for above					$ 5050

DESIGN WORKSHEET

Application: _____ Page: _____

System Components	Vendor or Manufacturer	Local Sales and Service	Remote Service	Remarks	Price

Bibliography

This is not intended to be a comprehensive bibliography containing every possible book, article, or report on educational computing. Instead, we have aimed at quality by providing the most recent and currently most significant documents in the field. We have divided the bibliography into sections and annotated each entry to make this more useful to you, as beginning computing educators.

COMPUTERS, COMPUTING, AND PROGRAMMING FOR BEGINNERS

Billings, Karen, and Moursund, David. *Are You Computer Literate?* Forest Grove, Ore.: Dilithium Press, P.O. Box 92, Dept. CT, 1979. This book discusses a number of computer literacy topics and suggests numerous activities to develop student awareness and understanding of computers.

Covvey, H. Dominic, and McAlister, Neil Harding. *Computer Consciousness: Surviving the Automated 80s.* Reading, Mass.: Addison-Wesley, 1980. This book provides a simple but extensive introduction to computer machinery and programming concepts. The authors approach computer systems step-by-step and explain in detail the key words of computer terminology. Numerous diagrams and cartoons enhance the understanding of the various concepts.

Dwyer, Thomas, and Critchfield, Margot. *BASIC and the Personal Computer.* Reading, Mass.: Addison-Wesley, 1978. This is a very useful introduction to BASIC on the personal computer. It demonstrates a number of computer applications including games, art, business, and simulation.

Luehrmann, Arthur; Peckham, Herbert; and Ramirez, Martha. *A First Course in Computing.* New York: McGraw-Hill, 1982. This is an excellent activity-oriented introduction to BASIC for middle school students and up. It includes both theory and practical applications in BASIC programming and is written to be used with any microcomputer.

Malone, Linda, and Johnson, Jerry. *BASIC Discoveries.* Palo Alto, Calif.: Creative Publications, 1981. This is an excellent book for middle school students and up, and is loaded with hands-on activities in BASIC coding and related subjects.

Willis, Jerry. *Peanut Butter and Jelly Guide to Computers.* Beaverton, Ore.: Dilithium Press, 1978. This book extends the information provided in Chapter 3 of *Practical Guide to Computers in Education.* It is written in a friendly, accessible style, yet provides a wealth of detailed information on computer hardware.

Willis, Jerry, and Donley, William, Jr. *Nailing Jelly to a Tree.* Beaverton, Ore.: Dilithium Press, 1981. This book simply and clearly introduces the reader to the basics of computer math and logic, to the various types of software in common use, and to the essentials of programming in machine, assembly, and BASIC languages. While not intending to produce skilled programmers, the book provides the information to enable the user to modify, enhance, and experiment with software already published.

COMPUTERS IN EDUCATION

Elementary and Secondary Schools Subcommittee (ES3) of the Association for Computing Machinery. "Topics: Computer Education for Elementary and Secondary Schools," ACM, SIGCSE and SIGCUE, Education Board, 1980. This is a collection of task force reports that are the results of several years efforts by hundreds of people across the country working on seventeen different subcommittees of the ACM ES3 from 1978 to 1980. Topics covered include: CAI, computer acquisition, teacher education, various subject area and level applications, use with special needs children, social and ethical issues, and computer literacy.

Hargan, Carol, and Hunter, Beverly. *Instructional Computing . . . Ten Case Studies.* Alexandria, Va.: Human Resources Research Organization, 1978. This book provides detailed descriptions of ten selected school districts, schools, and other learning places that have developed extensive computer applications. Each project description includes details of: organization, history, hardware and software used, costs, computer literacy and computer science programs established. A brief summary of lessons learned by each school or district is also included

Thomas, James L., ed. *Microcomputers in the Schools.* Phoenix, Ariz.: The Onyx Press, 1981. A collection of over thirty articles and appendices grouped under the following headings: selection considerations, hardware and software development, curriculum applications, and trends and issues. Articles are written by top educators and professionals in the field of educational technology. Annotated bibliography and appendices note further references for educators interested in classroom computer use.

CLASSROOM APPLICATIONS OF COMPUTERS

Ahl, David. *Basic Computer Games* and its sequel *More Basic Computer Games.* Morristown, N.J.: Creative Computing Press 1976, 1977. A collection of the classic computer games that have emerged from academic computer centers since the dawn of computing. The author has selected, annotated, and provided listings that run for each game included.

Anderson, Ronald E. "Computer Simulation Games, Exemplars," In *The Guide to Simulations/Games for Education and Training,* 4th ed. edited by R.E. Horn and A. Cleaves Beverly Hills: Sage Publications, 1980. In this article, the author provides brief descriptions of seventeen exemplary simulation games, primarily designed for use in higher education. He also discusses some of the theory, research results, and guidelines for evaluating simulations. A short bibliography is also included. The article could be of use to teachers considering computer simulations in the classroom.

Edwards, Judith B.; Ellis, Antoinette; Richardson, Duane; Holznagel, Donald; and Klassen, Daniel. *Computer Applications in Instruction: A Teacher's Guide to Selection and Use.* Hanover, N.H.: TSC/Houghton Mifflin, 1978. A good overview of computer applications with lots of examples and diagrams. Not detailed enough in any one area, but a good start. Includes four sections: the essentials of hardware, instructional uses of computers, selecting computer-based instructional units, and readings on computers in the curriculum.

Loop, Liza, and Christenson, Paul. *Exploring the Microcomputer Learning Environment.* Independent Research and Development Project Report No. 5. San Francisco: Far West Laboratory for Educational Research and Development, 1980. This is a report of the state of the art of educational uses of microcomputers. The report surveys existing educational computing projects, which are referred to as Computer-Augmented Learning Environments (CALEs). Besides developing a taxonomy by which to describe CALEs, the authors present clearly a summary of their findings as well as their recommendations.

Papert, Seymour; Abelson, Harold; diSessa, Andrea; Watt, Daniel; and Weir, Sylvia. "The Final Report of the Brookline LOGO project: Assessment and Documentation of a Children's Computer Laboratory." MIT LOGO Memo 53 and 54. Cambridge, Mass: MIT LOGO Group, 1980. This is a two-volume report of a federally funded project that investigated the learning of a group of sixth-grade students who had the opportunity to work with Logo. The report includes analysis of the subject matter learned by the students as well as descriptions of the individual learning experiences of sixteen students chosen to represent a wide range of academic ability.

"Popular Computer Games" *Popular Computing,* vol. 1, no. 1, November 1981. The staff of *Popular Computing* reviews its fourteen favorite popular computer games. Although none of the games is educational, the article can provide an insight into what turns people on about computer games. This knowledge could be helpful in designing educational games or in coping with the fallout in schools from popular computer games.

Roberts, Nancy. "Introducing Computer Simulations into the High Schools: An Applied Mathematics Curriculum." *Mathematics Teacher,* vol. 74, no. 8, November 1981. This is an article describing a new curriculum designed to introduce any student with a mathematics background of algebra to writing and simulating models of real-world situations on a computer. The curriculum development was funded by a grant from the U.S. Office of Education and will be published by Addison-Wesley in 1983.

Wagner, William J. "Microcomputers in the High School — Expanding Our Audience." *The Computing Teacher,* vol. 6, no. 1, September 1979. This was a talk given by Sandy Wagner of Mountain View High School and CUE. In it he identifies five different categories of students who might or might not use computers and then describes the courses, activities, and type of students who do not automatically seek out the computer. The article is very practical and inspirational for those just starting up school use of computers.

Watt, Daniel. "A Comparison of the Problem Solving Styles of Two Children Learning LOGO: A Computer Language for Children" Proceedings of the National Educational Computing Conference, 1979, University of Iowa, reprinted in *Creative Computing,* vol. 5, no. 12, December 1979. An introduction to the Logo computing language through the description of the learning experiences of two sixth-grade children.

Weir, Sylvia, and Watt, Daniel. "LOGO: A Computer Environment for Learning-Disabled Students." *The Computing Teacher,* vol. VIII, no. 5, 1981. The article describes a project in which Logo activities are integrated into the learning experiences of learning disabled students in grades 5 through 8. It discusses the benefits that these students gain by learning to program computers. The article also deals with the process of training teachers to integrate Logo into each student's individual learning plan.

Wilson, Charles. "Simulation: Is It Right for You?" *Personal Computing,* vol. 5, no. 2, February 1981. A brief introduction to simulations for people who might wish to use them in their work, whether in educational or noneducational settings. It provides some basic guidelines for construction of simulations without becoming too technical.

EVALUATING AND DEVELOPING EDUCATIONAL SOFTWARE

Hakansson, Joyce. "How to Evaluate Educational Courseware." *The Journal of Courseware Review,* vol. I, no. 1, 1981. This short review offers fundamental guidelines for the novice to use in approaching the task of evaluating courseware for the first time.

Heck, William P.; Johnson, Jerry; and Kansky, Robert J. *Guidelines for Evaluating Computerized Instructional Materials.* National Council of Teachers of Mathematics, 1981. A very useful overall set of guidelines. It is concise, well-documented, and oriented to educators who are new to the computers field.

Kingman, James. "Designing Good Educational Software." *Creative Computing,* vol. 7, no. 10. October 1981. This article covers the essential elements of the evaluation process in an easy-to-understand narrative format. Some of the computer terminology is not defined. The examples used in context are illuminating.

Kleiman, Glenn; Humphrey, Mary M.; and Van Buskirk, Trudy. "Evaluating Educational Software." *Creative Computing,* vol. 7, no. 10, October 1981. This is an article that specifies general criteria for courseware evaluation by explicating a set of questions to ask when reviewing software. It is easy to understand and fleshes out the guidelines offered elsewhere.

MECC Instructional Services. "Guide to Developing Software for the Apple II." Paper given at AEDS/MACUL meeting, Winter 1980. MECC is the founding parent of educational resource centers. Because of its preeminence in the field, its guidelines are often regarded as a model. This paper presents MECC's 1979 guidelines for authoring educational computer programs. Their current review criteria can be found in articles in other publications.

Peters, Hal, and Johnson, James. "Author's Guide: Design Development Style Packaging Review." Conduit, 1978. This *Author's Guide* is a superb reference that has been used as a model for establishing guidelines for developing and evaluating software. Some of it may be addressed to specific applications for microcomputer software, but the concepts presented can be easily adapted. Their sample review forms are particularly helpful. Reading this book requires some computer background.

Spitler, C. Douglas, and Corgan, Virginia. "Rules for Authoring Computer-Assisted Instruction Programs." *Educational Technology,* vol. xix, no. 11, November 1979. Concentrating on drill and practice, the authors offer a routine to use in developing CAI. The use of computer terminology assumes a basic understanding of how computer programs work.

ISSUES IN EDUCATIONAL COMPUTING

Anastasio, Ernest, and Morgan, Judith. "Study of Factors That Have Inhibited a More Widespread Use of Computers in the Instructional Process." EduCom, Interuniversity Communications Council, Inc., 1972. This study was carried out by the Educational Testing Service (ETS) under a grant from the National Science Foundation (NSF). The results of the study are presented in Chapter 8 of this book.

Anderson, Ronald; Klassen, Daniel and Johnson, David "In Defense of a Comprehensive View of Computer Literacy: A Reply to Luehrmann." *Mathematics Teacher*, vol. 74, no. 9, December 1981. This response to Arthur Leuhrmann's article "Computer Literacy: What Should It Be?" argues for a comprehensive view of computer literacy that includes many more objectives in addition to computer programming.

Johnson, David; Anderson, Ronald; Hansen, Thomas; and Klassen, Daniel. "Computer Literacy — What Is It?" *Mathematics Teacher*, Vol. 73, No. 2, February, 1980. This is a report of research supported by NSF and carried out by the Special Projects Division of the Minnesota Educational Computing Consortium (MECC). It consists essentially of a taxonomy of computer literacy objectives with only brief explanation and discussion. The taxonomy and short bibliography may be helpful to teachers and schools considering computer literacy courses.

Leuhrmann, Arthur, "Computer Literacy: What Should It Be?" *Mathematics Teacher*, vol. 74, no. 9, December, 1981. This article is a direct criticism of Johnson et al.'s "Computer Literacy — What Is It?" arguing that computer literacy objectives should be primarily to provide students with experiences in programming computers rather than memorizing information about computers.

————. "Should the Computer Teach the Student or Vice Versa." Proceedings of the American Federation of Information Processing Societies, 1972. Reprinted in *Creative Computing*, 1976 and in Taylor, Robert, ed. *The Computer in the School: Tutor, Tool, Tutee* (see below). This article makes a strong argument that educational use of computers should primarily concentrate on students learning to program rather than on computer aided instruction. Leuhrmann argues that learning computer programming provides important experiences that enhance a student's thinking abilities and, that not to provide the opportunity of learning programming to all students in our society would be to shortchange them on their education.

Malone, Thomas W. "What Makes Things Fun to Learn? A Study of Intrinsically Motivating Computer Games." Palo Alto, Calif.: Xerox Palo Alto Research Center, 1980. The author discusses the results of three studies: one on computer game preferences and two on students using two particular instructional games (Breakout and Darts). Also presented is a survey of the literature, a theory of intrinsically motivating instruction and a chapter on how to design instructional computer games. A useful set of references and appendices are also included. This report would be extremely helpful to teachers interested in using or designing computer instructional games.

National Council for Educational Statistics. "Student Use of Computers in Schools." US Dept. of Education 1981. Statistics on student access to computers in schools, cited in Chapter 8 of this book.

Olds, Henry; Schwartz, Judah; and Willie, Nancy. "People and Computers: Who Teaches Whom?" Newton, Mass.: Educational Development Center, Inc., 1980. A concise, descriptive, and explanatory document useful to educators who want to work with computers. It provides a model that could be implemented by others to encourage thoughtful discussions about the impact of computers in an educational environment.

Papert, Seymour. "Computers and Learning." In *The Computer Age: A Twenty-Year View*, edited by Dertouzos, Michael, and Moses, Joel. Cambridge, Mass.: MIT Press, 1979. A restatement and summing up of Papert's philosophy of education that has evolved over the past twelve years of work with computers and children at the MIT Logo Laboratory.

————. *Mindstorms: Children, Computers, and Powerful Ideas.* New York: Basic Books, 1980. This is the best seller of educational computing. It is a clearly written, inspirational exhortation to educators to use computers in radically new ways to provide a radically different kind of education. The book describes and discusses Papert's work using Logo with young children at the Artificial Intelligence Laboratory of MIT. Descriptions are delightful and filled with concrete examples. A must for anyone considering computer use in education.

Sheingold, Karen, and Billings, Karen. "Issues Relating to the Implementation of Computer Technology in Schools: A Cross-Sectional Study." Children's Electronic Laboratory Memo No. 1, Bank Street College of Education, 1981. This is a report of a study funded by NIE discussing three case studies of communities that have implemented the use of microcomputers into their schools. The study essentially consisted of documenting the innovation process in these towns through interviews and observations. At the end, the authors raise a series of questions as a result of their work, concerning the impact of microcomputers on education. This is a preliminary report.

Taylor, Robert P., ed. *The Computer in the School: Tutor, Tool, Tutee.* New York: Teachers College Press, 1981. A good solid compilation of nineteen essays related to educational applications for the computer by five pioneers in the field: Alfred Bork, Thomas Dwyer, Arthur Luehrmann, Seymour Papert, and Patrick Suppes. This book provides an historical perspective along with further food for thought to teachers interested in the issues raised in Chapter 8 of *Practical Guide to Computers in Education.*

U.S. Congressional Hearings: Computers and the Learning Society. Hearings, 1978. Order Number 052-070-04581-7. From: Superintendant of Documents, U.S. Government Printing Office, Washington, D.C. 02402. *Information Technology in Education: Potentials and Perspectives.* Hearings, 1980. Free from: Science and Technology Committee, 82-155 House Annex no. 2, Washington, D.C. 20515. Testimony by dozens of leaders in educational computing, describing numerous educational projects.

Resources

These resources were compiled by Newton Key of Intentional Educations as part of a much more extensive database of educational computing resources. Some of these entries and many others will be updated in the *1983 Classroom Computer News Directory of Educational Computing Resources*. Special thanks for assistance go to Vern Gerlach and Les Snyder at Arizona State University for some of the material on Continuing Education, to Karl Zinn for the use of Dataspan-produced information, and Francine Marchetti and Phyllis Caputo for starting the Intentional Educations/Classroom Computer News database. Also, a portion of the ERIC listings under Bibliographies and Indexes were produced by an ERIC search through the Dialog Information Services by Carla Hendrix, Lesley College Library. All addresses and phone numbers were correct as of publication, but may have changed since that time.

RESOURCES SECTION TABLE

OF CONTENTS

1. BIBLIOGRAPHIES AND INDEXES

This section is divided into two groups of materials containing references to the literature in educational computing: individual bibliographies (both annotated and unannotated) and regularly published indexes containing abstracts.

Bibliographies

The following four bibliographies can be ordered from the ERIC Document Reproduction Service (EDRS), P.O. Box 190, Arlington, VA 22210.

Computer-Based Education: The Best of ERIC, June 1976-August 1980
Keith A. Hall
(ED 195 288)
   This is an update of an earlier ERIC bibliography. About 200 reports, reviews, and conference proceedings are compiled in this annotated bibliography. The subject headings include: historical references, new technology, content area applications, teacher training, and developmental efforts such as PLATO.

Computer-Based Learning in Europe: A Bibliography
(ED 176 804)
   First published at Imperial College, London, in 1978, this bibliography lists 172 references on computer assisted instruction in Europe.

Individualized Learning Using Microcomputer CAI
John R. Hinton
(ED 196 409)
   This work reviews the literature on individualized instruction on microcomputers, submitted to the ERIC system between the autumn of 1978 and that of 1979.

Simulations and Gaming: The Best of ERIC
Don H. Coombs
   This is an annotated bibliography of sources published between 1972 and 1975 derived from a search of ERIC indexes. Sources are divided into sections including: social studies, language, business and economics, vocational education, and science and mathematics. The report is prefaced by a theory of gaming and a list of further information sources.

"A Beginner's Guide to Microcomputer Resources"
Albert L. Goldenberg
in *Audiovisual Instruction*, vol. 24, no. 8 (November 1979): 22-23
   This article presents a list of books, journals, and newsletters related to microcomputers as well as a list of manufacturers of microcomputers.

"Computer Literacy Bibliography"
Susan Friel and Nancy Roberts
in *Creative Computing* (September 1980): 92-97
   This is an annotated bibliography of over seventy books and articles. The references are divided into: computer applications and social issues, programming and computer guides, and teaching resources.

Computing Newsletter
University of Colorado, Colorado Springs, CO 80907
   The *Newsletter* annually compiles an extensive bibliography of computer-oriented books. The books are categorized by subject area.

1

"ERIC/RCS Report: An Annotated Bibliography of Readings for the Computer Novice and English Teacher"
Rodney J. Barth
English Journal, vol. 68, no. 1 (January 1979): 88-92
This report indexes 26 documents in the ERIC system dealing with computer applications in high school English.

"Recent Trends in Computer-Assisted Instruction"
P.O. Box E, School of Education, Stanford University, Stanford, CA 94305
This booklet contains abstracts of a number of reports, articles, and books relating to CAI.

Indexes

The following indexes provide abstracts of published material on computing, including educational applications of computers.

ACM Guide to Computing Literature
Association for Computing Machinery
Order Department
P.O. Box 64145
Baltimore, MD 21264
The *Guide* indexes current computer science publications. Educational listings are included, as is a separate Computing Reviews Index.

COMPendium
Epicurious
P.O. Box 129
Lincolndale, NY 10540
This monthly magazine indexes all non-editorial articles from about twenty personal computer magazines. Articles are categorized and briefly abstracted. Book reviews from the periodicals are separately indexed and computer-specific articles are cross-referenced. A classified section refers to product advertising in other periodicals.

Computer and Control Abstracts
The Institution of Electrical Engineers (IEEE)
445 Hoes Lane
Piscataway, NJ 08854
(201) 981-0060
The IEEE produces this monthly collection of abstracts of bibliographies, journal articles, books, and conference proceedings that are indexed by subject. Subjects include: CAI, educational administrative data processing, and other educational computing areas.

The Index
W. H. Wallace
Missouri Indexing, Inc.
P.O. Box 301
St. Ann, MO 63074
(314) 997-6470
This is a comprehensive reference index of articles in over 900 issues of computer publications. *The Index* is intended for bibliographic use by personal computer users and for reference to computer programs published in computer publications. Articles and programs are indexed by key words in the titles and are further grouped according to microcomputer system. A bibliography of publishers' addresses is included.

Microcomputer Index
2464 El Camino Real, 247
Santa Clara, CA 95051
(408) 241-8381
   This quarterly index contains abstracts of articles, reviews, and program listings from over twenty computing magazines. *Microcomputer Index* is now available on-line through the Dialog Information Retrieval Service (see On-Line Sources and Databases).

2. ON-LINE SOURCES AND DATABASES

Computer based information retrieval is a way of providing people with access to data and information of all kinds. On-line searches for information and related literature are available to educators through the following databases and projects as well as others listed in the *Directory of On-line Information Resources* below. While some of this rapid retrieval of information is relatively costly, CompuServe and The Source are personal information services at more affordable rates.

Directory of Online Information Resources
CSG Press
11301 Rockville Pike
Kensington, MD 20895
(301) 881-9400
   This twice-yearly *Directory* is not itself on-line. It is a guide to over 350 bibliographic and nonbibliographic on-line databases, most of which are for business and academic research, though more widely accessed sources (The Source) and educational databases (ERIC) are included as well. In addition to publishing the *Directory*, CSG has access to most of the databases listed and will perform information searches for users.

CompuServe Information Service
5000 Arlington Centre Blvd.
Columbus, OH 43220
(614) 457-8650
   CompuServe offers this connection to on-line wire services and newspaper news at a low rate on evenings and weekends (though the service is at a premium during the weekday working hours). The service also provides family information, entertainment, electronic mail, and personal computing services.

Dataspan
c/o Karl Zinn
Center for Research on Learning and Training (CRLT)
109 E. Madison Street
Ann Arbor, MI 48104
(313) 763-4410
   The Dataspan project, funded by the National Science Foundation, is developing an information bank on computer applications primarily for science and mathematics educators through interaction with local and national resource centers, teachers, publishers, and other projects. Dataspan has collected, indexed, and abstracted information on: reference materials, planning for computer use in classrooms, selecting computer systems, using local communications networks, local funding, professional associations, user groups, conferences, commercial organizations, public agencies, and in-print materials, among other subjects. The ultimate aim of the project is to link up

with other ongoing resource centers to assist them in providing information to their own constituents. To accomplish this, an on-line database package and the software to access it are being prepared by the project for dissemination to nationwide centers and groups interested in computer applications in education.

Dialog Information Services, Inc.
3460 Hillview Avenue
Palo Alto, CA 94304
(800) 227-1972

Dialog is an information retrieval service that links a terminal or microcomputer by telephone to a collection of on-line databases. Dialog, which has been used by libraries for over a decade, is now available to the personal computer user. Through a modem connection, the user can conduct on-line searches as well as order printed documents from the databases. The major large databases include ERIC (see below) and INSPEC (physics, computers, and electronics). The smaller databases available include Exceptional Child Education Resources (for special education) and National Foundations (funding sources). Order forms and other information are available from Dialog.

ERIC
Educational Resources Center
National Institute of Education
Washington, DC 20208
(202) 254-7934

The Educational Resources Information Center (ERIC) is designed to provide access to the findings of educational research. This nationwide information network is composed of clearinghouses across the country that abstract, index, store, and disseminate information about different topics in education. The particular topics covered by the respective clearinghouses may be obtained from the Educational Resources Center of ERIC at the above address or the ERIC Processsing and Referencing Facility (see below). The clearinghouses listed below are directly involved with information on classroom computer use.

ERIC Clearinghouse on Information Resources
Syracuse University
School of Education
130 Huntington Hall
Syracuse, NY 13210
(315) 423-3640

ERIC Clearinghouse on Elementary and Early Childhood Education
University of Illinois
College of Education
Urbana, IL 61801
(217) 333-1386

ERIC Processing and Referencing Facility
4833 Rugby Avenue, 303
Bethesda, MD 20814
(301) 656-9723

See the Bibliographies and Indexes and the Bibliography of this book for additional information on available ERIC-produced materials and sources.

The Source
Reader's Digest
Educational Division
Pleasantville, NY 10570
(914) 769-7000

The Source is an information and communications service that is geared towards home and business use but which is also applicable to classroom use for information retrieval and computer literacy. Hundreds of specific information services are possible through The Source including: UPI news, electronic mail, programming modules, and simple educational programs. Rates for prime and non-prime time differ for use of this telephone-linked computing service.

3. RESOURCE CENTERS

The following groups, places, and advisory services are designed to assist educators. While each computing resource center has specific interests and areas of expertise, in general they provide access to educational computing information, recommendations for specific educational computing applications, and workshops on computer-based education and programming.

Computers in Education as a Resource (CEDAR)
Exhibition Road
London SW7 2BX England
(01) 589-5111, ext. 1160

The CEDAR resource center maintains an information and advisory service for teachers interested in computer-based instruction. CEDAR also provides a resource file and a list of educational computing projects in the United Kingdom. Regular seminars on educational computing are held at the Imperial College center of CEDAR.

Educator's Hot Line
350 Union Station
Kansas City, MO 64108
(800) 255-5119

This toll-free hot line is a telephone-accessed resource center. Vital Information, publishers of *Educator's Handbook and Software Directory* and *VanLoves Apple II/III Software Directory* (see Software Directories), will answer questions about software and classroom or administrative computing applications.

EPIE Institute
P.O. Box 620
Stony Brook, NY 11790
(516) 246-8664

The Educational Products Information Exchange (EPIE) Institute is a huge educational advocacy group that provides detailed analyses of curriculum materials used in elementary and high schools. Along with the Microcomputer Resource Center (MRC) at Teachers College, Columbia University, EPIE has instituted a Microcomputer Software File, which reviews commercially available software programs. The EPIE Software File now has available reviews of six of the larger computer-based instructional programs as well as a number of microcomputer games. The Institute also publishes *EPIEgram*, an "educational consumers' newsletter" of equipment and materials, which identifies inferior or unsafe equipment including educational software and hardware. *EPIEgram* provides indepth reviews of information sources on computers in education. EPIE has also provided training seminars to help schools evaluate microcomputer software.

Microcomputer Center
San Mateo County Office of Education
333 Main Street
Redwood City, CA 94063
(415) 363-5472

The Microcomputer Center is a joint project of Computer-Using Educators (CUE) and the San Mateo County Office of Education. Besides maintaining Softswap (see Software Clearinghouses), the center has a variety of computers for educators to examine and a collection of commercial educational software for evaluation. The center primarily serves the teachers and administrators of San Mateo Couty, though educators from outside the county are welcome to use the center's resources on an informal basis.

Microcomputer Resource Center
Teachers College
Columbia University
New York, NY 10027
(212) 678-3740

The center, part of the "Computing in Education" program at Teachers College (see Continuing Education), is an excellent resource for teachers wanting to integrate microcomputers into their curricula. The center conducts seminars and workshops on curriculum materials and conducts field-based training for classroom computer use. It also serves as a clearinghouse for hardware and software information.

Microcomputer Education Laboratory at SUNY, Buffalo
QAL/MEL
217 Baldy Hall
SUNY at Buffalo
Amherst, NY 14260
(716) 636-2110

This laboratory was established to maintain information files on the purchase and application of microcomputers in education, available to the Buffalo area's educational community. These files include information on software, hardware, catalogues, and computer users services.

Minnesota Educational Computing Consortium (MECC)
2520 Broadway Drive
St. Paul, MN 55113
(612) 376-1101

MECC, supporting the nation's only statewide instructional computing effort, is organized to coordinate and provide computer services for the students, teachers, and administrators in Minnesota public schools and colleges. MECC provides inservice training, and curriculum guides, as well as developing and distributing educational software. They are an excellent source of software and written materials for use with Apple II and, to a lesser degree, Atari microcomputers. Both *Users*, a bimonthly instructional newsletter listing available materials, and their organizational newsletter, *Dataline*, are free upon request. Non- Minnesota customers to MECC pay extra for MECC products.

Technical Education Research Centers (TERC)
Computer Resource Center
8 Eliot Street
Cambridge, MA 02138
(617) 547-3890

The Computer Resource Center (CRC) of TERC houses information on microcomputer hardware and software and a library of technical and educational publications. It also maintains various microcomputers and educational software for inspection and sample use. CRC conducts workshops on classroom computer use which include: Logo use, Pascal programming, BASIC programming, the use of computers in educational administration, and computer use in math and science instruction. CRC membership is open to educators and other interested people for a nominal fee and allows use of the CRC facilities. CRC also holds an open-house once a week during which non-members may use the center.

University of Washington Computing Information Center
3737 Brooklyn Ave., N.E.
Seattle, WA 98105
(206) 543-5818

This resource center houses books, technical reports, audio cassettes, videotapes and periodicals covering all aspects of computing. It provides wide access to general computing literature as well as specialized bibliographies and reference services for educational computing. The center also publishes *CROP (Computing Resources for the Professional)*, a bimonthly publication that details current computing applications, including many in education.

4. RESEARCH AND DEVELOPMENT

The possibilities for uses of computers in education have expanded greatly, partially due to the activities of research groups such as the ones in this section. Most of these groups have developed and are developing numerous computer applications in education, some of which are mentioned in the descriptions below. Most of these organizations do strictly R&D, although some also provide direct services to educators.

Artificial Intelligence (A.I.) Laboratory
545 Technology Square
Massachusetts Institute of Technology
Cambridge, MA 02139

Workers at the A.I. Laboratory at MIT and at Bolt, Beranek, and Newman (see below) were responsible for the development of Logo, a child-appropriate interactive computer language. Under the leadership of Seymour Papert, the original Logo project at the A.I. Lab has extended this work by designing a wide range of educational applications for Logo. Versions of Logo for microcomputers are currently marketed by several companies. Research at the A.I. Lab is now developing new high-level computing languages for further educational applications.

Bolt, Beranek and Newman, Inc.
50 Moulton Street
Cambridge, MA 02138
(617) 497-3897

Bolt, Beranek and Newman has been active in the development of numerous educational computing applications, including Logo. Among their current projects is a language arts program for upper elementary grades that emphasizes teaching reading through microcomputers. The project is part of the NIE-funded "Center for the Study of Reading." BBN has also begun a microcomputer-based writing curriculum for upper elementary students, funded by the U.S. Department of Education.

Computer Literacy, Inc.
1466 Grizzly Park Boulevard
Berkeley, CA 94707
(415) 644-2400

Arthur Luehrmann's firm, Computer Literacy, Inc., provides courses in computing for teachers and others in the community. In addition to their efforts to promote general computer literacy for the community, this firm assists in curriculum planning for schools interested in computer education. Computer Literacy, Inc. concentrates on teaching BASIC and other general programming languages.

4

Human Resources Research Organization (HumRRO)
300 North Washington Street
Alexandria, VA 22314
(703) 549-3611

HumRRO is a behavioral science research organization that is pursuing several projects on CAI systems and materials. *Computer Literacy: Issues and Directions for 1985*, edited by Robert Siedel, Ronald Anderson, and Beverly Hunter, will be published shortly, and is based on a joint HumRRO and MECC Conference (sponsored by NSF) held in December, 1980. Beverly Hunter's "An Approach to Integrating Computer Literacy into the K-8 Curriculum" (October 1980), also available from HumRRO, is an initial report of the Computer Literacy Guides for Elementary and Junior High Schools Project. Professional papers outlining other research in computers in education are also available from HumRRO.

Intentional Educations, Inc.
51 Spring Street
Watertown, MA 02172
(617) 923-7707

This nonprofit organization has developed a wide range of educational materials, including educational software for use in schools and educational games for home use. In addition to publishing *Classroom Computer News (CCN)* and developing the Addison-Wesley Series on Computers in Education, Intentional Educations provides computer advisory services to schools including: teacher training and support, hardware information, and software evaluation. A complete directory of information on computer resources and materials is maintained and updated to provide the basis of the Annual *CCN Directory of Educational Computing Resources.*

Technical Education Research Centers (TERC)
8 Eliot Street
Cambridge, MA 02138
(617) 547-3890

In addition to their Computer Resource Center (CRC) and the *Hands On!* newsletter, TERC is active in the research and development of educational computing applications, primarily in science education. Efforts in this project include systems for the use of microcomputers as a tool for collecting data, plotting graphs, and monitoring experiments in lab instruction at the junior high, high school, and college levels. TERC also runs a series of national workshops on microcomputers in education. They have recently begun a series of NSF-funded workshops in New England for school decision-makers on educational computing applications.

WICAT
1160 South State Street
Orem, UT 84057
(801) 224-6400

This is a private company that has been active in developing computer-based instruction materials, including interactive videodisc/microcomputer materials.

Xerox
Palo Alto Research Center (PARC)
3333 Coyote Hill Road
Palo Alto, CA 94304
(415) 494-4000

The Learning Research Group at PARC developed the Smalltalk-80 interactive language, which promises to enhance many future educational programs. For information on the prospects for Smalltalk-80, see the special issue of *BYTE* (August 1981). The Cognitive and Instructional Sciences Group at PARC has developed detailed cognitive models for diagnosing students' misconceptions in skills such as arithmetic. The group is also interested in designing and using motivating educational computer games (see Thomas Malone's report in the Bibliography).

5. PROJECTS

The projects described below are but a few of the many ongoing networks, computer courses, and literacy projects to be found in educational settings. While many significant and successful projects are noted, descriptions of many more may be found in the *Microcomputer Directory: Applications in Educational Settings* listed below. Many state education departments have sponsored educational computing projects about which they can provide information. Those states most active in sponsoring projects include: Florida, North Carolina, New York, and Minnesota.

Microcomputer Directory: Applications in Educational Settings
Monroe C. Gutman Library
Harvard University Graduate School of Education
Cambridge, MA 02138
(617) 495-4225

This guide to schools with microcomputer programs and computing projects in traditional school settings and in alternative learning environments is a product of the staff of the Gutman Library. The first edition of the *Directory*, published in the spring of 1981, lists educational computing projects by state with descriptions included for each entry. The second edition, published in the spring of 1982 is expanded. Both are excellent guides to possible sources of information and ideas concerning applications developed by other educators.

Center for Computer Based Education (CBE)
308 Carroll Hall
The University of Akron
Akron, OH 44325
(216) 375-7848

CBE has been a viable part of the University of Akron's instructional delivery system since 1972. Via a campus network, faculty and students have access to 100 CBE courses which include a wide variety of subject areas. CBE is employed as part of the curriculum, for homework or extra credit and as an optional aid. The Center helps to promote the concept of the University as a community resource by supporting a network of computer terminals in over a dozen public schools in Northeastern Ohio. The Center provides educators with various workshops and seminars and publishes a quarterly newsletter. The CBE Center's role continues to expand into such areas as developing and selling courseware, helping community efforts for funding and operating CBE projects, and introducing all interested persons to the University's CBE system.

Educational Technology Center
University of California, Irvine
Irvine, CA 92717
(714) 833-7452

Under the leadership of Dr. Alfred Bork, the Educational Technology Center maintains several projects designed to develop computer based materials for all levels of the curriculum. For example, the Development of Learning Skills in Early Adolescence project is developing computer-based modules specifically for junior high school children, and the project on scientific literacy in public libraries is designed to improve public understanding of science. The center has also developed college-level science courses some of which will be distributed through Conduit (see Software Clearinghouses). Information on these projects is provided in their *Newsletter*.

EDUNET
EDUCOM
P.O. Box 364
Princeton, NJ 08540

EDUCOM is a consortium of colleges, universities, and nonprofit institutions connected with higher education. Its goal is to promote better application of computing and information technology in higher education. The EDUNET project is a model of communications and large-scale resource-sharing networking. Local access to EDUNET is available in over 300 U.S. and Canadian cities and in 30 other countries. Resources available through EDUNET include: CAI materials, simulation languages and models, graphics software, and database systems. The EDUNET project has also developed special software that facilitates the access and use of communications networks. While EDUCOM and EDUNET are concerned with higher education, many of their projects provide interesting models of the possibilities of educational computing applications for elementary and secondary schools as well.

Intelligent Videodisc Project
Computer Assisted Instruction Laboratory
Lindquist Center — Room 229
Weeg Computing Center
The University of Iowa
Iowa City, IA 52242
(319) 353-3170

The Intelligent Videodisc Project has developed and tested educational programs that link mini and microcomputers to videodisc players. Past programs have included information retrieval in art and testing in ballet, while current projects include pediatrics and communications and research into human factors in Videodisc interaction. Further information on the possibilities of precollege application of this technology is available in *Pipeline* (Fall 1980).

Logo

Division for Study and Research in Education
20C-109
18 Vassar Street
Cambridge, MA 02139
(617) 253-7360

Project LOGO
Lincoln School
194 Boylston St.
Brookline, MA 02146
(617) 547-3890

Lamplighter School
11611 Inwood Road
Dallas, TX 75229
c/o Texas Instruments (214) 995-7012

Lincoln-Sudbury Regional High School
390 Lincoln Road
Sudbury, MA 01776
(617) 443-9961 x-60

Under the leadership of Seymour Papert, the Logo Project at the A.I. Laboratory (see Research and Development) developed a wide range of educational applications for Logo, a child-appropriate computer language. The Division for Study and Research in Education (SRE) will provide memos from that original project and acts, in part, as a Logo information center. SRE is also developing further the educational applications of Logo, including a project using Logo with the education of the handicapped, the teaching of physics and math at MIT using Logo, and a Logo music project. The objective of the Logo project at Lincoln School is to enable students in grades 4-8 to use Logo to control and "teach" the computer. Students solve problems and do programming in the interactive setting that this project provides. The project at the Lamplighter School has been developed in cooperation with M.I.T. and Texas Instruments. Students have access to Logo through about fifty TI computers at the private open-plan elementary school. The Logo language, along with Pascal and LISP, are used at Lincoln-Sudbury Regional High School in a continuing project to teach students problem solving through computer programming.

Math and Computer Education Project
Lawrence Hall of Science
University of California, Berkeley
Berkeley, CA 94720
(415) 642-3167

This project features activities for student exploration of computing that are primarily used in workshops and classes held at the Lawrence Hall of Science (see Computer Learning Places). Programs for math education in grades K-7 are provided in classes, while outreach workshops provide K-12 mathematics and problem solving programs to classrooms in the area. The Computer Education Project staff provides these workshops as well as detailed programming courses in BASIC and PILOT to schoolchildren and the general public.

PLATO (IV) Project
CERL
252 Engineering Research Lab
103 S. Mathews Avenue
University of Illinois
Urbana, IL 61801
(217) 333-6500
Since the early sixties, the Computer Based Education Research Laboratory (CERL) has worked on the development of a computerized teaching system named Programmed Logic for Automatic Teaching Operation (PLATO). This system has utilized several different computer languages and at present is titled the PLATO IV program. The project has developed over 7,000 hours of instruction in 150 subject areas. The PLATO project is still being field tested with students, revised, and developed; over ten million hours of student use have been logged. The Control Data Corporation has been granted a license to establish regional PLATO systems that will eventually form a network available to educators. At present, CERL offers a list of available materials that pertain to the project.

Project Compute
Kiewit Computation Center
Dartmouth College
Hanover, NH 03755
A list of general and special purpose publications on educational computer use is available from the Computation Center. These materials were developed under Project Compute's program for free-access computing for college and regional secondary students.

SOLO/NET/Works
Department of Computer Science
312 Alumni Hall
University of Pittsburgh
Pittsburgh, PA 15260
(412) 624-6457
The Interactive Classroom Project, or SOLO/NET/Works, funded in part by the National Science Foundation, is a microcomputer-based learning environment. A network of low-cost microcomputers is being established, as is software, which will enable users at different microcomputers to communicate with one another. The aim is for local processes to be run independently at each microcomputer and for global interaction to take place among users of various microcomputers in the network. The project is to be built up in three phases and plans for development extend well into the eighties.

6. COMPUTER LEARNING PLACES

The following places are centers and projects in which the public, and more especially schoolchildren, may learn about computers. Many of these provide computers as part of simple exhibits as well as for educational or arcade-type games. Most of these places primarily provide exposure to computers, but projects such as CTUSA! attempt to facilitate community-wide computer literacy through various programming workshops and other seminars.

Capital Children's Museum
800 3rd Street, NE
Washington, DC 20002
(202) 553-8600

The museum includes within its exhibits hands-on computer facilities for children. Displays include innovative uses of microcomputers such as: a microcomputer weaving project, an interactive metrics game; and a communications exhibit that demonstrates graphics, text editing, electronic mail, simulation, and other applications of computers. The museum has weekend microcomputer workshops for children that provide introductions to computer operation and a chance to play computer games.

Children's Museum
300 Congress Street
Boston, MA 02210
(617) 426-6500

This museum has a series of terminals linked to two computers that provide simulations and games programs. These programs are preceded by an introduction to computers and their basic functioning.

Computer Camps

Computer camps are intended to provide children with general literacy in computer applications in society and to teach them programming in BASIC or similar languages. Computer summer camps are found in various localities across the country. Advertisements for such camps may be found in most of the computer magazines.

Computer Town UK! (CTUK!)

CTUK! is a nationwide network of computer literacy centers in the British Isles that are linked through a monthly notice board in *Personal Computer World* (see Computing Periodicals). Modeled after the computer literacy efforts of Computer Town USA! (see below), the centers are run by volunteer computer enthusiasts. CTUK! is intended to provide the public and especially schoolchildren with knowledge of programming and computer awareness.

Computer Town, USA! (CTUSA!)
Peoples' Computer Company
P.O. Box E
Menlo Park, CA 94025

A computer literacy project funded by the National Science Foundation, CTUSA! provides hands-on participation with microcomputers to the children and adults of Menlo Park, California. Courses and workshops centered around the resources of the Menlo Park Public Library are offered. The project is intended to be a model of educational computer uses that can be established using local resources. CTUSA! also publishes and distributes a monthly newsletter of the same name.

Lawrence Hall of Science
University of California, Berkeley
Berkeley, CA 94720
(415) 642-5132

The Lawrence Hall of Science is both a resource center for science education and an exhibit area for computer activities. Visitors have access to simple introductory computer programs and may rent supervised computer time on several different types of computers. School classes and other groups are brought to the hall for both ongoing and one-time workshops in subjects including: computers, math, chemistry, biology, astronomy, and physics. The hall is also the center for the Math and Computer Education Project (see Projects).

Sesame Place
100 Sesame Road
Langhorn, PA 19047
(215) 752-7070
This is essentially an entertainment park with a large computer gallery. About fifty Apple microcomputers are programmed with games and simple educational activities that are linked by a NESTAR network. Visitors pay an initial entry fee and then have access to the various computer-based entertainment and education programs. Although Sesame Place is modeled, in part, on the Lawrence Hall of Science, little education *about* computers is provided at the park.

7. USER GROUPS AND COMPUTER CLUBS

Most user groups and computer clubs are unlikely to be solely concerned with educational uses of microcomputers. However, the meetings of the various clubs and user groups do bring together people with a variety of expertise and interest in computing and so are good sources of information, assistance, and software exchange. There is likely to be a club or user group in your area. A partial list of national computer clubs is provided in *The First Book of Microcomputers* by Robert Moody, Hayden Book Company, Rochelle Park, NJ, 1978, pp. 105-13. Names and phone numbers to contact local computer clubs will generally be known at local computer stores. The following user groups are described simply as examples to illustrate various kinds of organizations, resource center backup, meetings, and workshops.

7

The Boston Computer Society
Three Center Plaza
Boston, MA 02108
(617) 367-8080
The Boston Computer Society is both a computer resource center and a consortium of user groups for most microcomputer systems and information utility sources, including: Apple, Atari, TRS-80, IBM, North Star, OSI, PET, Robotics, Sinclair, and The Source. Monthly meetings and seminars address home, business, and educational computer applications. The society produces a bimonthly, *Boston Computer Update*, which includes an educational computing column. *The First New England Microcomputer Resources Handbook* is also available from the society. Their Educational Resource Exchange provides information on funding, teacher training, equipment selection, and software availability.

Computer Education Resource Coalition (CERC)
Lesley College
29 Everett Street
Cambridge, MA 02238
This is a coalition of several organizations that provides services to teachers in the Boston area using educational technology. Their newsletter focuses on resources for teachers and includes a calendar of area computer-related events. CERC is sponsored by: Lesley College; TERC; The Boston Computer Society; MIT; Bolt, Beranek, and Newman; Harvard University; Educational Collaborative (EdCo); The Massachusetts Department of Education along with several local school systems. CERC hopes to expand its activities to include: supporting local conferences, lobbying for funding computer use in education, and developing a regional resource center

Computer-Using Educators (CUE)
c/o Don McKell
Independence High School
1776 Educational Park Drive
San Jose, CA 95133

CUE is a California-based users organization with members around the country. The organization seeks to improve school and college computer use. Activities include organizing major conferences, publishing a bimonthly newsletter, and jointly sponsoring Softswap (see Software Clearinghouses) with the Microcomputer Center at the San Mateo County Office of Education (see Resource Centers).

DECUS
One Iron Way
Marlboro, MA 01752

DECUS is the Digital Equipment Corporation Educational Users Group. Local chapters hold meetings to discuss hardware and to share software. DECUS has a large member-contributed software library. *EDU* is their educational users newsletter.

HP 3000 International Users Group (IUG)
SIG-Education
c/o Lloyd Davis
Director for Academic Computing
University of Tennessee
Chattanooga, TN 37401
(615) 755-4387

The Special Interest Group in Education of IUG currently distributes a newsletter and maintains a database on educational users of the HP 3000. They have taken over distribution of the contributed library of educational software for the HP 2000 and hold meetings twice a year in conjuction with the IUG. (Special interest groups also exist for users of other makes of computer. The national sales offices of these manufacturers should be able to provide some information on these.)

Northwest Council for Computer Education
Computer Center
Eastern Oregon State College
La Grande, OR 97850
(503) 963-2171

This group of computer educators sponsors meetings, workshops, and an annual conference, primarily for the educators of Oregon and Washington states.

8. HARDWARE

New product information is available in regular columns in nearly all computing magazines. *Curriculum Product Review* (see Software Catalogues) and the following catalogue also provide access to manufacturers' information.

Electronic Literature Review
Technical Information Distribution Service
40 West Ridgewood Avenue
Ridgewood, NJ 07450
(201) 444-8889

This free catalogue lists and describes several hundred industry publications that cover both individual components and complete computer systems. Most such publications are also free.

Rather than a comprehensive list of hardware manufacturers, the following is a sampling of the microcomputer manufacturers whose products are the most commonly used in schools. The number of microcomputer companies is large and growing fast, including many of the major mainframe and minicomputer manufacturers (e.g. IBM, Digital Equipment Corporation, and Hewlett-Packard) who are now entering the small computer market. However, at present, educational software is still limited for many of these new systems.

APF Electronics, Inc.
1501 Broadway
New York, NY 10036
(212) 869-1960

Apple Computer, Inc.
10260 Bandley Drive
Cupertino, CA 95014
Referral Number: (800) 538-9696
    The common Apple referral number can provide: the name and number of local dealers, literature on specific hardware systems, and regional sales telephone numbers for customer service inquiries.

Atari, Inc.
Bid Dept.: P.O. Box 427
1265 Borregas Avenue
Sunnyvale, CA 94086
Information: (800) 538-8547

Bell & Howell
Interactive Video Systems
7100 McCormick Rd.
Chicago, IL 60645
(312) 262-1600, ext. 248
    The Interactive Video Systems department provides documentation for Bell & Howell microcomputer systems and other related products.

Commodore Business Machines, Inc.
950 Rittenhouse Road
Norristown, PA 19403
    The following regional Commodore sales offices can provide local dealer referrals: for the Northeastern region (617) 938-0552; for the Mid-Atlantic region (215) 666-7950, ext. 343; for the Southeast region (404) 987-3311; for the South Central region (214) 458-1000; for the Midwest region (312) 595-5990; for the Southwest region (714) 972-1415; for the Northwest region (408) 727-4755; and for the New York region (212) 947-2767.

Compucolor Corp.
P.O. Box 569
Norcross, GA 30071
(404) 449-5996

Digital Equipment Corporation (DEC)
146 Main Street
Maynard, MA 01754

Exidy Systems, Inc.
1234 Elko
Sunnyvale, CA 94086
(408) 734-9831

Heath/Zenith
Benton Harbor, MI 49022
(616) 982-3200

International Business Machines (IBM) Corporation
P.O. Box 328
Boca Raton, FL 33432
(305) 998-6007

M/A-COM Office Systems, Inc.
c/o Ken Bolick
7 Oak Park
Bedford, MA 07730
(617) 275-3034
This was formerly Ohio Scientific.

Monroe Systems for Business
The American Road
Morris Plains, NJ 07950
(201) 540-7300
   Teachers should contact the Monroe Education Center at the above address.

North Star
14440 Catalina Street
San Leandro, CA 94577
(415) 357-8500

Radio Shack
National Bid Dept.
400 Atrium
1 Tandy Center
Forth Worth, TX 76102
Customer Service: (800) 433-1679
   A national bid department is maintained for hardware sales and service bids.
Educational questions may also be addressed to the national office. However, the
nationwide chain of Radio Shack dealerships is able to provide literature and sales
information as well.

Sinclair Research Limited
50 Stamford Street
Boston, MA 02114
(617) 742-4826

Texas Instruments, Inc.
c/o Jim Dugan
P.O. Box 10508
Mail Station 5890
Lubbock, TX 79408
(806) 741-2420
   Texas Instruments will provide sales and systems information for educators and
other microcomputer users at the above address.

Vector Graphics Inc.
500 N. Ventu Park Rd
Thousand Oaks, CA 91320
(805) 499-5831

Xerox
1341 W. Mockingbird
Dallas, TX 75247
(214) 723-0111

9. SOFTWARE

While the quality of most educational software currently is disappointing, a vast amount of it is commercially available. The number of software publishers is continually expanding and cannot be adequately represented here. See the *Classroom Computer News* Directory of Educational Computing Resources and the January to March 1981 issue of *AEDS Monitor* for a listing of particular vendors. Rather than relisting these, this section describes software directories and catalogues, software reviews, software clearinghouses, and a special group of software products: author languages.

The distinction between directories and catalogues is not hard and fast, and some publications that have been called directories by the publishers have been classified as catalogues below. In general, directories list and describe software from various publishers and usually cross-index the material by one or more of the following: subject area, grade level, programming language, type of instructional category, and microcomputer type. Catalogues generally list software from various publishers that can be ordered directly through the catalogue, or they provide access to noncritical manufacturers' information brochures. Catalogues and directories are available from the publishers at the address given unless otherwise described.

The following two publications do not fit neatly into either of these categories.

Courseware Magazine
4919 N. Millbrook, #222
Fresno, CA 93726
(209) 225-0953

Courseware is a printed magazine accompanied by cassettes or diskettes of documented, educational programs. Five issues per year provide usable microcomputer programs (usually two per issue) for use in K-12 curriculums. The text, including a teacher's guide, and the cassette or diskette are printed in three versions —Apple, PET, and TRS-80 Level II — for use with the respective microcomputers. The magazine also includes a calendar of educational technology workshops, and a list of computer camps.

Softside
Softside Publications
P.O. Box 68
Milford, NH 03055

Each issue of this monthly periodical has full documentation for several programs for the Apple, Atari, and TRS-80 microcomputers. With a cassette subscription, programs are provided on a tape similar to the *Courseware* format. Some packages are educational. Additional articles provide technical information for programmers.

Software Directories

The Apple Software Directory, Vol. 3 — Education
WIDL Video
5245 West Diversey Avenue
Chicago, IL 60639
(312) 622-9606

This directory lists educational software available from over 400 vendors. The programs are briefly described and are cross-referenced by subject matter. WIDL Video also publishes a directory of games software for the Apple; an Apple resource directory listing hardware, boards, and accessories; and *The Apple II Blue Book*, which includes all of this information in one volume.

Educator's Handbook and Software Directory
Vital Information, Inc.
350 Union Station
Kansas City, MO 64108
In addition to educational software listings for Apple microcomputers, this directory contains a special section of articles on using microcomputers in education. Software descriptions are categorized by subject area and grade level. The catalogue is also available from local Apple dealers.

Index to Computer-Based Learning, 1981 Edition
edited by Anastasia Wang
available from Instructional Media Laboratory
University of Wisconsin
P.O. Box 413
Milwaukee, WI 53201
The *Index*, available either as four paperbound volumes or on microfiche, lists over 4800 computer-based learning programs. Each is cross-indexed by source, programming language, central processor type, and programming category. Programs for primary and secondary school and universities are abstracted according to fourteen characteristics.

International Microcomputer Software Directory
Imprint Software
420 South Howes Street
Fort Collins, CO 80521
This directory lists thousands of software packages of all kinds, including some in most educational subjects. Listings are cross- referenced by application, computer system, and software publisher. Brochures on the directory are available.

1982 Swift's Directory of Educational Software, Apple II Edition
Sterling Swift Publishing Company
1600 Fortview Rd.
Austin, TX 78704
(512) 444-7570
This directory contains a selected listing of educational programs for the Apple microcomputer. The contents are divided into commercial and noncommercial publishers of educational software, and software is further classified by grade level. The directory is available from Sterling Swift and from some computer stores.

Reference Manual for Instructional Use of Microcomputers
Jem Research, Discovery Park
University of Victoria
P.O. Box 1700
Victoria, BC V8W 2Y2
(604) 477-7246
This directory indexes over 1000 educational software programs that are cross-referenced according to subject and grade level. In addition, over 200 representative programs are evaluated. The manual also includes: a listing of software publishes; a listing of distributors of computer-related products; and an annotated index of books, magazines, and journals on microcomputer technology and computer literacy.

School Microware Directory
Dresden Associates
P.O. Box 246
Dresden, ME 04342
This semi-annual directory includes software for Grades K-12 in most subject areas. Programs for TRS-80, PET, Atari and Apple II are listed and briefly described. Over 130 software suppliers are listed, and programs are indexed alphabetically and by grade level within subject/department. Separate listings for individual computer systems are also included.

The Software Directory
Software Central
P.O. Box 30424
Lincoln, NE 68503
This comprehensive guide to programs includes a category of educational software. The educational list is subdivided into programs for the various microcomputer systems. Programs are briefly described.

Starbeks Software Directory
11990 Dorsett Road
St. Louis, MO 63043
(314) 567-7180
Starbeks Directory describes over 1,000 programs for the Apple microcomputer. The list of educational software is divided by subject and includes programs for grades K-12. Programs are listed alphabetically by title and indexed by subject.

VanLoves AppleII/III Software Directory
Vital Information, Inc.
350 Union Station
Kansas City, MO 64108
This software directory includes an educational software section. Programs are listed alphabetically and by subject. A vendor list is also provided.

Software Catalogues

CIE Software News
Computer Information Exchange
Box 159
San Luis Rey, CA 92068
(714) 757-4849
This newsletter is a continuously updated directory of software, books, and hardware available directly from CIE.

Creative Discount Software
256 S. Robertson, Suite 2156
Beverly Hills, CA 90211
(800) 824-7888, no. 831
This catalogue lists programs for Apple II and TRS-80 microcomputers. A few of the programs listed are educational.

Curriculum Product Review
530 University Avenue
Palo Alto, CA 94301
Curriculum Product Review, published monthly August through April, lists texts, audio-visual materials, hardware, and software that may be of use to educators. The

descriptions of the different materials are linked to a readers service card for more manufacturers' information. With a special section on computer learning, this monthly is a good source of information on new commercial educational materials.

Huntington Computing Catalogue
P.O. Box 1297
1945 S. Dairy
Corcoran, CA 93212
(800) 344-5106
This free catalogue lists both educational and noneducational programs for the Apple, Atari, PET, and TRS-80 programs. Software can be ordered directly from Huntington Computing.

Instant Software
Peterborough, NH 03458
The publishers of *Kilobaud Microcomputing* offer this free direct mail catalogue. The catalogue, updated every few months, lists educational software, games, and simulations for TRS-80, Apple, PET, TI-99/4, and Atari 800 microcomputers.

K-12 Micro Media
172 Broadway
Woodcliff Lake, NJ 07675
(201) 391-7555
This free catalogue lists books and educational programs from fifty vendors for the Apple, TRS-80, PET, and Atari computers. Programs are listed by subject, including math, reading, language arts, science, and computer literacy. Software can be ordered directly through the catalogue.

Marck
280 Linden Avenue
Brandon, CT 06405
(203) 481-3271
This free catalogue lists educational programs by computer (Apple, Atari, PET, and TRS-80), subject area, and publisher. Subject areas include language, reading, history, geography, math, and science. Readers can order software and books about computing directly through the catalogue. All software listed is tested by Marck.

MECC
2520 Broadway Drive
St. Paul, MN 55113
(612) 376-1118
MECC produces a catalogue of Apple and Atari software it has developed. The programs are available through MECC.

Microcomputers Corporation Catalogue
34 Maple Avenue
P.O. Box 8
Armonk, NY 10504
(914) 273-6480
This free list of computer accessories and software includes many programs that are educational. Programs and accessories can be ordered through the catalogue.

Opportunities for Learning, Inc.
Dept. L-4
8950 Lurline Avenue

Chatsworth, CA 91311

(213) 341-2535

Educational software from elementary through college level for Apple, PET, TRS-80, and Atari systems is listed in this free directory. Listings are by subject, and within subject areas by grade. All software can be ordered through the catalogue.

Queue

5 Chapel Hill Drive

Fairfield, CT 06432

Queue is a catalogue of educational software available for Apple, Atari, PET, and TRS-80 microcomputers, grouped by subject and grade. Programs come from over forty educational software publishers but can be ordered directly through the catalogue. A monthly newsletter *Microcomputers in Education,* which lists new software additions to the catalogue, is available as well as short software reviews and resource information for computer-using educators.

Scholastic Microcomputer Instructional Materials

904 Sylvan Avenue

Englewood Cliffs, NJ 07632

(201) 567-7900

This free catalogue lists books about computing, computer accessories, and educational software for Apple, PET, TRS-80, TI-99/4, and Atari microcomputers. All products listed are available from Scholastic through this catalogue.

TRS-80 Software Directory

This catalogue, along with *Sourcebook,* is available from local Radio Shack stores. Both the catalogue and the booklet cover educational programs available for use with the TRS-80.

Software Reviews

As has been suggested, there is great variation in both the type and quality of commercially available software packages. The following sources of software reviews are listed to assist you in sorting through the various programs you might wish to use. Most of these are periodicals dedicated to software reviews. Other sources include: Conduit and MicroSIFT (see Software Clearinghouses) and EPIE's Microcomputer Software File (see Resource Centers). In addition to these journals, educational programs are regularly reviewed by various computer users groups; resource centers; and in periodicals such as *AEDS Monitor, Classroom Computer News, The Computing Teacher, Creative Computing, Educational Computer Magazine, Educational Technology, Electronic Learning, Personal Computing, Popular Computing,* and *Recreational Computing.* In the coming years, with the rapid increase in school computer use, we can expect to see the appearance of many more sources of software reviews.

Journal of Courseware Review

The Apple Foundation

2025 Mariani Avenue

Cupertino, CA 95014

(408) 973-2105

The *Journal* is published by the Foundation's Educational Program Evaluation Centre (EPEC) and it reviews commercial programs for Apple microcomputers. The *Journal* is a quarterly publication available from microcomputer dealers.

MACUL Journal
c/o Larry Smith
Wayne County ISD
33500 Van Born Road
Wayne, MI 48184
    The Spring 1980 *Journal* of the Michigan Association for Computer Users in Learning was a special issue that reviewed about 125 Apple, PET, and TRS-80 programs.

Peelings II
P.O. Box 188
Las Cruces, NM 88004
(505) 526-8364
    Peelings II is a magazine of Apple software evaluation published nine times a year. Commercially available programs are described in detail, including the systems setup, instructions, and documentation provided. Errors are noted, and a final evaluation of each program summarizes recommendations and criticisms. Occasional issues of *Peelings II* feature an education section.

Purser's Magazine
P.O. Box 466
El Dorado, CA 95623
(916) 622-5288
    Purser's began as one of the most complete listings of available software. Currently *Purser's* reviews programs and publishes separate issues for TRS-80, Apple, and Atari systems. Recent issues have published the results of readers' questionaires on microcomputer software and a guide to buying specific hardware systems. A brief Atari Software Directory is available from Purser's in exchange for a self-addressed, stamped, envelope.

School Microware Review
Dresden Associations
Box 246
Dresden, ME 04342
    Produced by the publishers of the *School Microware Directory* (see Software Directories), this periodical contains in-depth user evaluations of software programs for Apple, Atari, PET, and TRS-80 microcomputer systems. *School Microware Review* encourages teachers to submit courseware evaluations, and it contains useful critiques written by educators from around the country.

Software Review
Microform Review, Inc.
520 Riverside Avenue
Westport, CT 06880
(203) 226-6967
    This is a review of computer programs for library and educational applications. Besides reviewing software and computer-related books, *Software Review* also contains articles on software concepts and evaluation. The review is published twice yearly.

"Survey of Commercial Software"
written by Karen Jostad and Marge Kosel
available in AEDS Monitor (October-December 1980)
    This article is worth mentioning because of the size of the survey (1,225 software programs). The survey might also be useful to educators considering their first

microcomputer purchase. The reviews are categorized by: teaching strategies, program cost, subject area and grade level, and type of microcomputer system. The authors report their findings as to the costs and quality of software and document the number of programs available for different systems.

Software Clearinghouses

Several groups have recognized the need for quality educational software. The following group of commercial and noncommercial clearinghouses provide educators with useful information for determining software purchases, as well as being alternative sources for obtaining educational programs.

Conduit
P.O. Box 388
Iowa City, IA 52244
(319) 355-5789
    Conduit is both a software review and a software distribution center. Though primarily focused on software for higher education, some of the programs reviewed and distributed are appropriate for advanced high school math and science classes. Conduit has an ongoing project to convert mainframe and minicomputer programs for use on microcomputers, although only several dozen have as yet been completed. Their *Authors Guide* has been used as a model for establishing guidelines for developing and evaluating software. For an abstract of their biannual *Pipeline,* see Periodicals.

Microcomputer Education Applications Network (MEAN)
256 North Washington Street
Falls Church, VA 22046
(703) 536-2310
    MEAN aims to help educators to develop and sell software and to provide information on microcomputer applications in education. MEAN encourages software development in areas delineated by their members. For example, Modularized Student Management System (MSMS) is a pupil monitoring and IEP development package which runs on the Apple while SP ED READ and SP ED MATH software were developed to provide assistance in the creation of CAI for teachers with students having special difficulties in reading and math. These full programs are available to school officials and other interested individuals for purchase. MEAN publishes a quarterly newsletter, *MEAN Brief* which provides information on other software sources and industry news and contains a subscriber exchange of particular microcomputer applications and requests. MEAN also helps local districts and state agencies develop specific educational computing programs.

Microcomputer Software and Information for Teachers (MicroSIFT)
Northwest Regional Educational Laboratory (NWERL)
500 Lindsay Building
300 SW. 6th Avenue
Portland, OR 97204
(503) 248-6800
    MicroSIFT is a clearinghouse for K-12 software reviews. It focuses on establishing pro-cedures for the collection and evaluation of instructional materials and information. Reviews available from MicroSIFT are each done by several educators who review programs for content, instructional quality, and technical quality. Modeled after Conduit, MicroSIFT aims to distribute information about software availability and program evaluations. This information is to be established as part of the BRS database system.

Technical assistance to educational users is available. A quarterly newsletter, *MicroSIFT News,* is obtainable by writing to the above address.

Micro Co-op
P.O. Box 432
West Chicago, IL 60815
(312) 232-1984

Micro Co-op is a software cooperative that sells Apple and Atari software to their members at a discount. The membership fee covers a subscription to their bimonthly newsletter, which provides software listings and descriptive comparisons of programs.

Softswap
c/o Ann Lathrop
San Mateo County Office of Education
333 Main Street
Redwood City, CA 94063
(415) 363-5472

SOFTSWAP is a joint project of the Microcomputer Center of the San Mateo County Office of Education and Computer-Using Educators (CUE) (see CUE under User Groups, and Microcomputer Center under Resource Centers). Softswap receives donations of educational software, evaluates and refines the programs, and makes the programs available free of charge to educators who copy the programs at the Center. Further, SOFTSWAP operates as a software exchange. Any educator who contributes an original program on a disk may request any one SOFTSWAP disk in exchange. SOFTSWAP also sells disks (five to thirty programs per disk) for a nominal fee. Over 300 public domain programs are available on some 30 disks, including software for Apple, Atari, Compucolor, PET, and TRS-80 microcomputers. A complete catalogue and ordering information may be obtained by sending one dollar to SOFTSWAP.

Author Languages

Author languages were primarily developed to facilitate teacher construction of their own software. Author languages are not viable substitutes for detailed programming in a language such as BASIC. However, to build modules that present text, ask questions, respond to various expected and unexpected responses, and keep records of student programs, author languages are simple and effective. The most developed author languages, such as PILOT, allow ready access to graphics, sound, and utility programs in the construction of CAI materials by the teacher. Simple author languages, such as Shell Games, have fewer options and, critics claim, are not really languages at all.

Blocks
Available from Softswap (see Software Clearinghouses), from Margaret Irwin,California School for the Deaf, 39530 Gallaudet, Fremont, CA 94538; and from Ted Perry, San Juan Unified S.D., 2331 St. Marks Way, Sacramento, CA 95825.

Blocks, developed for Apple microcomputers, includes color and extensive graphics for lesson formatting. This program is widely used in schools and colleges, though much of the graphics available (for example, images of the fifty states and of traffic signs) is more appropriate for primary school children.

CAIWare
Available from Micrognome, Fireside Computing Inc., 5843 Montgomery Road Elkridge, MD 21227.

CAIWare is an author language developed for use with TRS-80 microcomputers. Lesson/testing formats available are true-false, multiple choice, and completion-type sentences. The program includes a CMI-type component that tabulates students' scores and skips to more advanced or more elementary lessons as needed.

GENIS
Available from Bell & Howell, Interactive Video Systems, 7100 McCormick Road, Chicago, IL 60645, and from Apple dealers.

Generalized Instructional Systems (GENIS) is a low-cost author language program designed for use with Apple microcomputers. GENIS disk based software facilitates the creation of curriculum materials and the retention and retrieval of grade reports and class enrollment. The basis of this CAI system is an extended version of PILOT (see below).

PILOT
Available from Apple dealers (version requires Pascal), from George Gerhold, Micropi Inc., 2445 N. Nugent, Lummi Island, WA 98262; and from Cook's Computer Co., 1905 Bailey Drive, Marshalltown, IA 50158 (an inexpensive Apple version).

Programmed Inquiry Learning or Teaching (PILOT) was the first microcomputer author language and is widely available in Apple, Atari, Radio Shack, and other versions. PILOT is less structured than Blocks, GENIS, or Shell Games, but its complexity makes it slightly more difficult to use than other author languages. Unlike most of the other author languages, PILOT is a true programming language that can also be used to allow students to write their own programs.

Shell Games
Available from Apple dealers.

This program is an inexpensive and simple way of formatting drill and practice programs for Apple microcomputers. In programs such as Shell Games, however, both teacher and pupil are constrained by the format; the teacher enters content material and test questions, and the student tends to be a passive recipient of information. Three lesson formats are available: true-false, multiple choice, and matching.

10. ASSOCIATIONS

Educational Technology

The following organizations are specifically concerned with educational technology.

Association for Computers in Mathematics and Science Teaching
P.O. Box 4
Austin, TX 78765
(512) 836-4378

10

This association is a professional organization for college and precollege mathematics and science teachers interested in educational uses of computers. Publication is *Journal of Computers in Mathematics and Science Teaching*.

Association for Educational Communications and Technology (AECT)
1126 Sixteenth Street NW
Washington, DC 20036
(202) 833-4180

AECT, an organization of media professionals, seeks to improve learning through the effective use of media and technology. It supports a special task force on microcomputers. Publications are *Educational Communication and Technology Journal*, *Journal of Instructional Development*, and *Instructional Innovator*.

Association for Educational Data Systems (AEDS)
1201 Sixteenth Street NW
Washington, DC 20036
(202) 833-4100

AEDS serves educators and data processing professionals at all levels of education. The group is composed largely of individual secondary level educators and is primarily concerned with administrative information systems and educational data systems. Activities include workshops and seminars on recent educational technology and programming contests for secondary school students. Publications are *AEDS Bulletin, AEDS Monitor, AEDS Journal,* and *AEDS Handbook.*

Association for the Development of Computer-based Instructional Systems (ADCIS)
ADCIS Headquarters
Computer Center
Western Washington University
Bellingham, WA 98225
(206) 676-2860

ADCIS membership includes elementary and secondary school systems, colleges, universities, businesses, and government agencies. The Association's purpose is to advance the use of computer-based instruction and/or management by facilitating communication between product developers and users. It seeks to reduce redundant activities among developers of CAI materials. ADCIS maintains several special-interest groups active in educational technology. Publications are *The Journal of Computer-Based Instruction,* and *ADCIS Newsletter.*

Computer Education Group
North Staffordshire Polytechnic Computer Centre
Blackheath Lane
Stafford, England

The Computer Education Group is an affiliate of the British Computer Society and provides information to teachers and others interested in school computer use. Its publication is *Computer Education.*

International Council for Computers in Education (ICCE)
Department of Computer and Information Science
University of Oregon
Eugene, OR 97403
(503) 686-4414

The ICCE is a professional organization for people interested in instructional use of computers at the precollege level. It has over 6,000 members and 24 organizational members. The ICCE has published a series of booklets on the instructional use of computers. Its publication is *The Computing Teacher.*

National Audio-Visual Association (NAVA)
3150 Spring Street
Fairfax, VA 22031
(703) 273-7200

NAVA is a trade association which advocates the educational use of various types of educational technology. NAVA provides information on funding for classroom computer use, both through the bi-annual *The A-V Connection: The Guide to Federal Funds for Audio-Visual Users* (see Funding), and through updates in their newsletter. Their annual *Audio-Visual Equipment Directory* provides details on microcomputer hardware and other technology. Its publication is *Action Facts.*

Society for Applied Learning Technology (SALT)
50 Culpepper Street
Warrenton, VA 22186
(703) 347-0055

SALT primarily serves professionals in the area of instructional technology. Though geared towards higher education and research, it is a useful source of information on technological innovations. Proceedings from SALT-sponsored conferences as well as books on microcomputers in education and educational technology are available from SALT. Its publications are *Journal of Educational Technology Systems*, and *SALT Newsletter*.

Computer Science

The following association of computer scientists, analysts, and social scientists involved with computers has significant interests in computer uses in education.

Association for Computing Machinery (ACM)
1133 Avenue of the Americas
New York, NY 10036
(212) 265-6300

ACM supports both local chapters in cities around the country and special-interest groups. Special-interest groups include: computers and society, personal computing, computer science education (CIGCSE), computer use in education (SIGCUE), and the ACM Elementary and Secondary School Subcommittee. Contact the New York office for information on local chapters and the special-interest groups. Its publications are *Communications, Computing Reviews, ACM Guide to Computer Science and Computer Applications Literature*, and *ACM SIGCUE Bulletin*.

Education

Most education associations have voiced some interest in educational technology. The groups listed below have continuing interest groups or produce periodicals particularly relevant to computer use in education.

American Educational Research Association (AERA)
1230 Seventeenth Street NW
Washington, DC 20036
(202) 223-9845

AERA is an organization of university researchers and has a special- interest group for members interested in computer assisted instruction. Publications are *Educational Researcher, Educational Evaluation and Policy, American Educational Research Journal*, and *Review of Educational Research*.

National Council of Teachers of Mathematics (NCTM)
1906 Association Drive
Reston, VA 22091
(703) 620-9840

NCTM actively encourages computer use in the classroom at all levels and has published a policy statement on educational microcomputer applications. One of its publications, *Mathematics Teacher* (see Periodicals), prints software reviews regularly and includes articles on theoretical issues in computer use in mathematics education. The NCTM's *Guidelines for Evaluating Computerized Instructional Materials* is a valuable guide to software review. Other publications include *Arithmetic Teacher, Journal for Research in Mathematics Education, Mathematics Student,* and *NCTM Newsletter.*

National Science Teachers Association (NSTA)
1742 Connecticut Avenue NW
Washington, DC 20009
(202) 328-5840

All NSTA journals seek articles on small computers in teaching. Projects initiated by NSTA include developing software for energy and interdisciplinary education. Computer-based science instruction is the subject of presentations at each annual NSTA conference. Publications are *Science and Children* and *The Science Teacher.*

11. PERIODICALS

The number of journals and magazines devoted to aspects of computing has grown enormously in the past few years, partially due to the needs of educators and other computer users for new information, and partially due to the enormous cash flow into this area. This section lists and briefly describes periodicals deemed most useful to educators interested in computer use and is divided into three groups: periodicals specifically directed toward educational computing, computing magazines that have frequent references to instruction or that publish special educational issues, and those educators' journals that have shown continued interest in computers.

The following two entries may be used as directories of periodicals dealing with small computers.

Micro . . . Publications in Review
Vogeler Publishing Inc.
455 Crossen Avenue
Elk Grove Village, IL 60007
(312) 228-0951

Micro . . . Publications in Review reproduces the table of contents of the latest issues of about seventy journals, magazines, and newsletters dealing with small computers. The *Review* includes a subject index divided into 26 major disciplines and a further index of lesser fields. Publishers' addresses are also listed.

"Special Interest Microcomputing Publications"
William L. Colsher
available in *On Computing,* vol. 2, no. 2 (Fall 1980): 60-67

This article describes journals, newsletters, and cassette magazines that focus on particular brands of computers or microprocessors. It includes a bibliography with publishers' addresses and rates.

Educational Computing Periodicals

ACM SIGCUE Bulletin
Computer Uses in Education
Association for Computing Machinery
P.O. Box 12015

Church Street Station
New York, NY 10249

The *Bulletin* contains a wide range of articles, reviews, and information resources useful for educators interested in computers. Practical guides to preparation of computer-based instructional materials and reports of research on the educational value of computer aided instruction are often included. The *Bulletin* presents interviews with leaders in educational computing and provides good coverage of conferences and current projects in this field.

AEDS Journal and *AEDS Monitor*
Association for Educational Data Systems
1201 Sixteenth Street, NW
Washington, DC 20036

AEDS Journal is a professional/academic quarterly publishing reports on original research, project descriptions and evaluations, and theoretical work relating to educational computer use. Articles often focus on problems in instructional design and administrative applications. Articles are prefaced by an abstract and a list of key words.

AEDS Monitor is a quarterly reporting on research on and various applications of computer use in education. Research and reviews from other groups such as ERIC and MECC are regularly included.

Classroom Computer News
Intentional Educations, Inc.
51 Spring Street
Watertown, MA 02172
(617) 923-7707

This bimonthly magazine provides educators with detailed descriptions of the possibilities and problems of classroom computer use. Articles linking computer-based learning with traditional instruction are regularly reported. Regular features include: a section on teacher-developed classroom applications, articles that contain original program listings, an interview with an influential computer educator, and a column of pointed opinion on educational computing issues. Also included are a regular series of annotated bibliographies for specific educational subjects, an extensive section reviewing software and books, and a section written for middle school children to increase their understanding of computers. An administration column suggests uses of computers in school organization, while a media column describes various approaches to the cataloging and retrieval of computer- based information. Manufacturers' information on new products and a calendar of computing workshops are listed as well.

The Computing Teacher
Department of Computer and Information Science
University of Oregon
Eugene, OR 97403
(503) 686-4414

Provided to individual and organizational members of the International Council for Computers in Education (ICCE), *The Computing Teacher* publishes solid general and technical articles on the instructional use of computers. It emphasizes precollege education and teacher training. Articles are provided mainly by teachers in the field. Included are programming corrections, suggestions, computing problems, and short software and book reviews. News items on conferences, projects, resource centers, and technological developments in computers are also regularly printed. *The Computing Teacher* carries articles on the use of calculators in education, as well.

11

Educational Computer Magazine
P.O. Box 535
Cupertino, CA 95015
(408) 252-3224

This is a bimonthly for educators using computers in the classroom. Feature articles regularly examine the possible benefits and problems of instructional computing. Each issue includes book and courseware reviews and a calendar of upcoming conferences in the field.

Educational Computing
MAGSUB (Subscription Services) Ltd.
Oakfield House
Perrymount Road
Haywards Heath
Sussex RH16 3DH England

This is a monthly British magazine reporting on the instructional applications of computers in schools, colleges, and universities. The magazine features detailed descriptions of new computing products and their possible uses in education. A regular school report describes computer applications in primary and secondary classes. A viewpoint column and interviews with leading computer-using educators make *Educational Computing* a good discussion forum for British views on educational computing. The publishers are a joint sponsor of the annual London Computer Fair.

Educational Technology
140 Sylvan Avenue
Englewood Cliffs, NJ 07632
(201) 871-4007

This long established monthly is oriented toward general educational use of technology. Each issue has columns on educational computer and media news that are primarily forums for professionals in these areas. Periodic special issues host a collection of articles examining specific facets of classroom use of technology. Included are detailed book, materials, and product reviews. *Educational Technology* seeks to draw attention to worthwhile commercially available courseware. Columnists comment on specific developments in educational technology, while theoretical articles discuss the *why* of educational computer applications.

Electronic Education
Electronic Communications, Inc.
Suite 220
1311 Executive Center Drive
Tallahassee, FL 32301
(904) 878-4178

Feature articles provide general introductions and nontechnical discussion of issues in the use of computers in education. News briefs note applications of educational technology. The magazine contains descriptive rather than critical reviews of computer systems and instructional packages.

Electronic Learning
Scholastic Inc.
902 Sylvan Avenue
Box 2001
Englewood Cliffs, NJ 07632
(201) 567-7900

This is a bimonthly providing nontechnical introductions to varied educational uses of electronic technology in grades K-12. News columns including a Washington report and international items report innovations and official receptivity to computers, video, and other technology in education. While feature articles are often noncritically enthusiastic about educational computing, the software reviews are useful. Commercial programs are evaluated by a group of educators who note the success of classroom applications as well as pedagogical and programming faults in the software. Regular features include: a primer for teachers with minimal computer literacy, teachers' suggestions for simple computer-based classroom activities, and guides to proposal writing and funding sources for the purchase of educational technology.

Journal of Computer-Based Instruction
ADCIS
Computer Center
Western Washington University
Bellingham, WA 98225
   The *Journal* is a professional quarterly of theoretical articles, lectures, and reports. The professional reports note findings of research and surveys in the field of computer-based instruction in elementary and secondary school systems, colleges, business, military, and government agencies.

Journal of Educational Technology Systems
Baywood Publishing Company Inc.
120 Marine St., Box D
Farmingdale, NY 11735
(516) 249-7130
   This quarterly is a technical educational journal primarily concerned with curriculum or program development. Articles discussing the models and structure inherent in educational programs are directed toward the developers of curriculum projects or instructional support systems.

Pipeline
P.O. Box 388
Iowa City, IO 52244
(319) 353-5789
   Pipeline is published twice-yearly by Conduit (see Software Clearinghouses) and features ideas for use in higher education and computer uses in education. Each issue contains descriptions and order forms for Conduit's latest reviewed and tested materials, some of which are applicable to secondary school curricula. Articles integrate discussions of educational technology, pedagogy, and curriculum content and are a useful resource for educators.

T.H.E. Journal
P.O. Box 992
Acton, MA 01720
(617) 263-3607
   Technological Horizons in Education (T.H.E.) Journal features general theoretical discussions and reports on applications of educational technology. *T.H.E. Journal* is published six times a year and is available free on a limited basis to qualified educators. Reviews of software, projects, and publications are linked to an inquiry service card so that additional information can be obtained from the publisher or manufacturer. Material included is geared towards promoting educational technology. However, much state-of-the-art information can be gleaned from the magazine.

Computing Periodicals

Magazines, and even weekly newspapers such as *Infoworld*, reporting on home and business computing news and application have proliferated. These magazines detail technical developments in microcomputing and they review software. Many are available at newsstands and can provide a quick summary of the state of the art. Reviews of educational materials, however, often are secondary to descriptions of game and accounting programs. More technical magazines, such as *Compute!* are very useful for programming techniques but presume a certain level of programming expertise.

Byte
70 Main Street
Peterborough, NH 03458
(603) 924-9281
This monthly contains detailed discussions of new microcomputer hardware and software. *Byte* offers very technical material for the home computer enthusiast. However, educators interested in developing their own programs will find this an invaluable source of information. An anthology of *The Best of Byte* is available from the publishers.

Creative Computing
P.O. Box 789-M
Morristown, NJ 07960
(800) 631-8112 and (201) 540-0445
  A monthly computing magazine dealing with a variety of computer applications, *Creative Computing* devotes some of each issue to educational uses of computers. Regular special issues on educational applications of computing include resource and software reviews. It provides both general and technical computing features. The magazine presents articles on programming techniques and applications, comparisons of high-level languages, listings of games, and discussions of the impact of computers on society. Two volumes of *The Best of Creative Computing* are available from the publishers.

Kilobaud Microcomputing
Subscription Department
P.O. Box 997
Farmingdale, NY 11737
  This is a monthly magazine emphasizing practical information for hardware and software enthusiasts. The material is both general and technical. Occasional special issues feature articles on educational uses of computing, though many of the articles and computer news briefs are for the home computer enthusiast.

Personal Computer World
c/o Steve England
41 Rathbone Place
London W1P 1DE England
(01) 637-7991
  This personal computing magazine contains in-depth hardware and software reviews as well as descriptions of British microcomputer applications. *Personal Computer World* publishes a monthly notice board, "ComputerTown UK! News," which provides an information exchange for the CTUK! network of computer literacy centers (see Computer Learning Places).

Personal Computing
P.O. Box 1408
Riverton, N.J. 08077
  This monthly features articles on home and business microcomputing. It is oriented

toward programming, applications, and hardware. An anthology of *The Best of Personal Computing* is available from the publishers.

Popular Computing
70 Main Street
Peterborough, NH 03458
(603) 924-9281

Previously titled *On Computing*, this monthly provides a nontechnical introduction to microcomputers and their various applications. *Popular Computing* is intended primarily for home and small business computer users.

Educational Periodicals

Most educational periodicals have in recent years devoted some attention to instructional applications of computers. However, only the two periodicals of the National Council of Teachers of Mathematics, *Arithmetic Teacher* and *Mathematics Teacher*, have consistently published reviews and articles on educational computing. This situation is likely to change in coming years, as interest in computer applications in other subjects grows.

Mathematics Teacher
National Council of Teachers of Mathematics
1906 Association Drive
Reston, VA 22091
(703) 620-9840

This journal emphasizes practical aids for the teaching of mathematics in secondary schools and junior colleges. It frequently includes articles on the uses of computers in mathematics education and reviews software programs. Special issues of *Mathematics Teacher* are devoted to the problems and the possibilities of classroom computer use (for example, see the November 1981 issue).

12. FUNDING

While state and federal grants to education have been extensive over the years, recently these sources have been curtailed due to changing political viewpoints and budgetary exigencies. In any case, no government agency has funds earmarked expressly for computer projects, although some government funding is available that may be used for such purposes. Rather than list government and private funding sources that are subject to constant flux, this section focuses on sourcebooks to assist in the process of seeking funds for computer acquisition.

Apple Educator's Information Booklet
Education Marketing Division, Apple Computer Inc., 10260 Bandley Drive, Cupertino, CA 95014; (408) 996-1010

In addition to general suggestions for using microcomputers, and specifically Apple systems, in the classroom, this booklet includes a guide to government funding, a listing of specific federal funding programs, and lists of private sources of grants and other sourcebooks. A free copy is available from the above address.

The A-V Connection: The Guide to Federal Funds for Audio-Visual Programs
NAVA, 3150 Spring Street,
Fairfax, VA 22031
(703) 273-7200

This bi-annual guide to federal funding of audiovisual materials and services published

12

by the National Audio-Visual Association, provides an explanation of federal program regulations, as well as tables, charts, and helpful suggestions for writing successful proposals. The guide includes examples of previously funded audio-visual projects.

Foundation Directory
Columiba University Press, 562 W. 113th Street, New York, NY 10025. Reference copies are available in virtually every public library.

The *Directory* is the most important single reference work on private and public grant-awarding foundations. The directory is published by the Foundation Center (see below).

Funding Report for Microcomputers
Bell & Howell Microcomputer Systems
Bell & Howell Interactive Video Systems, 7100 McCormick Boulevard, Chicago, IL 60645. Copies also available from local Bell & Howell dealers.

This free report contains extensive information on federal sources of funding. However, much of the information is dated.

The Grants Register
St. Martins Press, 175 Fifth Avenue, New York, NY 10010. Copies are also available in most public libraries.

This annually updated directory of funding organizations is extensive. Information on grants is provided for most such programs in the English- speaking world and many of the grants are related to education projects. Possible grants are indexed by subject.

Radio Shack's Federal Funding Guide and Proposal Development Handbook for Educators
Frank Johnson

This handbook is still available from Radio Shack dealers and is essentially an earlier and briefer version of the *Proposal Writing Guide* (see below). It outlines federal and state funding sources that are relevant to the acquisition and use of educational technology. A brief guide to writing a proposal — assessing needs, outlining objectives, detailing activities, and a summary evaluation — is also provided.

Radio Shack's Proposal Writing Guide
Norman T. Bell and Frank Johnson

This guide, also available from Radio Shack dealers, is designed to help individuals produce effective grant proposals for research and development of microcomputer materials. Intended for educators, software developers, and systems programmers, the guide assists in making definitions, assessments, and product delineation for federal and private grant applications. The writing of a proposal is presented step-by-step, from the identification of the problem and the bibliographic search of related materials to the final "process-product evaluation" of the process plan.

In addition to these sourcebooks, there are four funding-related organizations in particular worth mentioning:

The Apple Education Foundation
20525 Mariani Avenue
Cupertino, CA 95014
(408) 973-2105

The Apple Education Foundation seeks to provide support to new educational programs using low-cost technology. Funding is mainly in the form of microcomputer hardware and accessories. Primary and secondary school programs that have previously received grants include physics simulations, handwriting skills, micro English, adventure games, and word skills. A brochure is available describing previous grants and guidelines for funding applications for projects lasting up to sixteen months. The Foundation maintains the Educational Program Evaluation Centre (EPEC) (see Software Reviews), which reviews courseware and acts as a reference source for educational software. EPEC produces the quarterly *Journal of Courseware Review.*

Atari Institute for Educational Action Research
1265 Borregas Avenue
P.O. Box 427
Sunnyvale, CA 94086
(408) 745-2666

Guidelines are obtainable from the Institute for proposals for educational projects. Funding is primarily in the form of Atari hardware, with additional small cash grants for student research internships or travel for presentations at educational conferences or workshops. A major aim is to promote programs in model and alternative schools that illustrate the uses of computers in education. Grants will be provided for various model uses of educational technology, whether in regular institutions, in community programs, or in the home, though the Institute will want some evidence of expertise in programming.

Foundation Center
888 Seventh Avenue
New York, NY 10106
(212) 975-1120 or (800) 424-9836

The center maintains a network of reference collections on grant-awarding foundations for public use across the nation. Contact the headquarters for the collection nearest you.

National Science Foundation (NSF)
Washington, DC 20550
(202) 282-7930

In the past, the NSF has been responsible for much of the funding available for science education. However, recent budget cuts have curtailed their programs sharply. The NSF provides a *Guide to Programs* for each year and a monthly bulletin that describe the available funding.

13. CONTINUING EDUCATION

Computer literacy and programming courses have now appeared on the course lists of most institutions of higher education. However, many of these focus on aspects of data processing and programming languages that are not directly relevant to computer applications in education. This section lists only colleges and universities offering full-degree programs in educational computing.

Columbia University
Teachers College
525 West 120th Street
New York, NY 10027
(212) 678-3194

Teachers College offers a 32-credit master's degree program in computing and education.

Fairfield University
Fairfield, CT 06430
(203) 255-5411

Fairfield offers a full master's degree program in computers in education.

13

Lehigh University
School of Education
524 Brodhead Avenue
Bethlehem, PA 18015
(215) 861-3241

Lehigh offers a master's degree program in educational technology that is designed to train educators in the instructional use of microcomputers.

Lesley College
29 Everett Street
Cambridge, MA 02238
(617) 868-9600

Lesley offers a master's in computers in education and a certificate of advanced graduate study (CAGS) in curriculum and instruction with a concentration in computers in education. Both programs are designed for people without mathematics or science backgrounds.

Nova University
c/o Dr. Robert Burke
Office of New Programs
3301 College Avenue
Fort Lauderdale, FL 33314
(305) 475-7445

Nova offers a master's degree program and a specialist's program in computer education.

Stanford University
School of Education
Stanford, CA 94305
(415) 497-4793

Stanford offers a master's degree in Interactive Educational Technology which is for students interested in educational computing.

State University of New York at Stony Brook
Nicholls Road
Stony Brook, NY 11794
(516) 246-8427

SUNY at Stony Brook offers a master's degree program in technological systems with an optional concentration in classroom computer use.

University of Florida
College of Education
Gainsville, FL 32611

Florida is considering instituting a master's degree program in educational computing. Their doctoral program in education offers a minor in instructional computing.

University of Illinois
Department of Education
1310 S. Sixth Street
Champaign, IL 61820
(217) 333-0227 (Secondary Education), 333-2245 (Educational Psychology)

Both the department of Educational Psychology and the department of Secondary Education offer master's degree programs in educational computing. Further, the department of Secondary Education offers Ph.D. and Ed.D. degrees in Instructional Applications of Computers.

University of Oregon
Department of Computer and Information Science
Eugene, OR 97403
(503) 686-4408

Oregon offers a master's degree in Computer Science Education and a Ph.D. degree in education with an emphasis in computers in education.

Wayne State University
Detroit, MI 48202
(313) 577-3505

Wayne State offers master's and educational specialist degrees in computer applications in teaching.

Glossary

The words in this glossary are defined consistently with their use in the body of the book. Definitions of some terms may be different from definitions of those same terms in a more techinical work. Terms used within a glossary definition that are themselves defined in the glossary are *italicized*.

Acoustic couplers   See MODEM.

Address   In computing usage, the location of a computer word within the computer's *memory* or the location of a record on a *disk* storage medium.

Applications software   See *software.*

Artificial intelligence   A branch of computer science that has the aim of developing machines capable of carrying out functions normally associated with human intelligence such as learning, reasoning, self-correction, and adaptation.

Artificial intelligence language   Computer language used in *artificial intelligence* research.

ASCII characters   The American Standard Code for Information Interchange, an acronym pronounced "as-key," is a binary code using 8-bits to represent 128 text and control characters.

Assembler   A primitive language translator that facilitates giving instrucitons to the *central processing unit.*

Assembler languages   Sometimes referred to as low-level languages. These languages allow a programmer to instruct the *CPU* without using binary machine code.

Author languages   High-level languages that allow the user to program without having much knowledge of a computer language. Some author languages determine programming needs through the user's responses to a series of questions and then provide an appropriately formatted program. (See the Resources section: Author Languages for descriptions of some author languages.)

Backplane   see *Mother board.*

Baud rate   The speed at which *bits* are transmitted through *serial interfaces* measured in bits per second (e.g. 300 baud=300 bits per second).

Bit   Acronym for binary digit, a bit (zero or one) is the smallest unit of digital information.

Boot   Short for "bootstrap" which is the process of loading the *operating system* of a computer into main memory and commencing its operation.

Bug   An error in a computer program. The process of eliminating such program errors is known as *debugging.*

Bus   A set of wires and connections that links various computer components: *central processing unit (CPU), input/output ports, terminals,* and *interfaces.*

Byte   The number of *bits* required to store one character of text. A byte is most commonly but not always made up of 8 bits in various combinations of 0s and 1s that represent text and control characters in computer code.

Card cage   See *Mother board*.

Cathode ray tube (CRT)   Otherwise known as a *monitor* or video display unit, the CRT is an output device that is essentially a TV screen, although it will generally have much finer resolution than an ordinary television.

Central processing unit (CPU)   The "brains" of a computer. The CPU controls what the computer does. It contains the circuits that interpret and execute instructions.

Chip   A small (e.g. ¼" x ¼"), flat piece of silicon on which electronic circuits are etched.

Communications network   The connection of several individual computers so that files or messages can be sent back and forth between them. Communications networks can provide multiple connections to large information systems or connections to share ideas and programs between individual users.

Compiler   A computer language translator that translates a program in its entirety into machine code and stores it for later use. Compare with *interpreter*.

Computer   An electronic device that manipulates symbolic information according to a list of precise (and limited) instructions called a *program*.

Computer assisted instruction (CAI)   Sometimes called computer aided instruction. This term has undergone several changes in usage. Originally it was applied only to computerized tutorials. Now some people use it to refer to any instructional application of computers. We use it to mean those computer applications applied to traditional teaching methods such as drill, tutorial, demonstration, simulation, and instructional games.

Computer based testing (CBT)   Testing programs that use computers in any number of ways.

Computer hardware   See *hardware*.

Computer literacy   A term with many meanings to different people. We use it to mean the general range of skills and understanding needed to function effectively in a society increasingly dependent on computer and information technology. (See Chapter 2 for a detailed discussion of computer literacy.)

Computer managed instruction (CMI)   Primarily classroom management systems that use computers to help teachers to organize and manage teaching and record keeping for classes.

Computer software   See *software*.

Computer system   What most people mean when they say "computer." A computer system consists of a computer and all the *hardware* and *software* used in connection with its operation. A computer system requires at least a *central processing unit (CPU)* connected to *peripheral devices* for storage, and user *input* and *output*.

Courseware   Educational *software*, usually accompanied by a range of ancillary materials.

Cross-compiler or **Cross-assembler**   *Software* to convert programs written for one type of computer so that they can run on another type of computer.

Cursor   A position indicator on a video display screen that can be moved by various commands such as left, right, up, and down.

Database   A large collection of related data, often in several files generally accessible by computer, in which case it is commonly said to be *on-line*.

Data processing   Performing a programmed sequence of operations on a body of data to achieve a given result; also known as information processing. More commonly, a term used to refer to the manipulation of large amounts of data by a computer.

Debug   To find and correct errors in a computer program.

Dedicated (data line, terminal)   Refers to any component of a computer system set aside for a specific purpose or user only.

Dialects   Different versions of the same computer language

Digital signals   Electronic signals representing binary numbers (zeros and ones) used as codes for text or control characters in the computer.

Direct-connect modems   See *modem*.

Directory   A list of files stored on a *peripheral storage device* such as on a disk. Directories are usually obtainable from the *operating system program*.

Disk drive or **magnetic disk drives**   See *hard disk drive* and *floppy disk drive*.

Disk operating system (DOS)   An operating system for a disk drive. See *operating system*.

Distributed processing networks   Connections between a central computer and remote computers in which data is transmitted to a central computer (uploaded) for complex processing and then sent back to remote computers (downloaded) for review and more processing. Like *timesharing*, distributed processing networks share the cost and time of expensive central computers.

Documentation   The collection of manuals and instructions that explain the proper use and possible applications of a given piece of *hardware* or *software*.

Double-sided   See *floppy disk drive*.

Download   See *distributed processing networks*.

Dumb terminal   Input/output device without an internal *CPU*. Dumb terminals require host computers for operation, as compared with *intelligent* terminals, which have small internal *central processing units* to handle the terminal's functions and communications.

Emulator   A modified microcomputer containing *microprocessors* for other brands of machine which thus allow it to run programs written for the other machines.

Erasable programmable read only memory (EPROM)   See *programmable read only memory (PROM)*

Execute   The performance of the instructions in a program by a computer; synonymous with running a program.

Firmware   Programs that are wired into the computer by the manufacturer.

Floppy disk drive   A *peripheral device* for storing programs or other information on disks made of a thin flexible plastic with a magnetic recording surface (called a floppy disk or diskette). Floppies are more reliable than simple audio tape, but hold less information and operate more slowly than hard disks.

Flowchart   A chart or method of showing the sequence and branches of a procedure. Frequently used in designing computer programs.

Hardcopy printer   Synonymous with *printer*.

Hardcopy terminal   A terminal that uses a *printer* as its output device.

Hard disk drive   A *peripheral device* for storing programs or other information on disks made of rigid aluminum, coated with a magnetic recording surface (called hard disks). This is the most common form of storage on large computer systems due to the amount of information hard disks can hold, the speeds at which the disk drives operate, the ease at which information can be accessed, and their reliability.

Hardware   More properly called computer hardware, it is the collection of physical devices which make up a computer system.

High-level languages   Languages such as FORTRAN, BASIC, COBOL, Logo, APL, and many others that use English-like commands to keep the user from having to use machine code to communicate with the *central processing unit*. Typically, one high-level language statement will be equivalent to several machine-level instructions.

High-level language translators See *compiler* and *interpreter*

Input Information entered into the computer.

Input device A peripheral device allowing the user to enter information into the computer (e.g. a keyboard).

Input/output (I/O) device *Peripheral devices* that have both input and output components (e.g. video terminals).

Input/output ports (I/O ports) Electronic connections that link various *peripheral devices* to the *central processing unit.*

Intelligent (disk, terminal, or other component) Any component that contains its own *CPU* enabling it to execute instructions without the host *CPU*. Dumb components, on the other hand, require the *CPU* of the host computer to process all instructions.

Interface An electronic and physical connection between various electrical and electromechanical devices, the most important of which for a computer are between the *central processing unit* and the various *peripheral devices*. A serial *interface* transmits or accepts information one *bit* at a time, whereas a parallel interface transmits or accepts information one computer word at a time.

Interpreter A computer language translator that translates and executes a program, one line at a time, from a high-level language into machine code. Compare with *compiler.*

KSR (Keyboard send/receive) See *printer.*

Listing The actual lines of instruction making up a program.

Load To enter a program into the memory of the computer from some *peripheral storage device.*

Log-in or log-on A sign-on procedure for users of a timesharing system.

Low-level languages See *assembler.*

Machine-readable Information stored on a *peripheral storage device* in such a way that it can either be recorded by or played back to the computer.

Memory (also called **Main memory, core memory** or **main storage**) The integrated circuits of a computer in which information is stored that is directly accessible to the *CPU,* as opposed to peripheral storage which is accessible only via interfaces. See *random access memory (RAM)* and *read only memory (ROM).*

Menu A list of programs or files on a tape or disk.

Microcomputer A computer whose *central processing unit* is a *microprocessor.*

Microprocessor An integrated circuit that executes instructions. Also, a *central processing unit* on a single *chip*. Computers whose main *CPU* is a microprocessor are called *microcomputers.*

Modem Short for <u>Mo</u>dulator/<u>dem</u>odulator, this device provides communication between computers over phone lines by converting a computer's digital signals to audio tones and then back to digital signals for the computer at the other end. One type of modem called an acoustic coupler sends and receives its signals directly through the mouthpiece and earpiece of the phone, while direct-connect modems send and receive through wire connections to the phone.

Monitor see *cathode ray tube (CRT).*

Mother board Also called a cardcage or backplane, a printed circuit board containing slots onto which can be plugged various other circuit boards.

Networking The communication between or the sharing of resources by two or more computers. See *resource-sharing networks, communications networks,* and *distributed processing networks.*

On-line   A technical term referring to the location and connection of devices so that they are immediately accessible to the *CPU* of a computer. However, in common usage it has come to refer to information that can be accessed directly from a computer as compared with information from a book, radio, television, or other medium.

On-line database   See *database.*

Operating system   Systems software that manages the computer and its peripheral devices, allowing the user to run programs and to control the movement of data to and from the computer *memory* and *peripheral devices.* See *software.*

Output   The information reported by the *CPU* to any *peripheral device.*

Output device   A *peripheral device* allowing the user to receive information from the computer (e.g. printer).

Override   A provision in a program for the user to ignore or pass over elements of the program.

Parallel interface   See *interface.*

Peripheral devices   Devices for communicating with the *central processing unit* or storing data in *CPU* accessible form (e.g. keyboard, printer, disk drive.)

Printer   An output device that prints characters on paper. Many printers output only, but some may optionally be equipped with a keyboard for inputting as well. This option is known as KSR (Keyboard Send/Receive) and converts the printer into a terminal. The non-keyboard option is known as RO (Receive Only).

Print queue   See *queue.*

Program   The list of instructions that tells a computer to perform a given task or tasks; also known as *software.* Programs are written by programmers, and when a program is loaded into a computer, we say that the computer is programmed.

Programmers   See *program.*

Programmable read only memory (PROM)   A version of Read Only Memory (ROM) that can be programmed by the user. PROM may not be changed or erased once it is programmed. A version called Erasable Programmable Read Only Memory (EPROM) can be erased and re-programmed by a special process. See *Read only memory.*

Queue   A waiting line within a computer system for use of some component, e.g. several files waiting to be printed constitute a print queue.Queues most often occur in a time-sharing or resource-sharing system where there is contention for a device among several users.

Random access memory (RAM)   The computer's general purpose memory, sometimes called read/write memory. RAM may be written to or read from by the *central processing unit.* Information on RAM is usually *volatile;* that is it disappears when power to the computer is turned off.

Reading from memory   The process of moving data from *Random Access Memory* to the *central processing unit.*

Read only memory (ROM)   Integrated circuits on which are programmed special system programs that will be used often or will provide a set of simple commands enabling more powerful programs to be loaded. ROM has the following features: data may be read from ROM to the *central processing unit* but may not be written back into ROM; and data in ROM is fixed, not *volatile.*

Registers   Locations inside the *central processing unit* that store temporary results or intermediate calculations and are used repeatedly by the *CPU.*

Resource sharing   The sharing of one or more *peripheral devices* among several computers.

RO (Receive only) See *printer*.

Run To perform the list of instructions in a given program; when a computer is executing a program, we say the program is being run. Also, the command to run a program (RUN).

Save To store a program on a *peripheral storage device;* also a command to do so (SAVE).

Serial interface See *interface*.

Software Computer programs; the list of instructions that tell a computer to perform a given task or tasks. There are two basic types of software. Systems software enables the computer to carry out its basic operations. Examples include *operating systems*, language *interpreters*, or *utility programs*. Applications software consists of programs that instruct the computer to perform various real-world tasks such as writing checks, playing chess, or testing students.

Systems software See *software*.

Tape drive A *peripheral device* for storing programs or other information on magnetic tape.

Timesharing The concurrent use of one computer by several users. In general, timesharing is the connection of several users at different terminals to a shared computer. The connections are either through direct wires or through modems and telephone wires.

Timeslice A fraction of a second during which the *CPU* of a *timesharing* system is handling a user's request.

Upload See *distributed processing networks*.

Utility programs Systems *software* that enables the computer to carry out certain basic functions such as copying the contents of one disk onto another.

Video terminal A terminal that uses a video display unit (*monitor, CRT*) as its output device. See *cathode ray tube*.

Volatile Information that disappears from memory when the computer power is turned off.

Winchester techonology The principle for the storage and retrieval of information on hard disks, which has decreased the cost and increased the reliability of these devices considerably.

Word In computing usage, the number of *bits* processed and addressed at one time by the *central processing unit*. Personal computer manufacturers generally use an 8-bit word.

Writing to memory The process of moving data from the *central processing unit* to *Random Access Memory*.

Index

.